THE WORLD IS A

Home-coming. Calle, Helmuth (who met *Nordkaperen* at Dover), Poul, Knud

# *The World Is All Islands*

BY

CARL NIELSEN

*

TRANSLATED BY F. H. LYON



GEORGE ALLEN & UNWIN LTD
RUSKIN HOUSE
MUSEUM STREET LONDON

FIRST PUBLISHED IN 1957



*

*Translated from the original Danish*

JORDEN RUNDT MED NORDKAPEREN

*published by*

*Branner og Korchs Folrag*



PRINTED IN GREAT BRITAIN
*in 12 point Bembo type*
BY SIMSON SHAND LTD
LONDON, HERTFORD AND HARLOW

## CONTENTS

# ILLUSTRATIONS

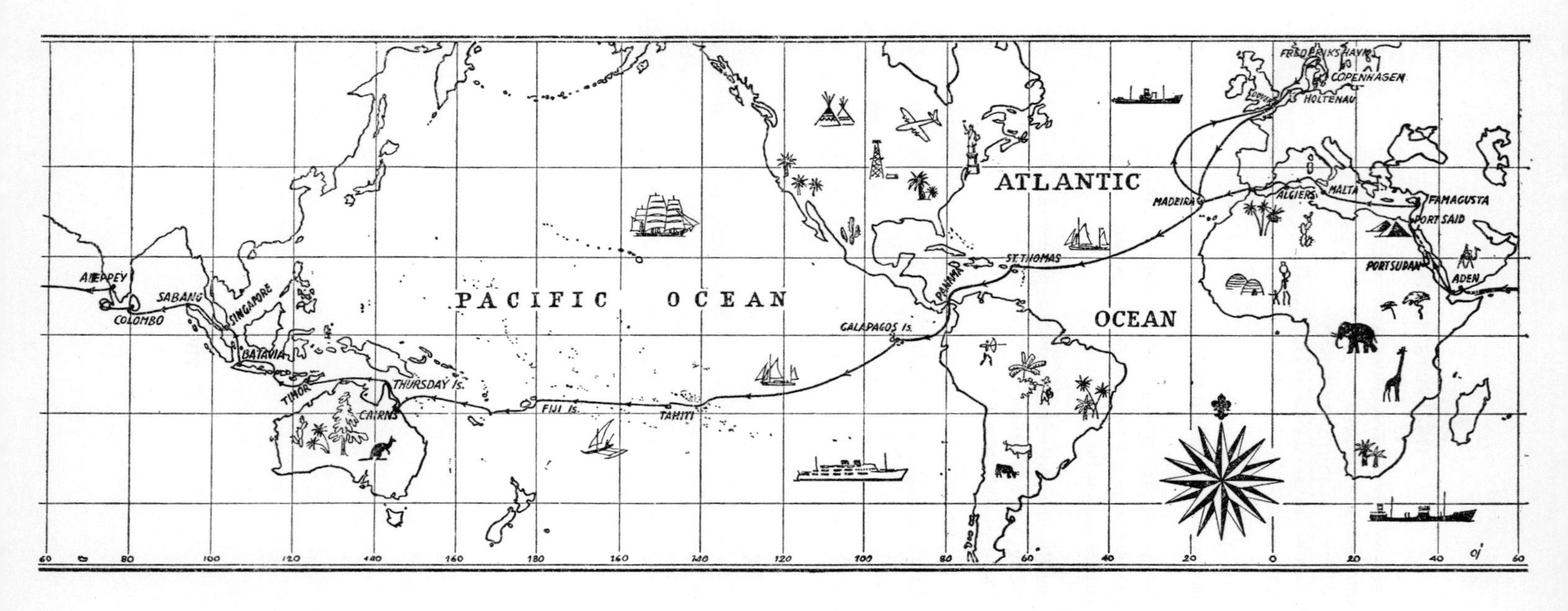

FREDERIKSHAVN
COPENHAGEN
DOVER
HOLTENAU
ATLANTIC
OCEAN
MADEIRA
ALGIERS
MALTA
FAMAGUSTA
PORT SAID
PORTSUDAN
ADEN
ST. THOMAS
PANAMA
GALAPAGOS Is.
PACIFIC OCEAN
TAHITI
FIJI Is.
THURSDAY Is.
CAIRNS
TIMOR
BATAVIA
SINGAPORE
SABANG
COLOMBO
ALEPPEY

CHAPTER I

# *We Buy a Boat*

'YOU'RE crazy!' said Knud and gave me a pitying look.

We were sitting in Niklasson's over a glass of beer, and I had just said something about sailing round the world in one's own boat. The casual words may have expressed a secret longing, but I did not mean them seriously.

After a pause I added: 'Theoretically it's quite possible.'

'Yes—theoretically one can fly to the moon,' Knud replied indifferently.

Knud Larsen was dark-skinned, almost like a Southerner. He was a man of few words and his friends called him 'the silent Dane'. But there was nothing Southern about his temperament. He was balanced and controlled to a degree which was exasperating. However, I must have fired his imagination. I detected a faint attention when he cleared his throat once or twice and finally asked if I could not explain my theory in rather more detail.

'Well, to put it in a few words, we'll buy an old boat, do her up, get hold of a third man, persuade my wife to give me a couple of years' holiday and look after my business, mug up what we've got to know, and then—well, we'll be off!'

'Yes, let's! Your best health!'

By this time Knud had recovered his balance. In a few words he pointed out to me the difficulties and obstacles.

'I quite see that,' I replied, 'but if——'

'If what?'

We took all the 'ifs' in turn, and I myself became more and more astonished at the new and favourable possibilities which disclosed themselves.

The first seed was sown. Next time we met we looked at each other eagerly. Did he mean now what he said last time, and did I? Yes, our interest had developed—we were simply fascinated by the plan. We took a deep breath, made our decision and promised one another that there should be no dilly-dallying. Now we were going to work!

This was during the Occupation—in the summer of 1944. The first boats we looked at were too dear for us, but we went on searching and at last found a boat at Elsinore. This we christened *Nordkaperen*. She did not at first seem up to our expectations, but the low price decided the matter. After repeated inspections we bought the boat—the die was cast—and we did not regret it afterwards.

The boat we bought was an 18-tonner, yawl rigged, specially built for regatta sailing in 1905. We found it an advantage that she was built of steel, as copper sheathing could not possibly be obtained at that time.

When we had the receipt and the ship's papers, we subjected our new property to a closer examination. (The words 'we' and 'our' must not be taken literally; the boat and the expenses were mine.) The masts, rigging and other gear we found either in the open air or in a shed near the quay.

As our examination proceeded we grew more and more disappointed. Their long exposure to the air had made both masts and rigging unfit for use on a voyage round the world. New masts, rigging and ropes were necessary—a sensible increase of our economic difficulties—not to speak of the extra work for ourselves. But this did not deter us—we were simply boiling over with energy.

When we had 'most humbly begged' the occupying Power to allow *Nordkaperen* to be towed to Copenhagen, work could be started.

The reconstruction would take a year, so we would be ready to sail immediately after the war. Our estimate of the duration of the war was correct, but we were quite out as regards the reconstruction, and we fixed our start for 1946—a year later than we had at first reckoned.

For the first part of the time *Nordkaperen* was lying in the Christianshavn canal, and we started the above-deck work at once. The engine was in a very worn-out state. We took it out to give it a general overhaul. It was placed up on the quay with a tarpaulin over it. Next morning it was gone. Its loss was not much lamented —it was worth little more than old iron.

Some of the woodwork looked rather rotten. We took it out and found that all the woodwork in the boat was rotten and spongy—with the sole exception of the half-deck. The boat was a deplorable sight when we had removed the spongy wood: only a few single deck planks were left here and there. But the cup was not yet full. One day, when we were knocking rust off the inside of the ship's bottom, a regular spring burst through. This was certainly not a bottom to sail round the world with!

Now our economic difficulties looked like outgrowing my resources. But we hauled the boat ashore before she could sink and began to take out everything suspicious. All that was left was the upper part minus woodwork, the sails and the keel. At that time I could still have sold the boat at a good profit, for the keel proved to be made of lead, which the former owner had overlooked.

But we would not sell our chance of sailing round the world, though many people tried to persuade us to sell and said we were mad. We turned a deaf ear and began to build resolutely. In the meantime the war ended, and the third man we wanted, my brother-in-law Poul Larsen, came home from Sweden as a corporal. Then a triple pact was concluded with a handshake—each for all and all for each.

Poul, who was half bald despite his youth, was one of those people who have a hearty approach. In good company he always had a song on his lips. To him the salt of life was sail, wind and water. Poul and Knud were very different types, but now, when the adventure is over, it is clear to me that one of the weightiest causes of the success of the voyage was the choice of personnel.

They were lads who could fill their places in a gale as well as in a drinking bout; moreover, they both had the rare quality of being givers rather than takers.

Luckily we could all use a tool, and none of us minded much about a scratch or two or sore hands from digging. The difficulties were great, as I have said, but not insuperable, and the work went steadily forward.

Knud, who was an engineer, was put in charge of the reconstruction, which meant that it was in the best hands. Minor injuries such as scraps of iron in our eyes or a torn-off nail could not be avoided. I myself scraped my shin-bone by treading through a loose deck plank. It meant ten days in hospital. Summers and winters passed with rain and snow, but we drew nearer and nearer to our goal.

We employed the dark evenings in brushing up our languages and studying the complicated ins and outs of navigation.

For two years the flame was kept burning, for two years we worked shoulder to shoulder in perfect collaboration which promised well for the execution of our plan. No one ever said: 'Oh, hang it, that'll do!' If the slightest doubt arose about the strength or efficiency of anything, it was taken out.

'The result depends on the preparations' became our slogan, and it accompanied us round the world. Situations enough might indeed arise the upshot of which would have to be left to chance.

But I must not lose myself in descriptions of the preparatory work. One fine day—and it was a fine day—*Nordkaperen* was ready, new in appearance and suitably fitted out. She was just as strong as—if not stronger than—on the day when she was launched forty years ago.

Then we tested the boat's sailing qualities by a number of trips in the Cattegat, preferably in hard weather. We altered the rigging a little, some trimming was done with the ballast, and at last everything seemed satisfactory.

The swarm of head-shaking sceptics who had followed our work had by degrees become markedly smaller. People began to show interest in us, but there were always some wearing 'knowing smiles' who would not give way. When their prophecies that *Nordkaperen* would never become a boat were not fulfilled, we were told, 'you won't get any farther than the North Sea!'

Through the active correspondence I carried on with my wife I learnt that these same people did not believe we should get across the Atlantic, and so on and so on, until we returned to Copenhagen. Not till then did they give way.

Our start was fixed for June 23 (my birthday), 1946, but before we sail I will give some details of *Nordkaperen's* construction.

*Nordkaperen* was, as I have said, built of steel, as stout as a barrel, and a very fast sailer. She had a flush deck, i.e. there were no deck-houses or cabins, a benefit in rough weather when there would be work to do on deck. At the same time less resistance was thus offered to the seas. Breadth and length were respectively 11 ft. and 50 ft.

*Nordkaperen's* great depth—about 8 ft.—gave her 'bite' in the water and less leeway. Above deck, taken all round, the chief considerations had been speed, safety and sailing capacity. There was not a scrap of comfort. This, however, was found below deck in the form of wide, soft bunks, padded cushions and pleasant surroundings.

One descended into the main cabin—the saloon—through the hatchway amidships, and had the little galley (Poul's laboratory) to starboard. On the port side was the lavatory. A little door led into the forward cabin, in which were two bunks. Poul slept here. From the forward cabin one came out into the forepeak, where sails and gear were stored. Thence, through a hatchway, one ascended to the fore-deck.

Aft there was a cabin with two double bunks. Here Knud and I slept. It was not always pleasant in the wide bunks. In a seaway we rolled over, unless we barred ourselves off.

Below the floor we had made room for a small engine. It was of course nicely out of the way, but it sometimes happened that it was filled with water. In the rest of the after part of the boat there was space for reserve supplies, tools, and fresh water and petrol tanks. We had plenty of reserve supplies, tools and handiness, and they were of help to us many times during our voyage round the world.

During the last days before sailing there was feverish activity on board. Supplies were taken on board—from matches to smoked sausages; medical stores, including sulphonamide and morphine; also navigation books, personal possessions, spare gear from copper nails to canvas, reading matter, playing cards, dice, chessmen, fishing gear, sporting guns, etc., etc. without end. The last thing we received on board was good wishes from the many who had come to take leave of us. Good wishes do not help very much, but they warm the heart.

## CHAPTER II

# *Through the Minefields*

THERE were hurrahs and hand-wavings as *Nordkaperen* glided slowly away from the wharf. My wife and some of our closest friends accompanied us for some way on board.

An elderly sail-maker named Jensen, an old sailing-ship seaman and a splendid fellow, had given us a hand just before we left. He gave us valuable support and confidence by saying, the first time he came on board *Nordkaperen*:

'I like this boat, she'll come through all right, I'm sure of that!'

Later, when I wanted to give this cheery optimist—a very poor man—some money for work done and for delivering some canvas, he said:

'I don't want anything till you come home. Let that be my contribution.'

He did get his money.

In talking to one another Knud, Poul and I were sure that we should come home again, but in our hearts we could not help imagining things that might happen.

We sailed up the Sound along the pretty coast of North Zealand, twice as pretty as usual that evening, and towards morning we called at Elsinore to land the first contingent of leave-takers. Only my wife and two of our friends accompanied us to the last Danish port, Frederikshavn.

We carefully followed the mine-swept channels up through the Cattegat, for although *Nordkaperen* was 'degaussed' there were other mines, not magnetic, to be avoided.

There was not much wind, and the weather was rainy, but we arrived at Frederikshavn on Tuesday morning.

Here our two friends helped us to put finishing touches to the gear, stow away provisions, sew cordage on to sails, get tackle ready, and so on, and on Thursday at midday the great moment came when we cast off from the last Danish harbour—from Denmark, from wife and children and friends, from secure existence. Then we realized with appalling clarity how mad our plan really was. On the whole that was a moment I do not care to remember.

We steered out into the Cattegat and went on waving so long as a human figure could be distinguished. Jutland grew faint on the horizon, then vanished into the misty air, and we were alone in our little world. We sat in silence for a long time.

'It's a queer feeling,' Knud said at last. We others would not deny it. We had now been working for two years to experience the great moment when we should be on our way to Madeira, and now we were not happy at all.

'I know what would do us good,' I said. And so did Poul, evidently. He was already going below to break the seals on our duty-free bottles.

He came up clinking glasses and bottles, and our glasses were soon full.

'May we stick together!'

We drank, and there was a short pause. Poul still had the bottle in his hand, and he refilled our glasses.

'Another toast—never give up!'

Poul still had the bottle in his hand. Then he threw it overboard.

'No more toasts?' asked Knud, licking his lips.

'I think such an excellent and important toast ought to be repeated,' said Poul, and no one protested.

At dusk the wind began to freshen and the sea rose. Knud, who had got the job of navigator, began to busy himself with his instruments, and Poul was clattering with cooking-pots and saucepans in preparation for our first dinner. The watches were arranged—four hours each all round the clock, and we began to settle down to long voyage routine.

Towards morning it turned bitterly cold, and the steersman had to put on all the clothes he possessed. We soon grew accustomed to doing a turn at the wheel at night while the others were asleep, but at first one felt lonely.

The Skagerak gave us our first test. We got a head wind and short sea and had to be continually tacking.

Our navigator was kept busy. The weather was rainy all the time and visibility bad. We could neither get a sight of land nor take any observations, and we had the greatest difficulty in keeping in the mine-swept channels. Now and again we had to cut across a corner of a minefield.

What made it all so much worse was that we were all more or less seasick. Poul, who had to stand in the little galley, with the smell of the Primus stove, naturally came off worst, and we wrinkled our noses suspiciously when he served us with hash.

All day we were on the look out for drifting mines: at night it was hopeless. We heard on the wireless that many drifting mines had been observed in the waters round us.

The fresh westerly wind increased in strength and brought with it more cold and rain. We consoled ourselves with the thought that we should soon be turning south-west, so that we could go ahead instead of ceaselessly tacking, but when that moment came the wind too shifted into the south-west, and we were just where we were before.

Knud was sitting quite blue about the nose one night when I came to relieve him. It was 2 a.m. We were tacking and should strictly speaking have gone about, but we agreed to cut off a corner of a minefield. Of course, we told Poul, and he had no objection. The danger from mines was not very great for *Nordkaperen*. She drew only about 8 ft., and experts had told us that the uppermost mines lay at least 10 ft. below the surface, but the feeling that the mines which were anchored to the bottom were swaying about, perhaps, less than two feet below us was not pleasant. We preferred, therefore, not to think about it. Nor, on the other hand, was it pleasant to be turned out every half-hour to go out on to the wet fore-deck and shift sail, which short tacks necessitated. That was why we cut off a corner of the minefield.

It was particularly cold that night. I crouched down at the bottom of the cockpit and only stuck the tip of my nose out once in a while to have a look round. It was slowly beginning to grow light over Jutland. . . . Two large gulls were playing round the boat. One of them rested on its wings for a moment, stood still in the air and then settled with a graceful movement on something close ahead which I was not in a position to identify.

For safety's sake I turned the boat a little to starboard so as not to strike the object. I stretched myself and was in the middle of a yawn when I discovered that it was a drifting mine. I agitatedly put the helm hard over to starboard, much more than necessary, but when one has been thinking for days on end about drifting mines, and the fearful destruction and loss of life they cause, one cannot avoid having a bit of a shock when one sees the horrible thing pitching in the waves only seven or eight yards away.

Of course I called Poul and Knud on deck. They gazed at the mine in silence. Not many words were exchanged on the subject, but we quickly agreed that it was certainly better to keep to the swept channels. I thought affectionately of the gull, went down and cut off a thick slice of smoked sausage and threw it to the bird. It dived down and picked up the smoked sausage, but dropped it again at once. A minute afterwards another gull did the same thing. That was all the thanks I got!

After four or five days' sailing we began to feel better in every way. The symptoms of seasickness had disappeared, and we discovered that *Nordkaperen* kept her course excellently without a helmsman. We made the wheel fast and could sit in shelter on the ladder down to the cabin and read, and keep an eye at the same time on what was happening.

We were looking for the Horns Reef lightship. There it lay,

where we expected to find it. We had gradually come out into waters which were clear of mines, but our pleasure was short-lived. It was not long before we were caught up in the minefields again. We had to go through a single channel, and tacked across towards Jutland to get on a level with it—the wind was against us all the time. When we had got into position to sail through the minefield, the wind dropped completely, and the sea was soon as calm as a mirror. We took it quietly: a little breathing-space did not come amiss, and we thoroughly enjoyed the delightful warm sunshine that accompanied it.

Then something remarkable happened. A fishing buoy with a blue rag on it came racing past us. We thought it a very curious proceeding. Was it, perhaps, being carried off by some sub-marine creature?

There was nothing wrong with the buoy; that was firmly fixed enough. On the other hand, *Nordkaperen* was being carried south-east by a strong current—right into the minefield.

There was nothing for it but to start the engine; it could be made full use of in the smooth water. One does not care about anchoring in a minefield! But wanting to do something and being able to do it are quite different things. The engine did not want to start. We did not worry; it was sure to be only something trivial. It started, sputtered a little and stopped again. This happened several times. Then Knud set to work to take the engine down, and when he does a thing it is done thoroughly. Screws, bolts, small and large parts of the engine were soon strewn all over the boat. It took four or five hours to put it together again, and in the meantime we were drifting rapidly south-eastward, into the minefield. The wind still showed no sign of giving us a helping hand.

When the engine was put together, it started at once, puffed and panted and stopped again. It wanted to show that it was not to blame—nor was it. A closer examination showed that despite all our care we had got the wrong fuel in our tanks—paraffin instead of petrol, and the engine refused to consume it. We had to save the little petrol we had to start the engine with, so there was nothing for it but let *Nordkaperen* drift and hope for a wind soon.

We had a flat calm for several days with blue sky and blazing sun. The windless days were spent in minor repairs and improvements. The sun was so hot that we could be almost naked: life would have been perfectly delightful had we not been going to Madeira—and if we had not been in a minefield!

When the bread question came up one day before we started, I had carelessly boasted that I could certainly bake a roll on the sea.

'Well, skipper,' Poul said one day, 'what about your baking some bread now? We've only biscuits left.'

There was no way out. I had to start baking on the Primus. When I had finished kneading, there was dough and flour all over the boat, and I matched my surroundings. However, the bread had been baked, and so far I had done what I had promised. But the culinary result was not so good. The bread was like ballast iron, black as coal outside, while inside it was full of all the lovely dough I had had so much trouble in kneading. Knud and Poul recoiled in horror. I had a taste myself, and felt a weight on my stomach. Resignedly I flung the bread to the gulls—and we did not see them again. That was the first and last time I baked on board.

When the wind came at last we welcomed it, even though it was variable, and we pushed on slowly but surely towards England. A violent thunderstorm surprised Knud one night when he was at the wheel. He got us up rather late, and we had to hurry to take in sail.

Flying jib, topsail and jib were taken in, and we raced through the darkness under the rest of our canvas like another Flying Dutchman. It thundered and lightened, the wind howled in the rigging, and the rain poured down, but luckily we went in the right direction. In an hour's time the whole thing was over, and Poul made us all a cup of strong coffee. The thunderstorm was replaced by a fresh fair wind, and when daylight came the English coast was in sight.

We kept on south and sighted the Newarp lightship. The wind was still fresh and our speed good, but our joy was short-lived: we met an adverse current and at the same time the wind disappeared again. The weather changed many times before we were out of the Channel, and several times we were in minefields, but we gradually came to take little notice of them. One evening a very fresh offshore wind came along and we agreed to snap our fingers at mines and wrecks and just get out into open sea as quickly as possible.

That night we sailed across the mouth of the Thames in pitch darkness. We logged 10.7 knots, and it was certainly a good thing we did not know how near we went to the hundreds of wrecks and mines which at that time made the Thames estuary unsafe. When we collided in the dark with some drifting object—this did happen—we jumped a foot in the air and waited anxiously for the explosion. We did not draw breath till a reasonable time had passed. I think that despite everything we had become fatalists.

*Nordkaperen* passed the historic cliffs of Dover, and arrived off Folkestone, which we passed four times, being driven back on each occasion by the strong tidal current before we were able to free ourselves.

One night in the Channel we were becalmed. *Nordkaperen* lay swinging round with no steering way; it was dark, although there was not a cloud in the sky, and several lighthouses winked cheerfully from the French coast.

There were plenty of pretty things to look at, but I preferred to spend my watch down in the cabin with a book. Soon my attention was attracted by a ship that was coming towards us; the thumping of her engines could be heard a long way off in the quiet night, and little as I wanted to I had to go on deck. A fair-sized motor-ship was approaching us about half a mile away; her masthead lights were in line, so there was no doubt that we were in her course. Our sidelights were lighted, but the boat was stern on to the approaching ship, so that they could not be seen. We carried no stern light, as we calculated the light from the binnacle to be sufficient, but I suddenly began to doubt this and tried to turn *Nordkaperen* head on to the motor-ship. She did not answer the helm at all. I hurriedly got hold of an electric torch and flashed it on the sails. Five hundred yards from us the motor-ship altered her course, and I drew a breath of relief, but too soon! For some reason or another she altered her course again and came straight for us. Now I grew really frightened. I flashed the lamp like a madman, but this had no effect. The ship's bows emerged from the darkness like a mountain and passed us at a distance of twelve yards. Her bow wave made *Nordkaperen* jump like a skittish horse, while sails, spars and rigging made a deafening clatter. They were no blessings I sent after the unknown ship, which unfortunately could not hear me.

At last the wind came, and we sailed across the Bay of Biscay before a fresh wind on our starboard quarter. We pressed on under full sail: the idle days had to be made up for.

It was with a feeling of relief that we came out into the open waters of the Atlantic. No confusing brooms, wreck buoys or light barrels not marked on the chart—and no minefields. The trip through the North Sea and the Channel had tried our nerves severely, but Knud's unshakeable calm and Poul's gay humour were a great support.

## CHAPTER III

# *Madeira*

We cannot confirm the evil reputation of the Bay of Biscay; it treated us well. Certainly the seas were high, and a fresh north-west wind increased their violence, but we were able to carry full sail—jibs included—even if it was a near thing in the strongest gusts. We moved swiftly towards our goal.

We became acquainted with phosphorescence and porpoises, and, as we were still green, we took a great deal of notice of them. When *Nordkaperen* plunged into a sea at night, a rain of sparks flew far and wide around us, and when we spat into the water it sounded—and looked—as if an electric spark sprang up from the surface. If one leant out over the bulwarks and looked at the keel, a glowing colossus seemed to be rushing through the water; our wake took a long time to disappear.

Dolphins and porpoises played around us by day and night, passing so close ahead of us that we often thought we had run them down. At night we could see their round and curved illuminated tracks long after they had gone.

We came into Spanish waters and could pick up small cuttle-fish from the deck several times a day. The seas had washed them on board. The Portuguese north wind—a fresh northerly wind which nearly always blows along the coasts of Spain and Portugal—was of help to us, even though we were three or four hundred miles from the coast. We met innumerable 'Portuguese men of war', a kind of jelly-fish with a narrow, transparent, semi-circular body that resembles a sail. They rode proudly on the crests of the waves with their three or four square inches of sail close-hauled. Their brilliant colours could not fail to attract the eye.

Our days were spent in doing repairs, reading, sleeping and watch-keeping. We began to feel the prison atmosphere of monotony, and the least interruption of the daily round was welcomed.

Sometimes we passed big Spanish or American fishing-boats lying on the banks fishing, but it was a different kind of fishing from what we knew. They had a very long outrigger towering up in the air on each side of the boat, and to it hundreds of fishing lines were attached. We had a bit of a chat with some of the fishermen; it amounted to very little, for we did not understand one another, but it was pleasant all the same to talk to a stranger; it enlivened our existence.

There were short periods when the wind dropped, and when that happened *Nordkaperen* pitched and rolled in the high seas so that sails, masts and booms—and we too for that matter—were nearly shaken off, Poul had to suffer for his carelessness one day when he had to do something to the main sheet. A sea striking us at an angle knocked the main boom out of place and it hit him on the forehead. He fell to the deck with a groan. It looked bad; he was bleeding severely, and we put him to bed. But circumnavigators are—and must be—made of special stuff. After a week's headache he was all right again.

We noticed that we were getting farther south. It grew warmer every day, and there was more and more work for us. We had to be ceaselessly patching to protect the expensive sails and ropes; halyards had continually to be renewed, and all falls had to be turned round or renewed. *Nordkaperen* had been under sail for three weeks, and they had unmistakably left their mark.

On Saturday, July 20, there were signs of a rise in spirits on board. It was our twenty-fourth day at sea, and about eleven next morning—if Knud's observations were correct—we should see the promised goal, Madeira, appear on the horizon. There was washing and brushing—with more or less good results; the boat was overhauled, brass-work polished, and so on. Early next morning—after a more or less sleepless night—we took it in turns to

Moderate breeze with a slanting horizon

PLATE II

Knud shooting the sun

Poul cuts steaks from harpooned dolphin

Into the clouds with the trade wind

PLATE III

Bound for America with a fresh breeze

ascend to the crosstrees to look out for land. But it was not till about noon that the long expected yell came from Poul:

'I see it, I see it, right ahead!'

And we others convinced ourselves that the distant blue shadows were mountains and not clouds. Yes, they were the mountains of Madeira. Great was our joy; all the hard, gloomy days in the North Sea and Channel were forgotten. Unfortunately distance, time and wind were not to our advantage. We reckoned that we should arrive at night, and we did not like that. We decided, therefore, to go west of Madeira, making a wide detour, instead of entering from the east, as had been our intention. We should thus be in port next morning.

Before darkness fell we had come so close to the mountains on the island of Porto Santo that we could make out valleys and shadows, and Madeira stood silhouetted in black on the southern horizon. About 8 p.m. the wind freshened, more than we cared for, and at the same time an awkward sea got up. The current, checked in its course by the proximity of the cliffs, eddied and churned up the seas against one another. They came from every quarter. *Nordkaperen* made unexpected leaps and bounds, and we had to hold on tight. The wind shifted and came from dead astern, and the mainsail swung right out, almost athwart ship. From the end of the boom a brace had been run out to the capstan on the fore-deck. The first time *Nordkaperen* rolled heavily a large part of the boom and sail went into the water, and as we were going at a good speed the brace snapped like a thread. We had a narrow shave of jibing. We set about repairing the damage at once, but we had only just completed it when *Nordkaperen* repeated the joke, and after three repairings we gave up using the brace.

Early next morning, when I stuck my head up through the hatch, I was astonished to see a high, steep mountain towering up out of the gloom close by. It looked as if it was going to fall down on us. In the course of the night we had come in very close under the coast of Madeira, and in the half-light of the early morning the distance seemed less than it was. We had been expecting green hills, terraces with vineyards and masses of colour, and instead we saw dark, dismal silhouettes of cliffs which resembled more than anything huge coal bunkers emitting now and then a thin streak of smoke.

But when the sun came and lit up the picture generously with his rays, the queen of the Atlantic lay before us in all her splendour, a feast of bright colours and dark shadows, the colours shifting and changing as the sun rose higher. The thin streaks of smoke came from little red-roofed houses which were strewn thickly over the mountain slopes and in the valleys.

We were still eight to ten miles off Funchal, the capital of Madeira—and then the wind disappeared. We had no choice but to start the engine. We were short of petrol and were afraid what we had would not be enough; so we set to work to mix a cocktail of spirits, paraffin and petrol, and the engine accepted this, despite occasional attacks of coughing.

For the last part of the journey we were busy shaving and washing and tidying up the boat. We circled round once or twice outside the harbour with the quarantine flag hoisted, and the pilot came out at once in a motor-boat. Soon afterwards we cast anchor in the first foreign harbour. We had sailed about 2,300 miles* and had been at sea for 25 days.

As soon as the anchor had rattled out, we were surrounded by motor-boats containing people who offered their services for various purposes or wanted to sell strange things—from casks of Madeira wine to canary birds. We were too inexperienced to keep them off, but luckily the doctor, Customs officials and police came, and they knew how to get rid of them!

The examination and stamping of our papers was got through in the time taken to consume three or four glasses of schnaps. The Danish liquors made the officials friendly and accommodating, and we had difficulty getting rid of them again—one man had almost to be put overboard but, of course, we were unwilling to cast a slur on our reputation for hospitality. When we hauled

* Miles at sea in this book are always sea miles.

down the quarantine flag there were swarms of inquisitive visitors all over the boat, and we were kept busy answering questions.

One or two ship-chandlers saw their chance of selling provisions and other things a ship needed. There must be money to be earned on board a millionaire yacht like ours, and they at once invited us to Funchal to see the town by night—it would not cost us a shilling! We had plenty of provisions on board and were far from being millionaires, so it would be a dead loss to them, but we thanked them and accepted.

Gradually darkness fell. The last visitors were put overboard, we put on our shore clothes, and our watchman took us ashore. Our hosts were waiting on the quay, and soon after we entered the cheerful town. Life was good, and we were guests.

It was a wonderful night. The ship-chandlers, thinking us an easy prey, took us from dance-house—or brothel, if you like—to dance-house. There were many temptations for sailors on a long voyage, and one of them was the delicious iced drinks. The ship-chandlers filled us with whisky, gin and beer, and were surprised at their apparently having so little effect on us. At last they gave up trying to influence us, in one direction or another, and staggered home astonished, blear-eyed and richer by one experience.

We were alone, and had to manage for ourselves as best we could.

Through winding streets paved with slippery cobble-stones we came to a house where there was life and music. 'Casanova' was on a board outside. We must go in there. We had the greatest difficulty in keeping at their distance a gang of dusky beauties in low dresses who descended on us like a swarm of wasps.

We met some British ship's officers and were soon in good company. A band of five men were making such a racket at one end of the oblong room that we had to shout to hear each other. Poul was dancing vigorously with a little Spanish girl called Maria. He was living in another world already—in a pair of large, black, seductive eyes. We noticed that he disappeared, but thought no more of it till I was presented with a bill for a bottle of champagne which we had not had. On my protesting the waiter explained by gesticulations and grimaces that the champagne had been served to one of my friends somewhere else in the house. Then I realized the position, and paid. It turned out that the girl (without Poul's knowledge) had ordered the champagne in our name.

We left the haunt of vice to the great sorrow of the girls, but on our way to something new and exciting Poul disappeared again, simply vanished into the earth. Knud and I became almost sober with nervousness, and we looked for him in the nearest streets, but with no result. He had gone and was still gone. We searched in the nearest taverns—hopeless.

Two or three small boys sat down in front of us and took hold of our legs. They wanted to clean our shoes. Then two more boys came who wanted to sell us papers—those of the day before. The little disturbance attracted more young sharks. We could very well spare a few coppers or a cigarette, they thought. I thought I could save the situation by throwing a few coins and cigarettes to the crowd, but this I should never have done. A moment later Knud and I were at the head of a long procession moving at top speed up and down the steep streets. At long last, after prayers and threats, we got rid of our tormentors and sank down exhausted on a doorstep in a side street. There another mannikin appeared before us. 'Me show your friend—come,' he said in English. We followed him with interest. The gods alone know how he knew about us and our sufferings, or how he knew Poul. This was never explained.

We went through a great number of streets, over a bridge, through still more streets, and just as we were beginning to think we had fallen into a trap, we discovered Poul. He was standing outside a house which a brilliantly illuminated sign proclaimed to be a dance-hall named 'Tivoli'. He was engaged in a cheerful conversation with two policemen: they were all thoroughly enjoying themselves, slapping each other on the shoulder and telling funny stories. How they managed to laugh in the right places was a mystery to us, for Poul was talking Danish and the policemen Portuguese.

On our way down to the harbour, to our amazement, we met the watchman who ought properly to have been on board our boat. We asked him what he was doing, and he cheerfully replied:

'If you only pay for a watchman, we don't steal anything.'

This was our first encounter with port gangsters.

We quickly got into touch with the Danish Consul, P. Mathiassen, who had a pile of letters for us, and the Swedish Consul, Chr. Andreasen, who, by the way, also was a Dane. The acquaintance of these two warm-hearted, helpful men was a great pleasure and was also most valuable to us.

Chr. Andreasen was the manager of a wine company, and he invited us several times to taste the four million gallons of Madeira he had to keep house with. We went through the different years' vintages thoroughly, but in the end we could not see much difference. One day Andreasen showed us a bottle of wine which was 150 years old. The wine being such a rarity, the glasses were filled only half full. We raised our glasses ceremoniously, drank with closed eyes and savoured the wine for a long time, as the Consul did.

He looked at us eagerly. Poul and I could not see any particular difference from any other wine, so we said nothing. But Knud saved the situation by having recourse to an old joke.

'Well, what do you think?' There was a triumphant ring in Andreasen's voice.

'Well,' Knud replied slowly. 'if I may give my candid opinion, it's rather small for its age!'

We had another glass at once.

Our friends the ship-chandlers, who had attacked us in vain, came near having their revenge in the end. The firm they represented had a monoply of all sales of petrol in the port and could fix the price themselves. We were in a hole, for we should need petrol. We approached them reluctantly. They demanded more than twice the price charged at the pumps in the town. The agents' expenses were evidently to be covered.

We asked for time to consider the proposition.

Down by the harbour a Customs official stood dozing in the strong afternoon sun. I placed myself by his side, as though accidentally, offered him a cigarette and opened a conversation. He was interested in circumnavigators, but nevertheless had time to look round sharply to make sure that nothing illegal was going on—that is, nothing he did not know about. I was thinking on the same lines. A note and two packets of cigarettes changed hands, our watchman arranged the rest, and soon petrol was flowing down into *Nordkaperen's* tanks. We had saved some twenty pounds.

It was necessity which made us law-breakers, but we did not regret it—least of all when we saw the ship-chandlers' astonished faces when told that we did not want any petrol. (Moreover, we had the blessing of a senior official!)

Poul had one of his greatest wishes fulfilled in Madeira. He acquired a guitar. It cost him his wrist-watch, but when he was singing and playing—which he nearly always was—he paid no attention to the passage of time.

We had begun to long to be at sea again.

After a stay of eight days we sailed on the afternoon of Tuesday, July 30. Our next destination was the West Indies on the other side of the Atlantic, about 2,900 miles away. It was a cordial farewell, with many presents in the form of cigarettes, tobacco, wine, embroidery and other souvenirs.

We were wished a prosperous journey and au revoir. We had promised to come back to Madeira to complete the encirclement of the earth.

## CHAPTER IV

# *Atlantic Crossing*

The sea was like glass and there was no wind, not even a cat's paw, when we left Madeira. The sun shone from a cloudless sky. The engine was running queerly: that is to say, there was a curious knocking noise in it which we could not locate. Late in the afternoon the noise became louder, and a thorough examination disclosed that a cardan bearing on the shaft had seized up. We had no spare parts and had thus no possibility of repairing the damage. The engine was useless to us.

'It's that damned black market petrol,' said Poul, and talked of Nemesis.

Fortunately none of us wanted to discuss the cause of a disaster or the responsibility for it. We were more interested in putting it right, so Poul's idea found no response.

We had no wish to go back to carry out repairs, and decided instead to wait for the wind which would carry us across the Atlantic. For a whole day and night *Nordkaperen* lay turning round on herself. She wanted to have her bows pointing the wrong way, towards the queen of the Atlantic, which lay about thirty miles away. In the afternoon of the day after we had started, a light breeze came from the north-east. All the sail we had was crowded on to *Nordkaperen*, even the studding-sail under the main boom. The faint breath gradually became a steady breeze, and next morning it became a fresh breeze, which carried us quickly towards America . . . Madeira was long out of sight. We had caught the trade wind.

For the first four days at sea we kept an average speed of 150 miles a day (the 'dud' day included) and we began to discuss the possibility of a record passage across the Atlantic.

At Madeira we had met an elderly Dane, Captain Schlanbuch, who was very much interested in voyages round the world, and was in touch with everything which happened in that time. Among those whose praises he sang was a Nova Scotia man who had sailed his boat from Madeira to St Thomas in twenty-seven days, a really fine performance. His boat had been no bigger than *Nordkaperen*, but he was a professional and a splendid navigator, Captain Schlanbuch added by way of explanation.

We agreed to have a race and prepared for it. All sail was to be carried by day and by night, the log was streamed and studied every time the watch was relieved. We wanted to see who was doing most knots.

Twenty-eight miles in a four hours' watch was something. thirty-two was very good, and when we got up to thirty-six there was joy on board. The fresh breeze increased in strength, and after a week's sailing it could almost be said to be blowing hard, but it kept steady, and the gigantic seas were regular. All sail must stay up. Record-breaking had got into our blood.

The big seas heaved us forward as they thundered and roared about us. It was regular surf-riding. There were prospects of a fine record, but all good things have an end.

We had our first scare at 3 a.m. on Thursday, August 8. Our overload of sail took its revenge.

Knud was at the wheel. He heard a sharp crack from the rigging and tried to discover the cause with an electric torch. Great was his astonishment when he found that *Nordkaperen* was sailing with a regular lateen sail. A one-inch bolt in the gooseneck had broken, the boom had broken away from the mast, had slipped halfway across the deck and had at the same time torn the lowest mast-hoops away from the sail. The whole mainsail was in great danger of being torn to ribbons, and accordingly Knud called Poul and me. We set to work to repair the damage at once.

It was a difficult task, for we could not let *Nordkaperen* run into the wind. For one thing, the sail, hanging loose as it was, would be destroyed and would involve other things in its own destruction if it was allowed to remain flapping about in the strong wind; for another, a closer acquaintance with those gigantic seas broadside or head on was not an inviting prospect.

Further, the pressure of the wind made it impossible for us to take in the sail. It must be repaired while it was up.

With Poul as an alert helmsman—for in the event of a jibe it would have been very dangerous to be near the mast—Knud and I began the laborious repair work. First we fixed up emergency lighting, and then spars and strong tackle had to be found. The boom had to be got into place with the wind pressing on the sail. After three hours' work the boom was forced into place and made fast to the mast fitting with many lashings of thin wire.

It was light when we had finished. Poul made a cup of coffee, and we continued the wild chase.

The first half of our crossing of the Atlantic I remember as a splendid time, when we often covered about 200 miles in twenty-four hours. Both time and boat sped on. In the dark nights the man at the wheel saw nothing and heard only the eternal roaring of the seas round *Nordkaperen*. What a good thing it was that the rigging was so strong! The breaking strain on all the wires was 50 per cent more than necessary, and that gave a delightful feeling of security. The boat steered herself—she held well on her course with filled sails in the regular swell. We did not touch the wheel for three days on end.

If *Nordkaperen* got slightly off her course she put herself right again. The big jib, which ran from the end of the long jib-boom, was hauled sideways amidships and acted as a spinnaker. When a sea let us go or caught us, *Nordkaperen* could lie at an angle of 45 degrees with bow or stern pointing up at the scurrying trade-wind clouds. There had been much repairing of sails and rigging on the voyage from Denmark to Madeira, but now all our spare time was spent in taking out and splicing ropes, making matting to prevent chafing and patching torn sails. We worked almost all round the clock, and it was a severe strain on our reserve stocks.

One good thing was that much work made the time pass quickly, so that the monotony was less noticeable.

The topsail was the weak point in our canvas. Although it was new, it had to come down for repairs every day. It was constantly splitting this way and that. The topsail halyard was also an enemy of ours: it was continually having to be renewed, and it was a nasty job getting hold of it, for the halyard block was right up under the truck. It was just as trying to the helmsman's nerves. He had to keep his eye on the high, irregular seas and warn his comrade who was hanging on tight up at the masthead. Mast and rigging were whining to and fro with a list of more than fifteen feet on each side. Poul and Knud were never afraid to undertake this job.

One night the down-haul of the topsail snapped, and I realized how much strength was needed to hold on when one was being flung thirty feet backwards and forwards through the air. With a rope's-end between my teeth I climbed up the mast-hoops to the crosstrees, got control of the flapping topsail and, holding fast with one hand and 'by the eyelids', I made the down-haul fast with the other hand and my teeth. When I stood on the deck again I was trembling all over with weariness, and I had only been up to the crosstrees.

On the tenth day we had completed half our voyage. There was a great opportunity of making a fine record sail.

On Tuesday the 13th, we experienced *Nordkaperen's* first jibe. Knud was to relieve Poul at 2 a.m. The wind was particularly fresh that night, and a big sea struck the boat and made her dip her boom deep into the water. She swung round like a fly with one wing, the wind got hold of the leeside of the sails, and we jibed with a crash. The braces snapped, the topsail blew down and the aerial was smashed, but luckily both mast and boom held.

It took an hour of our night's rest to repair the damage.

The only living creatures we saw in mid-Atlantic were flying fish. Every morning we were able to collect from the deck some of them which had flown on board in the course of the night. Our largest take in one night was sixteen. We ate them, but none of us seemed to care for them much. We always had quantities of good food on board anyhow.

We wound our way forward towards America, sometimes with our boom in the air or under water, and with the mast where the boom ought to have been. *Nordkaperen's* violent pitching and leaping made life hard for our cook Poul. He sometimes gave an extremely comic performance in the galley.

If the weather continued as it had begun, we had no doubt that we could cross the Atlantic in twenty days—a unique record—but it was not to be.

The steady trade wind gave way to uncertain squally weather, and a series of misfortunes began. Thursday the 15th was our first squally day, and in my watch from 10 p.m. to 2 a.m. the weather played tricks with us.

We were still under full sail, with headsails set full and main and mizen booms swung out with braces on them. The wind had been uncertain all day, but we thought it would pass and kept all sail up. About midnight black clouds came up from the west, and soon the moon was covered. The rain could be heard long before it came. It was a cloudburst, and with it there came several violent gusts of wind from the north.

I changed course quickly, so that we should run before the wind due south in order not to have the sails torn to pieces. Luckily the heavy rain kept the seas down, and *Nordkaperen* sped along with her forepart under water up to the bulwarks. I doubted whether I ought to wake the others, but reckoned that the storm would soon pass over. When we had raced along for a few minutes both wind and rain suddenly stopped. I heaved a sigh of relief but did not feel completely reassured. *Nordkaperen* had been lying and turning round for a minute or two with no steerage way on her, when the wind returned with renewed force, this time from the south. The sails snapped and crackled like machine-guns until I got the boat round, and then we went back in the direction from which we had come. Another calm interval, and then the storm came back, but this time I was ready to receive it. I had got the boat turned round, and this time we went off to the south-east. The rigging creaked and *Nordkaperen* shovelled her way through the water, which came smoking past us on a level with the bulwarks. Now and again a little came on board. In the middle of our chase a strange thing happened; the moon broke through the clouds and cast a ghostly light over the rain-swept sea and over ourselves. Seldom if ever have I so longed for my relief as that night, and when Poul turned out at 2 a.m. I was soaked with rain and perspiration.

When it grew light we looked to see if the rigging had suffered from the wild ride of the past night. We could see from the deck that the topsail halyard had snapped, and Knud climbed up to take it down. On the way down he discovered that the peak halyard and foresail halyard were also in a bad way—only one strand held them together.

Our emergency stores were examined, but there was not much left. We rolled cigarettes and held a little council of war.

'If it goes on like this, we shan't have any rope left when we get to St Thomas,' I sighed.

'Can't we take the ends of the best and splice them together?' suggested Poul.

Knud did not think the different thicknesses of rope would work well together, and proposed that we should strike the topsail and use the topsail halyard as foresail halyard.

'Yes, and use the foresail halyard to repair the peak halyard with,' I put in.

We all had good ideas, and after many involved calculations we found a fairly acceptable solution. We went up on deck to make a survey of the damage.

The question settled itself, however—and in rather a different manner from what we desired or expected. A gigantic sea came rolling up from westward, a regular wall of water that came crashing across the line of the other seas. We had certainly seen a tidal wave like it before, but not such a big one. Possibly it was caused by an earthquake.

Before we could do anything to mitigate the effects of the tidal wave, *Nordkaperen* was lifted up in the air, turned half round and jibed with a deafening crash. We had flung ourselves to the deck to avoid being struck by the boom and to be able to hold on. The starboard rail was under water. *Nordkaperen* was not getting off so lightly this time!

Of course the braces snapped, the topsail split from one end, the mainsail came down, the foresail fell into the water, our temporary repairs to the boom could not hold; the boom went its own way and tore off most of the mast-hoops; the aerial had ingeniously and carefully twisted itself in among halyards and stays. The deck was covered with ropes and sails, half of them overboard and loose ends were flying about our ears. It was complete chaos: in fact a regular bird's nest. *Nordkaperen* had laid herself broadside on to the seas, and we had to set the main trysail as quickly as possible as a square foresail to get the course right and the boat moving. Then we set about the laborious work of clearing up. The gear that was hanging overboard was hauled in, the boom was put in its place, and we tried to get all the loose ends into order. One man had to go aloft to clear the aerial from the ropes and wires in which it had entangled itself.

We had run to the wheel in turn to straighten out the course when *Nordkaperen* threatened to go right off. Once when it was my turn I got into trouble.

In the bottom of the cockpit stood a rusty oil-can; I knew quite well it was there, but a pair of oilskin trousers invidiously covered the long point, which went through my shoe and a good inch up into my foot, when I was running down to take the helm. I did not notice any special pain at the moment, and got the boat on to her course again before I began to pull the oil-can out. Unluckily the point broke off in my foot. Knud came along with a pair of pincers and pulled out the stump. After a temporary dressing had been put on I took the wheel for a couple of hours while Knud and Poul went on with the clearing up on deck. Then I had to give up and was put to bed.

Our attempted Atlantic record was now in danger. The weather had become very uncertain, so we gave up repairing the mainsail and set the trysail in its place. The result of this was that our average speed was reduced from 7-8 knots to 3-4 knots. A crew of three for *Nordkaperen* had been precious little, and it was a hard job to run her with two men. For the seven days before we reached St. Thomas Knud and Poul sailed her alone. They sailed, repaired, slept, cooked and nursed me.

My foot swelled up, and I had severe pains and a temperature. We kept a watch out for inflammation, and Knud sharpened a knife in case it should be necessary to make an incision. In addition to his other good qualities he was a capable surgeon. To be on the safe side I took a large dose of sulphonamide, and on the fourth day after this I felt pretty well and could sit on deck for an hour on end.

On several nights Poul and Knud had to be on deck at the same time, when violent thunderstorms passed over us, and I was not comfortable feeling the boat pitch under the heavy wind pressure, seeing the flashes of the lightning through the skylight or hearing Knud and Poul cursing and stamping on the deck when things were troublesome. I wanted to be with them and felt my helplessness twice as much as usual.

During the last days at sea *Nordkaperen* dragged herself along like a pinioned duck, but at last the day dawned when we might expect to see a light or land. This happened on Wednesday the 21st at 2 a.m., and Knud's words were like music to the ear:

'Light ahead, skipper!'

It was the lighthouse on the advanced post of the West Indies, the little island of Sombrero. The first gleam of light we had seen in three weeks was bidding us welcome. At 5.30 a.m. the island was abeam and we were now only a day's sail from St Thomas. The usual preparations for landing were made, and we hoped that the engine would take us into port despite the seized-up bearing, but we made the annoying discovery that it was full of water. Some cock or other had failed, and the engine was not much more than a mass of rust.

At dawn next morning several small islands appeared, and when we approached St Thomas we hoisted the Danish flag on the flagstaff and the quarantine flag in the shrouds. A motor-boat manned by negroes in uniform came out to meet us. I nearly tumbled into the water with astonishment when the dusky gentlemen asked us of what nationality we were. I thought our flag must have fallen down.

'Don't answer the fools!' growled Knud, but we were bound to give them an answer.

'We're Chinese!' I shouted.

They looked bewildered, turned their boat and went back. So it was left to us to get ourselves into a strange port without mainsail or engine.

But we managed to tack into the harbour, luckily kept clear of rocks projecting from the water and cast anchor at 9 a.m. close to the quay at Charlotte Amalie.

St Thomas's capital and only town, Charlotte Amalie, has a harbour in a good sheltered position, surrounded by mountains on all sides.

We had arrived in the hurricane season, which explained the disturbed weather conditions. Fortunately serious hurricanes only visited the islands at intervals of years, but when at last they came they were fearful. One of our first acts was to write to Captain Schlanbuch and tell him that we had crossed the Atlantic in 22 days and 18 hours. His Nova Scotia man might as well go home and to bed.

A book we had with us gave us another standard by which to measure our record. It was about the voyage round the world of the Swedish cutter *Fidra*. *Fidra* was of 44 tons, *Nordkaperen* 18. *Fidra* had a professional crew of eleven, *Nordkaperen* was sailed by three amateurs. *Fidra* carried nearly 5,400 sq. ft. of sail, *Nordkaperen* 1,500 sq. ft. *Fidra's* average speed on the same route was 5.19, *Nordkaperen's* 5.3 knots.

Had we not good reason to feel proud?

## CHAPTER V

# *Caribbean Interlude*

We were whirled into a round of parties and sociability with the Danish colony, which numbered about a hundred, and we never had an evening to ourselves. The severe heat of the tropical climate was not good for us, and we had to have recourse to those medicines called whisky and rum, which are agreeable, if not necessary, forms of nourishment.

The negroes of St Thomas had not much sense of orderliness or capacity to make themselves comfortable. Their houses and their surroundings were like dumping grounds, and we never accustomed ourselves to the peculiar smell which hung about them. We resorted for the most part to the pretty, well-kept houses in which the Danes lived outside the town.

Nowhere else in the world had we a more cordial reception than in the former Danish possession St Thomas. We got to know the island by motor trips in every direction through the mountains and along the coast—every Dane has a car—but unfortunately we were there in the dry season, and the withered, stunted vegetation was a miserable sight.

On our first walk through the steep narrow streets of Charlotte Amalie, between neglected, tumble-down houses, we were amused to see that many streets still had Danish names—Strandgade, Kongensgade, etc. One restaurant had a Danish name, Elverhoj, and there was much else that was Danish about the town. We passed one or two churchyards, whose appearance shocked us. Most of the tombstones had fallen down or were leaning at a sharp angle, while dead leaves and boughs, paper, empty bottles and jampots were lying about everywhere. Goats—and in one place a cow—were grazing peacefully among the graves. It was an example of the St Thomas negroes' complete lack of energy and orderliness. The island looked like—and was—an American poor-house.

Some bright-coloured coca-cola advertisements attracted our attention. They were affixed to a crazy shed. The sound of voices and music issued from its semi-darkness, and our thirst compelled us to enter.

We had lost our way in the town. All the customers were negroes; no one showed any sign of serving us, and we had to fetch three iced Pilsners from the counter ourselves. The drinks were shoved across to us in a perfunctory manner.

In one corner of the room stood an automatic player, which made no appeal to us. It played so violently that the whole machine shook. When fed with five cents it played almost any of the popular tunes of the day that was wanted, and its noise was ceaseless. The negroes stood in a regular queue to get to it. When a negro had offered his five cents to the idol he stood before the machine fascinated and full of pride—this was his music.

It was a consolation in our sufferings to catch the words 'Your health!' in Danish swirling through the disturbed air around us. An unshaved negro, grey with age, wanted to show his compatriots that he remembered a bit of Danish. He tottered towards us—he was a tall man—and addressed us in a mixture of Danish and nigger's English.

Was it we who had come from Denmark in a little boat?

Yes—it was we.

He told the others about our voyage, and we modestly enjoyed the gaze of many admiring eyes.

'Do you know what you are?' he continued.

'No,'—assuming the demeanour of modest heroes.

'Silly idiots!'

We paid and went out, followed by suppressed titters. No doubt those words had often been said to him in the past, but we consoled ourselves with the thought that perhaps he did not know what they really meant.

Our refreshments had cooled us—particularly the last episode —and we went on in the blinding sun.

The leading Danes in the West Indian Company invited us and *Nordkaperen* over to the company's wharf on the opposite side of the harbour, and they helped us with words and deeds during the prolonged repairs to the boat. Those were hard days for us, as long as the work went on. The sun blazed mercilessly and the heat was almost unbearable. We could not work in the middle of the day between eleven and two, and as it grew dark early, our working days were short.

Through Captain Mylner, the harbour-master, we got into touch with the St Thomas pilot. His name was Jimmy, and his acquaintance gave us much pleasure. His brother had once tried to sail round the world, but had given up. However, his charts were stored in Jimmy's office, and we might take what we liked—for nothing, too. When we had finished sorting them out we called Jimmy, and he had a shock when he saw that the 500 charts had been reduced to about 50. We excused ourselves by saying that it was easier to sort out those which we could not use. He looked crestfallen, but a promise was a promise, and he congratulated us on the result. We reciprocated by inviting him to the Elverhoj.

We now actually had charts for the whole of our voyage round the world, which relieved the strain on our finances.

When we returned to *Nordkaperen* and the charts—transported in a lorry—had been taken on board, an invitation came from the Danish Consul, Mr E. Höpfner, and his wife to a reception on King Christian's birthday.

*Nordkaperen* was dressed with signal flags as soon as it was light. We put on white duck suits and were driven to the Consul's fine big house, 'Danmark Hill'.

The reception was followed by a cheerful evening among Danes and in between the food and the many drinks there was time for a game of poker. I won two and a half dollars—a good day taken all round.

As the work proceeded on the repairs to *Nordkaperen*, we found that she was in a worse state than we had at first expected. The engine was taken away to a workshop, where it took Knud several weeks to get it into order again. He also made new bolts and other metal parts. In the meantime, Poul and I were occupied in repairing the rigging, painting and polishing. The bottom of the boat also received partial treatment. She was turned over on her side with the help of a steam crane which was placed at our disposal, but we could not do anything to the part of the keel which was continually under water.

At long last we grew acclimatized and were able to stand the heat. We could even go about in the sun stripped to the waist. We hung mosquito nets in front of our bunks, so that we could sleep at night undisturbed. St Thomas swarmed with creeping things of all kinds. The worst were huge poisonous spiders and land-crabs, which lived in holes in the earth.

At last *Nordkaperen* was ready for sea, and we decided to make a combined trial and pleasure trip to another little island, St Jan, which was close to St Thomas. We had more than twenty-five guests on board and spent a delightful day on the island.

St Jan was almost uninhabited, and of the sugar plantations we saw nothing but ruins of refineries and negroes' houses. The island had once had 12,000 inhabitants; only 800 were now left. It had been the breeding-place of the terrible negro rebellion years ago.

We came into contact with an American lieutenant, twenty-eight years old, who wanted to sail with us. His name was William Schell, and he was ordinarily called Bill. He had flown from California alone to get a chance of joining us. He only knew *Nordkaperen* by reputation, but we liked him and he liked us, so he became cook instead of Poul.

Bill was a regular adventurous type and had been through the whole of the war in the Pacific. The only condition we made was that he must pay for his own food and necessaries and sign a paper stating that neither he nor his family could make any claim for compensation in the event of accident or death.

Life on board became more agreeable, and Poul was more pleased than anyone because he got off cooking.

The embroidery we had obtained by barter—or been given—in Madeira we exchanged for a big load of American canned goods.

We left St Thomas on October 10, after a stay of six weeks. Our next port of call was Cristobal, at the entrance to the Panama Canal. We had the crossing of the Caribbean Sea, 1,100 miles, ahead of us. It was still the hurricane season, and during our first days at sea we often looked uneasily at the barometer. The West Indians' fear of hurricanes had slightly infected us: we had been filled with so many frightful stories. When black clouds appeared on those first days we hurriedly took in our jibs, but when we realized by degrees that the clouds were comparatively harmless, we ceased to worry about them.

One day the barometer fell heavily, and we looked for signs of the arrival of the hurricane. The air became tense with a stifling, oppressive warmth. The sails were made ready to be struck at once, and we saw that our safety gear was in order. Four pairs of eyes anxiously followed the pointer of the barometer. A slight gust of wind made it fall a little lower, but to our great joy it began to rise again at sundown, and we breathed a sigh of relief.

Bill bellowed an American soldiers' song for sheer joy that the tension was over. He served us with four large glasses of rum punch—we had received a small cask of West Indian rum as a farewell gift from St Thomas.

When Poul has a little rum in him he enjoys playing the guitar, but the nice guitar that had cost him his wrist-watch in Madeira came to a sad end.

One evening while we were lying at St Thomas we had a large Danish party on board. Poul sang the melancholy songs of his native land to the guests and drew sobs from his guitar. But he was faithless to it; it was flung down into a corner on deck and forgotten. Next morning—after a refreshing tropical shower—it no longer resembled a guitar. All the fastenings had come unstuck and it looked like a garden broom. Poul spent an hour or two at its death-bed, but he could never bring it to life again and swore that he would never drink any more. The rest of us consoled him with ill-concealed satisfaction.

That was the story of Poul's first guitar—the stories of three others are similar. We remained in the cockpit while it was getting dark, and while we were enjoying the rum and each other's society, the whole northern sky was covered with coal-black clouds. Soon we were in the midst of a furious thunder squall, such as none of us has experienced either before or since. The rain splashed down on us in cascades and one flash of lightning followed on the heels of the last. The thunder was deafening; we spoke only in single words and half sentences. Sharp cracks like a pistol and deep resonant thunder combined to produce an inferno which sounded in our ears long after the storm was over. What troubled us most were the gusts of wind of hurricane force that came from all sides, and, of course, we had not taken in one sail. Luckily we had no braces on and could go about as the situation demanded. All four of us were fully occupied in shifting backstays and sheets, veering and hauling again and again. For a time we were afraid that a hurricane was developing, and we began to take in sail, but we got no farther than trying—the wind pressure was too strong. If the sails were to come down they must come of themselves.

Bill was standing on the fore-deck shouting something to us, but we heard no more than the first words: 'Shall we—' The rest was drowned by the thunder. This happened several times. Then he grew furious and shouted out into the dark:

'Oh, stop that God-damned noise!'—shaking his fist as he did so. It had some effect. There was a short pause.

'Shall we have a rum punch?'

We were in the mood for it, especially while the pause lasted. While I was standing in the cabin mixing rum and sugar and lemon, I felt the boat pitch violently. The storm had begun again. Before I could get up again, there was an ear-splitting crash, and a sail began flapping and banging about noisily.

Three faces, lit up by flashes of lightning, were gazing in consternation at a cracked boom. It had been unable to withstand the sudden squall; it may have had a hidden defect from its time in the Atlantic. While we were busy hauling in the sheet, the wind dropped and the weather cleared up in a few minutes.

Mainsail and topsail were taken in; the latter was damaged, and when Poul went on to the fore-deck to clear up, we heard him shout:

'Where the devil is our flying jib?'

We looked up; it had gone. When such a storm is raging that one has no idea what is happening, one can be excused for not noticing a sail being blown into the sea. Luckily the sheet had held: we found the sail trailing in the water astern.

This was really the only wind we had on the crossing which put any strain on our newly repaired engine. Every night the lightning flashed all round the horizon, but it was only the cold tropical lightning. We had no more thunder, and the horrible black clouds which came up did no harm, even if they seemed to predict the end of the world.

We had quickly fallen into the old groove as regards watches; only Bill was allowed to spend every night in his bunk, and in return we got our meals at the proper times. The little engine worked faithfully day after day. We had entered a calm belt, and the sea was as bright and flat as a dancing floor.

*Nordkaperen* quickly became an intermediate landing-place for many different kinds of birds. One night great black shadows were flickering noiselessly round us, settled often only three feet or so away from us, and then flew on. In the daytime swarms of small birds came to visit us—swallows, various pretty song-birds and one single hawk. Our first regular passenger was a swallow, which

A bird in the hand—our pet Olsen

PLATE IV

Funchal in Madeira, our first foreign port

*Nordkaperen* careened for bottom-scraping

American ketch *Alone*, lost with all hands on voyage round the world

PLATE V

Knud at the wheel—comfortable steering

stayed with us two days, and then a fair-sized flock of swallows came and settled down on the ship. They jabbered and twittered and generally behaved as if they owned the boat. After a couple of hours the whole flight took off, and our solitary swallow went with them.

Of all our feathered guests a little green bird was the most popular. We christened it Olsen.

Olsen came dipping along over the surface one morning, and swooped down gracefully on to *Nordkaperen*. He settled on the railings and looked round with satisfaction. When he had studied the local conditions sufficiently he hopped down on to the deck and began to hunt flies and other insects which had come with us from St Thomas. During the chase, which greatly preoccupied him, he ran between our feet. We sat reverently and did not dare to move. Gradually he became bolder and would sit on our arms and shoulders. He sometimes flew away for a couple of hours or so, but came back again. One evening when Poul was washing the deck he overlooked Olsen, who was hunting under a petrol-can. He was washed across the deck, but just shook himself, cursed a little—and all was forgotten. On the third day he flew through the cabins, pecked at us during our siesta, and did not mind hopping about on the table at meals. He would sit on the cheese or the liver patties or on the spoon one was raising to one's mouth. Olsen wanted to examine everything. He naturally became our pet, and there was sorrow on board when his end came.

During his usual morning hunt on deck he got in the way of a sheet that was swinging in the air. When the sail pulled the sheet tight, Olsen was caught between the edge of the sail and the sheet. He fell on his back with a cheep of pain and was engaged for two hours in a struggle for life which we had to watch in silence without being able to help. We hoped to the last, even if he was only quite an ordinary little bird. We shall never forget Olsen.

Our next visitor on board was a sparrow-hawk. It sat in the crosstrees for a whole day, looking evil. When we discovered that it was after our little friends we fired a few shots to frighten it, but it would not move, even when the bullets were whining past close by. Not till we threw various things up at it did it clear off.

A day or two later some small birds' feathers came floating down on top of us. The hawk had come back and was consuming its prey. We chased it away again, but when, next time, I saw it come back with a live bird in its claws, I lost patience. It was Nature's law no doubt, but that was not going to run on board my ship. I climbed the mast with a pistol in my pocket, got within certain range of the busily occupied hawk, pressed the trigger and sent it tumbling down through the air stone-dead. After that our amusing little birds came to visit us again.

But creatures bringing violent death in their wake exist also under the glittering surface of the sea. One day Bill was washing a frying-pan. He was holding it overboard, but suddenly recoiled with a yell. A big shark had glided up to our port side. Knud hurriedly rigged up a shark-hook while I fetched the rifle. Meanwhile Poul had a lot of trouble to save the log-chip. The shark went for it again and again, but when we were at last ready for the execution the criminal had gone. Our estimates of its size varied, but the average guess was about 14 ft.

We had counted on catching a lot of fish to supplement our provisions, but after fishing for three days without result we gave it up. Only Bill went on pegging away at it. We could not understand how he could fiddle about with a hook and line all day, and he had to put up with a good deal of ironical chaff, but we looked very small when on the fifth day he hauled on board a great fat 20 lbs. dorado. Seldom had so much delicious food been eaten on board *Nordkaperen*. The rest of us started busily fishing again.

The night watch was never bored in the quiet night. Great fish splashed and gambolled in the water, and migrating birds passed through the air over his head. We felt well with Bill's luxury food inside us, the engine thumped cheerfully and we glided through the leaden sea.

The weather became rainy when we approached Cristobal, and even if the temperature was 84 degrees F. the air felt cold. On

Saturday the 19th it rained hard all day, and the usual cheerful atmosphere on approaching land was totally absent. Next day we anchored at Cristobal. It was raining steadily. It was mid-afternoon—the Caribbean had been crossed in ten days without any great excitements. We had dreamed of foaming into harbour with all sail set in fresh, fine weather. Instead we came crawling in like a louse on a chip of wood—in torrents of rain and with a cracked boom!

## CHAPTER VI

# *Panama*

It was Sunday, and the streets near the quay were empty. Our spirits, already far from high, sank below zero when we were told that we should have to pay 45 cents per foot a day to lie in Cristobal harbour. That would mean for *Nordkaperen* about 25 dollars. We had just got rid of the authorities when a little white motorboat came shooting out toward us.

The president of the local sailing club came on board, and we could have embraced him when he said that he only came to invite *Nordkaperen* and her crew to lie at the club's landing-stage as welcome guests for so long as we should stay at Cristobal—free of charge!

The joyful tidings were celebrated in West Indian rum in the company of the charming president and his companions. Spirits in the cabin rose till they nearly dented the deck above.

The sailing club lay well hidden behind the coaling harbour in pleasant surroundings, and when we approached the club-house, which was surrounded by bushes and low palms, we heard voices, music and singing. By now our ill-humour had completely disappeared, and soon after, when we sat in cheerful company among hospitable, hearty Americans, we did not care if there was rain or sunshine.

We had meant to have made a new boom, but the practical Americans speedily conjured up a steel tube which could be used as a sheath in which the broken boom could be put together. We were not even allowed to repair the boom ourselves. The tools were almost taken out of our hands, while they fought one another to get at them. The Americans also gave us fishing gear, whisky, cigarettes and home-made cakes.

On one of the first days we had a good look at Cristobal and Colon. Walking in the outer parts of Cristobal, one felt oneself in a zoological garden. The wooden houses were built on high posts, and there were mosquito nets in front of the windows and verandahs, so that the houses reminded one of large cages for birds or animals. The spaces under the houses were washing and drying places, garages or play-rooms—taken all round pleasant family homes.

Through pretty well-kept streets we reached the centre of the town, which astonished us by the elegance of its buildings—not least the public buildings. Cristobal is inhabited almost exclusively by whites, and in it English is spoken, but in Colon—literally across the street—live negroes, Chinese and every possible shade of half-breed, and there Spanish is the language. It is astounding that two towns which have, so to speak, grown together to form two parts of one town can show such great differences in architecture, language and races.

We walked through Colon's narrow, picturesque streets, whose pavements run under the galleries of the houses. We were surrounded by noise and riot. Hundreds of Navy men filled the streets, and they were nearly all drunk. There were indeed many temptations—variety shows and bars one after another all along the streets. They enticed the passer-by with music and song and pictures of more or less clothed prima donnas.

When it grew dark, Colon lit up its cascades of many-coloured neon, and life became more intense, both in and out of doors. The street traders' noise was quite bewildering. It was dangerous to stand still outside a shop window; immediately a couple of dubious-looking coloured merchants came rushing out and hauled one inside willy nilly. They jabbered and chattered and used their arts of persuasion as they flung on the counter articles of the most diverse kind, from plaster Christs to dirty pictures. If one had the courage to go out without buying anything, one was sure to have a torrent of obscene words hurled at one's retreating figure.

We turned down a dark, quiet side street to rest our tired nerves, but there was not much rest there! Behind every pillar, in every niche or doorway black, yellow or pale beauties stood in wait for us. They came running out like spiders and were in no way behind the other Colon traders in enterprise. Only they did not know our ignorance. We were counted on as certain customers, so they outdid one another in advertisement and exhibitionism, abusing one another, turning up the whites of their eyes and lavishing honey-sweet smiles on us. Bill enjoyed himself vastly. He entered into the fun of the thing and began to treat with a whole swarm at once. But this was a mistake. When the birds of paradise realized that we were having a game with them, they were swiftly transformed into hissing furies. Accordingly we had to turn about and began to work our way out of the narrow street, but suddenly discovered that there were only three of us—Knud was missing. From the darkness behind us came the noise of a struggle, interrupted by Knud's raised in violent protest:

'Let go . . . let go, you damned black bitch . . . let go, I tell you!'

An affectionate, persuasive voice—that of a six-feet tall negro matron—endeavoured to calm Knud. We hastened to the rescue to tear Knud out of a pair of fat arms. He had been caught without our noticing it as we went past a dark door.

We had to fight a regular battle to save our navigator. The negress received help from her colleagues, and some sulphurous language was flying about in the dark. At last we got free and fled from the spawn of Sodom—Knud, of course, far ahead of the rest of us, but Bill was choking with laughter for a long time afterwards and for that matter we all found it hard to contain ourselves.

We stayed at Cristobal for just on a fortnight and had a good time among the members of the sailing club. We had soon seen enough of the two combined towns. The great moment came when we were to go through the Panama Canal, from one world ocean to the other in the course of a few hours. The canal pilot came on board. We should pass through three locks to get up into the artificially raised Lake Gatun, which lies 85 ft. above the sea. After crossing this lake we should go through three more locks—this time downhill—and then should be in the Pacific with a saving of many thousands of sea miles.

*Nordkaperen* entered the lock with a fair-sized steamer and a little motor craft carrying bananas. We looked pretty small in company, and as for some reason we could not get up speed with our engine and were in difficulties with the strong current, we were hooked on alongside the banana boat, which took good care of us.

When the great lock doors began to slide to behind us, *Nordkaperen* gave a violent start. The water was beginning to eddy fiercely as if a subterranean earthquake was in progress. *Nordkaperen* pulled and struggled to get loose from the banana boat, but she held us tight, and we ascended 28 ft. Twice more the gates were shut behind us, and twice more the water rose in boiling rings. At last we were in Lake Gatun. From the uppermost lock we had a splendid view over the Caribbean coast region.

So that our lock companions should not wait too long for us in the locks on the other side of the lake, the banana boat took us in tow. Lake Gatun was an interesting spectacle. Trees—whole woods indeed—stood out in the water, and fish were playing about among the branches like birds. It was obvious that the lake had been artificially raised. To get into the lock with the steamer, which was faster than we were, we had—under the pilot's direction—to take short cuts through narrow straits and wind our way among little green islands. There were no houses or signs of habitation at all, but the islands lay so close together that they continually obstructed our view.

When the pilot told the one-eyed captain of the banana boat to steer straight towards a wood, we imagined that he had gone crazy, but just as we thought a stranding inevitable, a narrow channel opened among the trees. This happened several times. For the last part of the crossing, before we reached the locks on the Pacific side, we passed through a narrow canal which had been dug and blasted between high, gloomy cliffs. On the sheer cliff was a memorial tablet: the pilot told us it was for the 30,000 men who lost their lives in the making of the canal.

When we approached the locks, *Nordkaperen* was again hooked on alongside the banana boat. The steamer was there already and waiting for us. We entered the lock, the gates were shut, and we sank rapidly—in three stages—and were again at our normal height. This time our boat behaved properly and we had her freed from the banana boat's embrace. We paid for the tow with a bottle of rum, which the negro captain raised to his lips immediately. We could now just see the Pacific despite the failing light. The voyage through the canal had taken about seven hours, and we were at Balboa.

The president of the Balboa sailing club came on board *Nordkaperen* and piloted us to the guest's buoy off the club-house. We had received an invitation in advance and much enjoyed the great hospitality of the members.

As elsewhere, invitations streamed in, to both parties and outings. On one of the outings we went to old Panama, plundered and burned long ago by the pirate Morgan. The shattered ruins were preserved with studious care to testify—our host told us—to the lawlessness and ruthlessness of the old days. After the last war, however, the ruins may have lost some of their value as an attraction for tourists.

On other expeditions we went through jungles and over mountains and came to know the surroundings of the Panama Canal pretty well.

*Nordkaperen* had got a thick layer of barnacles on her bottom on her voyage across the Caribbean, and it had to be scraped to keep up her speed. The sailing club's slip was too small for *Nordkaperen*, and we therefore decided to make use of the high tide, which rose to about 18 ft. At 2 a.m., when the tide was highest, we carefully sailed the boat ashore. The slight swell made her strike the bottom several times, but luckily no big ships whose wash could have damaged us came past. When at last the tide began to fall, we lashed the boat fast to some bollards and made ropes fast from the masthead to some strong points in the neighbourhood, abeam of *Nordkaperen*. About 5 or 6 a.m. the water had fallen so much that we could begin scraping barnacles and snails off the bottom, and before the tide rose again the boat was cleaned and painted with red-lead. We got her off later without any great difficulty.

The night after we repeated the experiment to get the bottom painted with anti-fouling paint, and then *Nordkaperen* was ready for the South Seas as far as her bottom was concerned. It was a Sunday morning when we were painting her bottom, and a crowd of interested spectators followed the work—especially when we were going to float her. An on-shore wind had sprung up, the seas were fairly high, and it took all our ingenuity and capacity to get her off intact, but the good, strong boat was not damaged by the hard bump she received.

This is a comparatively cheap and easy way of getting a boat's bottom scraped and painted, but it can be dangerous.

The days passed in preparations for our South Seas voyage. The dinghy had not survived the crossing of the Atlantic. We had left it at St Thomas and secured a rubber boat in its place through the military in the Panama zone. We also obtained spare water containers, wire, fittings, rope and special fishing tackle which would help us to eke out our provisions.

We increased our knowledge of the inhabitants of the South Sea islands, their fish and animal life generally from borrowed books, or we took the advice of experienced people. Rigging and sails were carefully examined, repaired and strengthened. The engine and lighting were inspected, we saw that we had extra batteries for our wireless and electric torches, and finally, we provided ourselves with the most suitable clothing.

Bill and I worked hard to secure provisions and utensils. In short, everything we could do with our few dollars for our own security was done. We were about to start on the longest lap of our voyage round the world—about 5,000 miles from Panama to Tahiti with a short call at the Galapagos islands, where supplies for a long voyage could not be purchased.

Cristobal and Colon were Siamese twins with quite different characters, and so were Balboa and Panama. But we preferred Panama to Colon. Where *Nordkaperen* lay we had a good view of the ships from all the world that passed through the canal, from small local traders and tugs to huge cruisers and aircraft carriers. In the three weeks or so that we lay at the guest's buoy we saw only two Danish ships pass. At long last we were ready to sail, and after a farewell party given for us by the sailing club, we headed out through the Gulf of Panama on the morning of November 27—bound for the desolate, mysterious Galapagos islands.

CHAPTER VII

# *Into the South Seas*

THE tide helped us out of the bay, and as soon as we were clear of the land we set our course, but unfortunately the wind was right against us, so we started tacking.

We held a council of war at which we discussed the question whether we should sail straight towards our destination with many short tacks, or do the whole voyage in two stretches, going far south first. We agreed on the latter, as we should then have the benefit of the ocean current when we turned and stood out. From Panama to the Galapagos was about 900 sea miles, a long distance to cover by tacking.

With the wind to starboard of us and sheets hauled taut we went south for some days, right down to the coast of Ecuador, and when we were about 40 miles from Esmeraldos we turned and set a course for the Galapagos which we hoped to be able to hold.

The wind was continually shifting for some time, holding us up and helping us on. We alternately blessed and cursed the clerk of the weather. Luckily we ended by blessing him. *Nordkaperen* put up a good show, most of the time without a helmsman. She covered a distance of 1,200 miles in ten days and six hours, all the time close-hauled.

For the first three or four days we had continual rain—the rainy season from the Panama zone accompanied us—but the gusts that came with it helped us well on our way. We carried all sail for the whole crossing, and the deck was ceaselessly under water. When we reached the Humboldt current the water and air grew cold, and though we were roughly on the equator we were miserably cold and had to put on thick jerseys. The warm zones we had just left had coddled us to such a degree that we were frozen with the thermometer at 68 degrees F.

We managed to catch some large dorados which were excellent eating, but for the most part the fish were too big; they broke the lines and carried off the hooks. On account of the high sea we could not run into the wind when we got a bite, and had therefore to haul in the fish even if *Nordkaperen* was doing six or seven knots. We needed strong lines for that.

We were towing a 100 ft. line with a dummy fish as bait behind us, and when the watch shouted 'Fish!' there was a busy time on board, hauling and easing. We hoped every time that the fish would not be too large, but every other time it went off with bait and line. In this way we lost nearly all our fishing gear, but had some delicious fish dishes all the same.

One evening Bill produced quite a new form of distraction. When we were assembled in the cockpit as usual after enjoying the sunset, and darkness had fallen, Knud asked if anyone had seen our one and only electric torch. He found it immediately by the after hatch and turned it on to go and read the log. In some way this must have escaped Bill's notice, for to our great astonishment we saw him crawling on all fours round the binnacle as if searching for something. We found it hard to keep our faces.

'Turn the light just here,' he said to Knud, 'the torch must be here.' He was astonished at our peals of laughter. At last, when Knud had flashed the light in his face a few times, he realized what we were laughing at and then joined in vigorously himself. For several days—and nights—afterwards he was liable to burst out laughing suddenly when he thought of it.

In the Atlantic we had taken the seas on board mainly from astern, but now we made the acquaintance of the great deep sea billows from ahead as well. We had lashed the wheel fast, and *Nordkaperen* herself followed the rhythm of the seas excellently. She raised herself gently on to the top of the sea and slid safely down on the other side of the mountain of water. Occasionally, however, the rhythm was broken. The boat's bows hammered into the seas several times running, and she stopped and lay with the water pouring over the deck, but she was able to get under way again, slowly but surely. In the worst case, when an unusually high and steep sea came, the bows might hang for a moment in the air, after which she fell into the trough of the sea with a crash and lost her course. Then a helping hand was needed.

It was exciting to be on watch in the moonless part of the night. One could not see two yards ahead of one in the dark. It was like tobogganing with one's eyes shut. *Nordkaperen* was lifted up—and up—and up, and with a feeling as if one's inside was being drawn out one went down again—down and down. When the water ran away under her, and she fell down from a sea and the next wave outwitted us, one did not know which was bow or stern of the boat. One could only hear the water, bubbling and seething as it ran off the deck or splashed from one side to the other—and one might notice that one's rubber boots were full of water.

The last night but one we were at sea we were in collision with some drifting object with a crash that was felt all over the ship. We all woke and rushed up on deck to see what we had run into, but it had disappeared into the darkness astern. Fortunately the boat was undamaged. And so came the last night before we reached the mysterious Galapagos.

We crossed the Equator at 3 a.m. on December 7, and I was so busy writing that I missed the great moment. It had been intended that all the boys should have been called so that we might have a little glass of something, but now we had missed the baptism with all its ceremonies—the little glass, however, we had next day.

When I had finished my writing I went up on deck to see a new day begin. Hardly any two dawns are alike. Sky, clouds, and sea change from day to day, and if it is grey or rainy weather, there is a delicious sense of relief in seeing the first faint grey succeed to the oppressive darkness of the night. Perhaps the fact that the morning watch will soon be over makes the feeling still more cheerful.

It is the duty of the watch to examine sails and rigging for any damage they may have sustained in the course of the night. He has to throw small creeping things and flying fish overboard, read the log and barometer, put out the lights and make various entries regarding the strength of the wind, etc., in the log-book.

Meanwhile the time had advanced to 6 a.m., and Knud, who had the next watch, was called. The cook Bill too was hauled out of his bunk, and he at once set about making the morning coffee and served biscuits and marmalade. I could not turn in till I had got this inside me. But it was not easy to fall asleep when we were to make a landfall the same day. We sighted Santa Cruz, one of the largest islands of the Galapagos group, and soon several small volcanoes appeared on the horizon. Three or four hours later we landed in a little bay on the western side of the small island of Baltra, where we knew there was an American military base. We counted on getting fresh water and petrol there. As soon as we had anchored the deck was swarming with soldiers in bathing drawers. Our arrival was a pleasant diversion in their dreary life. Baltra was a flat monotonous island, consisting only of lava and ashes. The plants and trees which composed the island's vegetation could be counted. There was also some cactus and mangrove scrub.

We got fresh water—tasting strongly of chlorine—but petrol was not to be had for love or money.

The young colonel was stiff and disobliging.

'If one person has it the next must have it too, and then I should have my hands full,' he said.

Perhaps one sailing vessel a year calls at Baltra.

He turned his knife in the wound by ordering some thousands of gallons of aeroplane fuel to be thrown into the sea while we were there. It had grown too old, he said.

The soldiers' sympathies were on our side.

So we became law-breakers for the second time. One moonlight night we stealthily approached the landing-stage with a borrowed dinghy and took twenty gallons of a petrol from a drum which stood by a shed (the spot had been pointed out to us!). Two armed sentries helped us to keep a look-out. They had been ordered to do so by a superior, but they were more nervous than we were. They also helped us to fill up. While this was being done a military car came by, and we had to take cover hurriedly behind the shed. The sentries in their nervousness nearly did the same, but recovered their poise at the last moment.

We had a narrow shave of capsizing the dinghy and her precious cargo. A sea-lion suddenly came up blowing between the wharf and the dinghy. The shock we got infected the dinghy; she rolled over till her bulwarks were under water, but we got her on an even keel again.

On the morning of Tuesday, December 10, we started to sail to Academy Bay, on the southern side of Santa Cruz. We had heard, among other things, that there was a little Norwegian colony there. To avoid sailing right round Baltra—a long detour—we decided to go through a narrow strait between Santa Cruz and Baltra—the Itavaca Channel. We had a chart which showed that the fairway and reefs were marked with brooms, but we were bitterly to regret having tried to save ourselves a couple of hours' sailing.

When we approached the entrance to the strait we discovered that the chart had lied. There were no brooms or sea-marks. We held a brief council of war. We were in favour of forcing the straits, or at any rate having a try at it. The sea was calm, so I did not hesitate for a moment. The thought of saving fifteen miles was alluring.

All sails were struck and the engine started. Poul stood in the bows on the starboard side and took soundings uninterruptedly. Knud sat at the helm, and I crawled out to the end of the jib-boom to study the bottom and give warning of reefs or rocks. *Nordkaperen* glided forward at the lowest possible speed.

Despite the close look-out we were keeping we found time for a peep at the incredible life which was stirring in the water. Turtles, rays, large and small fish in all the colours of the rainbow were moving round the boat in the clear water. Several times I was so engrossed by what I saw that I only noticed at the last moment a coral block sticking up from the bottom.

The first reef approached, and we could see a faint line of surf across the channel. We endeavoured with great caution to find a way through at a place which appeared to be navigable. It was not—we were ashore! But luckily we got off again by putting the engine at full speed astern. Cautiously, keeping a close look-out, we glided along the reef, and at last we found a gap through which we succeeded in passing.

Now we were in the straits themselves—we had entered the trap.

We advanced with infinite slowness, while Poul called all the time: '9 ft.—13½ ft.—9 ft.—22 ft.—barely 3 ft.' and so on. Now and again I interrupted with 'starboard—more starboard—port again,' and suddenly yelled:

'Astern—astern for God's sake!'

And Knud went astern till the boat shook all over. The bottom had risen up before us to form a coral reef, just visible on the surface of the water.

But the way on the boat, combined with a strengthening current running our way, put *Nordkaperen* gently but decidedly on the reef. We swung out the boom and got a bit of a list on, set the engine full speed ahead, and at the same time shoved her off forward with loose spars and booms, and once more luck was with us. We got over the reef. We had now all begun to regret having tried to save ourselves the detour, but now there was no way back. We were still only halfway through the strait.

Once we were moving along at a snail's pace, really only drifting with the current, but about three ship's lengths farther forward we were ashore again. I had given warning, but the current was too strong, and we could not turn. Coral blocks rose on both sides of us.

This time all attempts to get off were vain. The engine was put full speed ahead and astern, we swung the boom out again and with ballast iron lashed to the end of it, so that the boat took a heavy list. We poled for all we were worth, but *Nordkaperen* would not move.

We had used a couple of hours more than we had calculated. The water had begun to fall, and the increasing current was pressing us farther and farther in on to the reef. There was a rise of six feet in the tide in the fairway round the islands, so the situation was critical.

If the water fell so much that *Nordkaperen* was lying right on her beam-ends, it was doubtful whether she would right herself when the water returned. We gave up all attempts to get her off and began to work with all our might to meet the dangerous situation which would arise if the boat turned over.

Bill was set to pump up the rubber boat—a wearisome job, but he called song to his aid. We others found rope, wire and other gear. The spinnaker boom and a spare boom were sacrificed. They were sawn into suitable lengths and put into place as temporary shores from the bulwarks to the reef.

Next, when the rubber boat was ready, an anchor was carried a long way out to starboard—the list being in the opposite direction—and a long thick rope was made fast from the throat halyard at the masthead to the anchor. *Nordkaperen* had gradually taken a heavy list, the water had fallen rapidly, and the shoring up was not effective, as the booms slipped on the coral bottom. We hauled carefully on the rope via the throat halyard, and to our joy *Nordkaperen* righted herself, but we squeezed the lemon too hard. The boat had been standing on the edge of a coral block, and when the mast had almost risen to a perpendicular position, she slipped down off her foundation, fell several inches, stood swaying for an instant as if not knowing which way to fall—and then tumbled over the wrong way with her bulwarks under water.

All our work had been in vain, and now the situation was worse than before.

The water was falling visibly from minute to minute, and round us the reef was beginning to appear above the surface. We had been working quickly before, but now we worked feverishly, and our work showed the marks of haste. The biggest anchor we had was carried out to port at top speed. It could not be placed in the rubber boat and was therefore lashed fast to an empty petrol container, which formed a pontoon. In our haste the lashings were not properly done, and when Poul and Bill had almost reached the right place with the anchor, it fell off the pontoon and sank in six feet of water. Unfortunately the rope had not yet been made fast. There was nothing for Bill and Poul to do but to jump into the water. Bill went under with a rope and fastened it to the anchor, while Poul stood by. Knud and I followed the course of operations eagerly from *Nordkaperen*. The water had begun to wash up on to the deck.

The very moment the shout of 'Ready!' came we began to haul hard on the rope that ran to the masthead, and a few exciting seconds followed. To begin with the anchor slipped once or twice, and the boat fell back again, but at last it caught and she rose inch by inch, despite the acute angle formed by the mast and the surface of the water.

We could see that Poul and Bill climbed into the rubber boat with unusual speed, and also heard them shouting something, but we had other things to think about. Not till they came closer and we saw their excited faces could we understand that something unusual had happened.

A shark had cruised round them and passed close to them, but fortunately had not detected them till they had finished their work.

Next time we wanted to see if an anchor was all right we could damned well dive in ourselves, they said.

Despite his excitement Bill wanted to give us an idea of the shark's size. 'It was as thick as that!' he said, throwing out his arms, and nearly tumbled backwards out of the rubber boat. Only a comical and acrobatic manoeuvre saved him.

*Nordkaperen* had gradually risen to an almost natural and safe position. So far she was saved.

While Bill was cooking breakfast, Knud and I went for a row up the strait to find a navigable way through.

It was anything but a pleasant sight to see the countless rocks and reefs lying in wait below the surface of the water. When we came back, *Nordkaperen* stood fairly dry and erect in her prison, but the water had ceased to fall. After our meal we all took a siesta to shorten the time of waiting, and while we slept the water rose.

In the afternoon the tide was high enough to float the boat, and our anchors did good service. We put the rope from the big anchor on the capstan, and slowly but surely we warped her afloat.

While we were salvaging ropes and anchors, we saw a motor-boat approaching us from the other end of the strait, and from her changes of course we could see that she had local knowledge. There were four men on board, two Germans and two South Americans, all with long hair and long beards. They came from Academy Bay and were bound for the military base. They said that there certainly had been seamarks and brooms in the strait, but that the military had removed them and prohibited sailing through the channel because several of their own craft had had their bottoms ripped up when they tried to do it.

They warned us against entering Academy Bay after dark on account of the many rocks and reefs, and offered to pilot us out of the strait—an offer which we gladly accepted.

We zigzagged out and soon had deep water under our keel again, which reassured us. We thanked our new friends for their pilotage and good advice, and took leave of them. We cast anchor in the shelter of a neighbouring point, as we could not land at Academy Bay in daylight. *Nordkaperen* now lay in a good sheltered position, close under high, steep cliffs on the eastern side of Santa Cruz.

We all sat on the bulwarks and looked at the coast. Great blocks of lava lay at the foot of the cliffs and formed breakwaters. We felt we should like to try whether the cliffs could be ascended from the sea side, and went in to the coast in the rubber boat to have a closer look. After an hour's search we found a spot which was suitable for an attempt at landing. The ascent was not so high as elsewhere, and the lava blocks which were piled on each other formed a sort of flight of steps nearly up to the top. Only the last bit seemed to offer problems.

Knud stayed behind with the rubber boat while we others began the climb. We crawled in open order so as not to have loose stones—or each other—falling on our heads. This was a good plan, for pieces of lava rained down ceaselessly in our tracks.

We tested each new lava block carefully to see if it was firm. When I had got halfway up I had a scare. The flat block I was standing on moved a few inches out towards the drop, and I had to jump quickly farther in on to the rock to restore the balance. It was with some caution that I bade farewell to my uncertain foothold. We could see Knud in the rubber boat far below, just a little dot. He had moved away from the cliffs, out of the way of fragments of lava. Bill had a special facility for sending these greetings down into the depths. He seemed to be enjoying himself greatly.

The last twenty or thirty feet caused us difficulties. There were no lava blocks and hardly any projections on which to support ourselves. Poul got up first, but in a short time we were all standing on the edge quite blown, and looking out over a singular piece of country. Rough black lumps of lava lay scattered about on a wide plain. In the background was the top of a volcano partly hidden by dark clouds. Leafless trees and bushes grew sparsely among the lava; their greyish-white naked branches veiled the landscape behind them. A few giant cactuses stood up here and there like crosses.

It was very quiet: not a bird or animal was to be seen or heard. 'I believe we've come to the moon,' said Bill.

We found each other talking in subdued voices—the stillness of the landscape affected our speech: involuntarily we looked about for skulls. Some twelve yards from where we stood the ground was cut by a few long, deep crevasses about six feet across, to the bottom of which we could not see. They marked the edge of the next landslip.

Having looked long enough at the moon landscape, we began the descent, which was almost worse than the ascent. Time after time Bill sent whole cartloads of fragments down in a thick cloud of dust. We called to him anxiously and were not reassured till we got an answer. When he had got halfway down he had to go up again. He had destroyed his own route, with the result that he reached the bottom long after the rest of us. On board *Nordkaperen* we had a busy time patching up the scars derived from our cliff-climbing.

Next morning we weighed anchor and continued our interrupted voyage to Academy Bay.

We got a head wind when we rounded the point, and had to tack the whole way to our destination. In the afternoon we met a strong adverse current, and even with a fresh wind we made hardly any progress. After an hour of this we moved cautiously nearer to the coast to avoid the current. We knew it was a dangerous coast and therefore kept far enough out not to be—all events according to the chart—in any kind of danger.

On one tack towards the coast Knud was at the helm, while we others were below. Suddenly a crash and shock made the boat quiver. *Nordkaperen* had run aground.

Poul, Bill and I were in such a hurry to get on deck that we stuck fast in the hatchway, but finally agreed on an order of precedence.

We were far from land and had felt ourselves immune from surprises of that kind, so there was, putting it at the lowest, slight confusion on board. *Nordkaperen* was indeed lifted off at once by the big swell, but all the same . . .

We must have got inside a reef and now wanted to find our way out again. A few tense minutes followed in which we expected a crash, but nothing happened.

The most mysterious thing was that Poul, who had begun sounding at once, did not find bottom, even with a line nearly 100 ft. long. *Nordkaperen* must have struck a submarine mountain-top or a drifting wreck. The chart showed nothing. The boat had sprung a small leak and was taking in a little water. but this ceased in the course of a few days. To be sure of reaching Academy Bay before it grew dark, we started the engine, and at 6 p.m. we reached our destination and dropped anchor as near the coast as we dared.

## CHAPTER VIII

# *The Galapagos Islands*

A FEW rowing boats came out to us at once. They were manned by a miscellaneous collection of people differing widely in appearance, age and nationality. We had difficulty in understanding each other, as they spoke only Spanish, but they all eagerly accepted the wine and cigarettes we offered them, and they were as delighted as children when we let them see our pictures.

Among the visitors was a young, slightly intoxicated South American, wearing a faded old uniform and wooden shoes. He grabbed hold of our passports and ship's papers several times, and each time I took them away from him again amiably but firmly. He smiled apologetically, pointed to himself and then at the list of the ship's company. I shook my head and shut the papers up in a locker. Whether he wanted to travel as a passenger or be taken on as a seaman, there was nothing doing at any rate on board *Nordkaperen*. He poured out a flood of drunken rubbish which I did not understand. The visit became prolonged and the visitors showed no sign of disappearing. On the contrary, they sent a man ashore to fetch more.

When the boat came back, there was a Norwegian in it. His name was Graffe, and him we could understand.

I cannot deny that I felt a trifle sheepish when Graffe presented the South American wearing wooden shoes as the commanding officer on Santa Cruz, whose duty it was to inspect and stamp our passports and papers. Fortunately he was neither offended nor triumphant, but smiled apologetically when I respectfully handed him the file-cover containing our documents. Among the papers, by mistake, was a receipt for some charts we had bought in Denmark. It was thoroughly examined, and then taken ashore with the other papers for stamping. His ideas about ship's papers were generally speaking pretty vague. He did not seem to know the difference between a Customs clearance certificate and a tram ticket.

Graffe told us that the commanding officer on Santa Cruz had under him only a force of six soldiers—and they were all in the cells! Two of them were let out every evening to play cards with the C.O. or make palm wine for him. For that matter the whole force was sent home to Ecuador while we were there.

This side of Santa Cruz, by the way, was more inviting than the one we had encountered on our first landing. Here there were earth and vegetation—if not much—and pleasant little huts peeped out from among palms and other greenery.

The whole island was inhabited by about a hundred souls, of which the Norwegian colony amounted to a good twenty. Most of the Norwegians lived up on the mountain slopes and supported themselves by farming.

Other nations were represented, but by far the greater part of the population were Ecuadorians, who could not conceal their descent from the South American Indians. Their way of life was extremely primitive, but anyone wishing to live a carefree life without much to do could find a paradise on this island.

The men could, and most of them did, hang about all day without lifting a finger. Their only clothing was a pair of shorts. Their beards and hair ran wild. There was nothing in the way of taxes—except in name—no health insurance or club subscriptions, no bills, no doctor, no midwife, no priests, no police, no interference from the authorities.

There was a sufficiency of fish, fruit, vegetables, tea and tobacco plants. Wild cows, horses, pigs and asses could be captured or shot with ease up in the mountains. The only communication the inhabitants had with the mainland was a small steamer which came from Ecuador three or four times a year. We were fortunate enough to witness the little Government steamer's arrival. The whole district was decorated with flags, the male inhabitants shaved and put on clean shirts. The C.O. was actually sober and came out to us with an Ecuadorian flag, which we finally had to fly as a visitors' flag. Although he did not say it, we understood that he would appreciate our wearing white. A great event was impending!

Graffe had told us that the Ecuadorian fleet consisted of one small steamer, 86 years old and of 200 tons or so. She always had a list to port.

It was a real experience for us to witness her arrival. The intense excitement relieved itself in general cheering when a cloud of smoke appeared on the horizon. The steamer brought mail and other good things.

She was indeed a shabby old grey steamer with a long thin funnel, and she had too, as we had been told, a heavy list to port, or, as Knud said, 'She's pouring water out of her ear!'

When she came nearer we saw that all the passengers were standing up on the bridge with the white-clad officers. There was hardly any room for the man at the wheel. On deck a crew, three times as large as necessary, was milling about in confusion. The steamer passed our anchorage slowly, and Poul suddenly jumped into the air with a shout:

'Why, good Lord, she's dipping to us!'

He just managed to dip the Dannebrog quickly while the officers of the Ecuadorian fleet were busy studying *Nordkaperen*. They ought never to have done this. There was a bump, and the steamer was on a reef. The engines were put full speed astern—so hard that the old tub creaked and rattled, and she shook herself off the shoal pretty quickly. She backed right out of the bay, steamed round for half an hour and approached for the second time—in a more correct manner. We had a man by the ensign ready to dip, in case they should think of doing it again. They did not.

Among the few inhabitants of the island who lived in a pretty, well-built house, and who made anything out of life from an economic standpoint, was a Norwegian fisherman called Stampa. He owned a large fishing-boat and a few smaller craft. Although he had four or five Indians in his pay, he worked hard and energetically himself, and was—according to what others told us—a capable and successful fisherman. He went to sea for five or six days at a time and returned with a kind of cod he called *gubbe* (old man). They were cleaned and salted and then had to be dried.

When the steamer came from the mainland Stampa had collected a fine pile of dried fish, which brought in a good deal of money.

He had come to the island with a Norwegian expedition in 1929. It consisted of about thirty Norwegians who wanted to fish and run a canning factory on the shore of Academy Bay. They had brought machinery and materials, and all went well for a year. But then the post of manager fell vacant, and nineteen Norwegians laid claim to it. The result was that the whole thing collapsed, and when the factory was burnt down shortly afterwards the last spark of life in the undertaking, on which so many dreams had been built, was extinguished. Only a little Norwegian colony and a heap of old rusty machines were left to recall the enterprise.

We heard this story at a party given one evening by Stampa and his wife. This party was very international; no fewer than six nations were represented—Danes, Norwegians, one solitary Swede, Germans, Ecuadorians (who spoke Spanish), and Bill, who was an American. We exchanged views in a roundabout manner. Thus a question had to be addressed to Stampa, who passed it on to a Spanish-speaker, who in turn passed it on to the German to whom it was addressed. The answer came back by the same roundabout route.

It was half an hour's walk to Stampa's house from the place where we usually landed. Our route was along sandy tracks, through mangrove scrub, along the edge of the shore and between lava blocks and cactus, and it was hard to find our way in the dark. The house lay on the edge of a quiet little lagoon, where his boats were at anchor. The entrance to the lagoon was very difficult and complicated. There were reefs and rocks on either hand, and *Nordkaperen* unfortunately could not get in.

I was standing on the edge of the lagoon one morning and wondering at the shifting colours of the mirror-like surface. Stampa came up to me:

'Would you like a sail round the lagoon?' he asked. I was a little surprised, as the lagoon was apparently no larger than a football field. I could see everything from where I stood. So I answered politely, but without any great interest: 'Yes thank you, that would be very pleasant.'

We waded out to a little open motor-boat and started it, and our round trip began.

On the eastern side of the lagoon there were rocks and reefs, on the south side steep cliffs; elsewhere it was surrounded by mangrove scrub. Stampa steered the boat in among rocks and ledges that projected from the water. We went at full speed, but I felt quite safe. I knew that he knew the channel inside out, like his own pocket, but when he steered steadily at full speed right towards a cliff, I thought he had gone mad. I looked in alarm at his quiet, weather-beaten face, but there was nothing abnormal to be seen in it—just a little smile that puckered the corners of his eyes. When we were a couple of boats' lengths from the rough cliff, I detected a narrow opening into a channel about 200 yards long. It was only six or nine feet wide and had presumably been caused by an earthquake. It bore the northern name of Lake Ocland.

Stampa was still going at full speed when he steered into it. It was a curious natural phenomenon that revealed itself to us. The sheer cliffs, as high as houses, threatened to close over the boat. Plants with bright red flowers grew here and there on the cliff-side, shining out on the perpendicular wall like little lanterns in the gloom. Crabs of every possible colour, from sky-blue to dark red, sat in great numbers on the wall. They plunged into the water frightened at the noise of the engine as we came along. When one looked straight up one could see a narrow strip of sky between the menacing overhang of the cliffs and isolated silhouettes of the prehistoric-looking iguanas, lizards more than three feet long, which abounded on the coasts of Santa Cruz. Many kinds of fish were darting about ahead of the boat. There were still sharks and rays among them—certainly little fellows, but they contributed to the tense, mysterious atmosphere which brooded over the ravine. Up till now Stampa had not said a word, but had allowed me to study the surroundings unobserved.

At last he said:

'There are one or two Indians here who declare that they have seen a giant cuttle-fish in this channel.'

He said this very quietly. I, on the contrary, looked down uneasily into the dark bottomless depths and moved a little farther back into the boat. Suppose a gripping arm were to come up out of the water and capsize the boat!

'But,' Stampa added, 'I haven't seen any cuttle-fish in the seventeen years I've lived here.'

I breathed a sigh of relief.

At last we reached the end of the channel, which terminated in a kind of circular basin. Here there was more light and more plants and the walls were hardly as steep. It was a very pretty scene. We turned the boat with difficulty and sailed out again. When we stood on the edge of the lagoon again I looked back at the cliffs, but was quite unable to locate the opening leading into the mysterious channel.

The evening we arrived at Academy Bay we passed a small island about a mile and a half from the coast. It was called 'Jensen's Island'.

We had seen through the telescope a number of sea-lions on the beaches. This was something which merited closer inspection.

The inhabitants warned us against attempting to land on the island, saying that the boat would be dashed to pieces by the breakers. We did not doubt that this was so, but we did not intend to use an ordinary boat; on the contrary, we should use our tried friend, the rubber boat, which we were sure would stand the test.

Poul and Knud had been for a tiring walk in the hills the day before and did not want to come, so Bill and I started alone on the wearisome pull out to the island.

The current and wind were against us, and it took us an hour and a half to get out there. We became rather dubious when we saw the mighty Pacific breakers rolling in upon the island from every side, and we made a circle round it—at a respectful distance—to find the most suitable place to land. At last we decided, took a few quick strokes till a sea took hold of us, and went rushing in towards cliffs and lava blocks. We shook off the surf just as we reached land, and before the next sea came we had secured a foothold in a comparatively safe place. But we were soaked up to the waist. In a breathing-space we got the rubber boat up on to dry land.

We jumped from stone to stone to get farther into the island, but came to a piece of water that barred all further advance. Although we had looked carefully at the place, we had not seen that what we had landed on was a separate little island. We had therefore to go back again and had a lot of trouble in getting out into open water. When a sea drew back, we flung the boat out. Bill jumped in first and rowed with all his might till the next sea had shattered itself against the cliffs. Then, in the interval, he came in and took me off. There was only room for one at a time on the narrow ledge from which we jumped.

I got on board safely, but this time Bill failed to get the boat clear of the surf. We were flung up on to a lava block in a cloud of spray and water, hung there for a moment and then bounded off again. A good thing she was not a wooden boat—if she had been only a few dozen fragments would have remained!

Even though we were in a bit of a mess, Bill had presence of mind enough to row out at once, and we just got through.

This experience, however, had not quenched our desire to make another landing, and we landed on the right island as successfully as before—certainly drenched, but with our cameras dry. The island was about 300 by 400 yards, covered with mangrove, and the beach consisted of large irregular lava blocks. Only on the east side was there a little strip of sand.

We leapt from stone to stone and were suddenly confronted with our first sea-lion. Bill nearly jumped over it, but discovered his mistake at the last moment. It was a full-grown bull—and it was fast asleep. We threw a few pebbles at it, and it opened its eyes in bewilderment. I have always supposed sea-lions to be friendly, sociable creatures, so I tried to attract it as if it were a dog, calling 'come on, old man!' and slapping my knees.

It did come—but not in the way I had expected. It sprang straight at us with its yellow teeth bared, growling and barking. Bill and I tumbled down in our attempts to escape and both fell off the rock into a foot and a half of water. Up again and away! The sea-lion, however, must have thought we had been scared enough. It made its way slowly back to its sleeping-place, but followed us with its eyes and growled as we passed, making a wide detour to avoid it.

We proceeded along the north side of the island and now and again came upon similar sea-lions, but they were timid and ran away from us. There were also many pelicans, which sat with an omniscient and reflective air. We were almost within touching distance of them before they took wing.

The great surprise came on the eastern side of the island. There countless sea-lions lay basking on the sand and rocks. There were light grey, dark grey, reddish and shining black specimens—all cows, with their roly-poly babies close round them. They were apparently all asleep. On the rocks which rose above the little strip of sand sat groups of marine iguanas; they were, without exaggeration, in thousands.

'One can't starve here,' said Bill, stopping and gazing at them in astonishment.

We had heard that the ugly black iguanas were delicious eating. Where there was a little room left on the shore gulls and pelicans sat, but none of these creatures took any notice of us. We had to push the iguanas off the rocks to find somewhere to put our feet. Having made quite sure that no bull sea-lion was concealed in the crowd, we tried to entice cows out into the water to get some photographs. But none of them paid any attention to our shouts and yells; they slept on undisturbed. We awakened them one by one by tickling their sides. They opened their clear, beautiful eyes, looked at us calmly—and shut their eyes again. They had had this little island to themselves for many generations and knew nothing of the wickedness of men. But now a subconscious fear complex did spring up in them. They opened their eyes again and fled in panic towards the water, calling anxiously to their children, who waddled whimpering after their mothers.

We were still engaged in waking the sleepers when an ominous growling and barking made us turn round. And up out of the water shot a big sea-lion—such a magnificent fellow that we were near forgetting to make tracks for sheer admiration of him. He was a colossus. The end of his muzzle was on a level with our chests, and his splendid black shining body was propelled towards us at a clumsy gallop, while his fearful teeth were bared in an ugly snarl. Then we woke up and fled into the midst of the iguanas, which flung themselves down from the rocks in terror. If we had known that sea-lions could be so dangerous, we should have brought fire-arms with us for use in self-defence.

The chief, however, soon grew tired of pursuing us, and when the coast was clear we crept stealthily back. He was now busy nosing round all his wives and seeing if they or their children had suffered any injury. The whole colony was in an uproar, but he soon rallied his troops, and the harem now lay in safety at the water's edge.

We had noticed that individual sea-lions had emerged from the mangrove scrub. This had to be looked into. After several vain attempts to photograph the great bull, who rushed furiously at us every time, we went into the scrub. We followed narrow tracks made by the sea-lions and at last reached the centre of the island. Here there was a crater filled with sand, an open space about twelve yards across cleared of mangrove. This was the centre, or place of assembly, of the colony, and from it countless tracks, like rays, led out to the water. It looked too as if it had been a battle-ground, where internal disputes between the bulls had been decided. Many skeletons of well-grown sea-lions suggested this. They had lost their lives in contests for the ownership of the harem. There were many depressions and holes in the shelter of the scrub, and we found most of the skeletons in there.

When we had looked about in the scrub for half an hour, we went back to the strip of beach. On our way to the boat we came upon quite a small sea-lion cub, lying quite alone and looking curiously at us. Bill was determined to photograph it, and knelt down to take a close-up. I was standing with my back to the scrub, when there was a crashing and creaking just behind me. I had just time to jump to one side when a large bull sea-lion burst out of the scrub. It brushed my left arm without noticing me and made straight for Bill, raging and snarling. Bill had to run for his life. The photograph of the cub was never taken. We fled in different directions, but found one another again.

The sun was now low in the sky, and we must hurry home before darkness fell. We found the rubber boat, and now the same performance began—we trying to get on board and clear of the surf. After the third attempt we were afloat outside the reef and rocks, drenched to the skin.

The mist of spray flung up by the surf over the island was conspicuous in the rays of the evening sun. So it was, unfortunately, when we had our photographs developed.

One more little excitement was in store for us before we got home to *Nordkaperen*.

We were halfway there when we thought we saw the dorsal fins of two sharks following the boat at a distance of a few yards. I wanted to slash at them with an oar to chase them away, but restrained myself. They were not like ordinary sharks!

Bill rose up in the boat to see better, but subsided again quickly with an expression of consternation on his face.

'Christ, they're not sharks, it's a huge ray!'

I raised myself a little to see if Bill was right. He was.

It was the ray's side fins that now and again came up above the water. Never before or since have I seen such a thumping fellow, though rays were common in the Galapagos islands. It was a good nine feet across.

We knew that it was a very dangerous fish, and the minutes in which it followed our yellow rubber boat were not pleasant ones for us. Bill and I whispered to one another. We dared not row either faster or slower, or we might make the monster more inquisitive. Sometimes it was only a few inches from the boat's stern, and each time I cautiously moved a little forward. It was an ugly customer to have at one's back!

Stampa had told us that a year before a giant ray had attacked his fishing-boat and tried to capsize it. We could not help thinking of that now, and Bill whispered:

'Do you think it can upset us?'

Its back was as broad as two rubber boats!

'No, no,' I whispered back, though with no great conviction.

Bill began to giggle out loud, and I hurriedly told him to be quiet. He caught a crab with one oar, and the irregularity in the boat's rhythm attracted the ray and brought it closer. It continued to show an uncomfortable degree of interest in the strange yellow fish, but at least it must have discovered that the 'fish' was not edible. Then it turned away. It was not till several minutes afterwards, however, that we began to breathe freely.

Supper was an hour late that day. When Poul and Knud heard about our adventures they wanted to go and see the island, and we planned another landing, but nothing came of it.

However, Bill and I were out again in search of adventures a few days later. A little way up the coast, north-east of where *Nordkaperen* lay, there were some reefs about half a mile out in the water. They were visible at low tide. The inhabitants had told us that lobsters were to be caught there, and this absorbed Bill entirely. He had been an expert in lobster-catching in California,

His method was simple enough; he just dived and caught them with his hands. The Pacific lobster has no claws like its northern brethren, but a pair of gloves was necessary all the same, for the lobsters pricked horribly.

He persuaded me to go over the reef with him. We landed on the north-east side, and all went easily and smoothly. Bill was soon ready for the hunt. He had on watertight rubber goggles, swimming fins and a pair of thick gloves.

We had learned that sharks were never seen round the reef, so that side of the matter did not trouble us. Further, Bill was only a few yards from the reef and could reach dry land quickly if after all a shark should show itself. He was soon busy diving and hunting, and I only saw him now and then, when he came up to get a breath of air. Bill was a very good diver. He could go down to a depth of twenty to twenty-five feet and hold his breath for an incredibly long time.

I passed the time of waiting in studying the water-holes round about on the reef, and was in a continual state of amazement at the strange, swarming, brilliantly coloured life which displayed itself in them.

I had, with some trouble, fished up a pretty green water-plant to look at it more closely, when to my astonishment it began to crawl down into the water again. I let it crawl, and fished it up again in a little while to discover the mystery. I found that the plant was growing on the back of a shell-fish which reminded me strongly of a star-fish. In the same water-hole I prodded with a little harpoon at a queer creature which at intervals stuck out its head from a crack between the stones. It had a head like a giant smoked herring which gaped. The length of its body I never ascertained; the fellow was always too quick for me.

Bill returned—with no lobsters—for a rest. The tide had begun to get fairly high, and I proposed that we should make a start soon, but Bill wanted to have half an hour more, and when that was up just a quarter of an hour more, and then another quarter of an hour. But all the time not a sign of a lobster. I wondered at his energy. He dived and puffed and blowed, and sometimes I could not distinguish between him and some hugh turtles which were swimming about in the neighbourhood.

The water had covered almost the whole reef, when at last there came a yell from Bill. He had caught no fewer than two lobsters at once, but now the communications between us were cut. To get over to him on the other side of the reef, I must go in the rubber boat, row clear of the reef and make a wide detour outside the breakers.

Everything went very well, till I had practically reached him. I was occupied in finding a good landing-place when Bill pointed out to sea and shouted:

'Hallo! look there! good luck!'

I turned round and saw what I had feared: several huge tidal waves, a wall of water from six to nine feet high, were on their way in towards us. The seas came shouting and stumbling like drunken men who have lost their balance. They looked anything but pleasant.

There was only one thing to be done; I must row to meet them and take them on the rise and, in general see that I got as far away from the reef as possible. Bill had crawled up on the highest point of the reef and was following my movements with a malicious grin.

I managed the first wave fairly well. I rowed to meet it as hard as I could, and the rubber boat was lifted up as by a giant's hand and flung up in the air, while cascades of water poured on board. I succeeded in keeping the boat upright and got clear of the surf with a few vigorous strokes. The rubber boat had inside pockets, and my camera was in one of these. The water was washing about on the level of the pocket, so I took the apparatus out and put it inside my jacket. During this manoeuvre, which had to be executed rapidly, I lost the starboard oar, and a desperate attempt to recapture it failed completely. I succeeded in putting together the spare oar, the separate parts of which were in another pocket, but I was unable to get the boat straight and the next wave hit her broadside on. The boat was whirled for some way with the wave before I became master of the situation, and was now full of water and unmanageable, so that when the third and biggest wave came, I was a defenceless victim. Though I tried with all my might I could not get the boat out of the surf. She was swept in towards the reef at a dizzy speed. The boat gyrated like a merry-go-round; now my legs were sticking straight up in the air, now I had to press my back against the bottom of the boat in order not to overbalance. As if by a miracle the sea freed me and the boat some twelve yards from the reef, and luckily I had kept a firm grip of the oars, so I could row westward as fast as the waterlogged state of the boat would allow. The seas that followed were not so tremendous.

But what about Bill?

I had had an opportunity in the intervals between the seas of seeing how he was faring. He was convulsed with laughter at my acrobatic exercises. Correspondingly, one of the reasons for my failure to cope with the last wave was my amusement at his manner of taking things.

The first wave went high over his head and washed both him and the lobsters and the malicious grin for a considerable distance. But when he came up again, God bless my soul! he had still got both the lobsters, nor, so far as I could see, had the grin disappeared.

The second wave treated him in the same way, but he still held the two lobsters triumphantly in his hands. The grin had now become uncontrolled laughter. When he saw me surf-riding on the last wave, his laughter became a regular paroxysm, and he let himself fall backwards into the water before the sea reached him. First the lobsters bobbed up above the rocks, as in a Punch and Judy show, followed by the still grinning face.

The water had become rather disturbed after the passage of the tidal wave. It was difficult to reach the reef from the sea side, especially with a waterlogged boat, and I was a long way out. My camera had been soaked and demanded immediate inspection.

so I preferred to row home to *Nordkaperen*, empty the boat of water, and then go back behind the reef and take Bill off. He agreed.

'O.K.,' he shouted back, 'then I'll catch one or two more lobsters.'

I was curious to know how he was going to catch more lobsters and at the same time look after the two he had already, but he managed it very neatly. He placed the lobsters between two stones and began to dive again, this time behind the reef.

When I reached *Nordkaperen* we emptied the rubber boat, and Poul rowed in behind the reef to fetch Bill, while I myself tried to save my camera. Unfortunately it had got more water into it than it could stand.

Bill had really succeeded in catching another lobster, so our supper was something out of the common.

The hour of our departure from Acadamy Bay was approaching, and we received farewell visits. The Norwegians up in the mountains brought us farewell presents—fruit of all kinds, vegetables and dried fish. They were well-disposed towards us and it was a pleasure to them to make these gifts, but we got four times as much food as we could eat before it went bad. There were, among other things, four huge sticks of bananas, papaya, pineapples, smoked and dried fish, eggs and many other good things. They entreated us to stay over Christmas, but unfortunately we had to say no thank you. We had no time.

We sailed on the morning of Friday, December 20, and it was our intention to visit Tagus Cove, a little rocky harbour on the western side of Albemarle, another large island in the Galapagos group. This intention never materialized.

There was not much wind, and we used the engine for several hours. When at last the wind came, it was against us. It disappeared again at dusk, and we had got no farther than the little island of Tortuga, about forty miles from Academy Bay. We tried to slip past the island with the little wind there was, but a strong current forced us in towards it. We were short of petrol and could not afford to start the engine, so we went about and stood out to sea. *Nordkaperen* took what seemed to us an endless time to get away from this dangerous neighbourhood. In the dark we could no longer see Tortuga, but only hear the thundering of the breakers. Next morning we were not much nearer our destination and there was still very little wind. It looked as if we had entered a windless zone.

After long consideration I altered our sailing plans. The boys were much disappointed when I told them that we were to miss Tagus Cove. Bill was grumpy for several days.

I understood their disappointment, but we had before us a stretch of about 4,000 miles to Tahiti. We were short of water—we had only brackish water from Academy Bay—and we had hardly any petrol. We could not be at all sure of having our stocks renewed on Albemarle, an almost uninhabited island. Another important reason was that we had no special chart of the waters round Albemarle, only an old general chart.

We had felt the atmosphere of mystery and excitement in the air over the Galapagos, and we all hoped to see the islands again.

As we gradually worked our way out into the south-easterly trade wind, things began to move. A fresh breeze on our port quarter carried us swiftly towards Tahiti. Now and then we did daily runs which we never achieved before or since despite our best efforts.

Thus, from noon on December 25 to noon on December 26 we sailed 222 miles, an average of 9.25 knots. The following days were not much worse, so we were in high spirits and already dreaming of a record voyage. But this was not to be. Our speed gradually decreased again—190 miles, 180, 165, and so on, till we got down to 51, our lowest day's run.

But none of the wind that came was wasted. Whether it was fresh or light, we were continually at work and experimenting with the sails. We set every imaginable combination: big jib as flying jib, storm-sail as jib, little jib as studding-sail under the boom, storm mizen as square sail on the mainmast, etc. Where there was the slightest possibility of a breath of air getting through a sail was set.

'It's like a rag-shop,' said Bill.

But the many rags carried *Nordkaperen's* sturdy little hull through the high, long foaming Pacific seas at a good speed.

In the waters two hundred miles south-west of the Galapagos whalers would have had a good chance. There were swarms of whales round us day and night, small and large. Sometimes we sailed through crowds extending farther than the eye could reach. One morning at sunrise, when I was on watch, I sighted a large school of little whales. The men were fast asleep, and I thought I would demonstrate my efficiency by surprising them with a whale steak. I altered course to starboard, right into the school; I got out the big harpoon, fitted wire and rope to it and was ready to attack. *Nordkaperen* kept on her course towards one of the biggest whales, and I stood ready for action on the fore-deck.

As the whales gradually came nearer, they increased alarmingly in size. There was presumably a good deal more of them under water than above, and I began to revise my ideas of little whales. When we were a few yards from the first, which lay right across our bows, I realized its dimensions for the first time. It was about thirty feet long and as thick as an elephant.

I flung the harpoon down, rushed to the wheel and the boat answered her helm at the last moment. We just avoided running into the colossus, and I had to show the utmost alertness to get out of the school again. The whales showed no fear of *Nordkaperen*. I was certainly more frightened than they were. The harpoon and gear were quietly put away again, and I did not mention the episode till a long time afterwards.

On Christmas Eve we all shaved, and the cook Bill had an evening off. Poul took over the post of cook and gave us a Danish supper with *biksemad** and rice porridge. Bill decorated a banana stick as a Christmas tree and made a Father Christmas of pineapple and melons. He had a few old socks round him, and in these

* A kind of hash of chopped meat and potatoes.

were the presents: cigarettes which Bill had stolen from us, razor blades, a roll of toilet paper and things of that kind. In Knud's sock was a small tin of grease with an inscription on the lid: 'For greasing the keel when *Nordkaperen* goes over a reef.'

We had subjected Knud to some harmless and cheerful teasing because he happened to have been at the wheel every time we had run aground.

It was a Christmas Eve beyond all expectations, and our last bottle of rum was used to wash down the *biksemad*.

Then came the moment we had long feared. All the half-ripe bananas we had brought from the Galapagos became ripe at once. We went about with swollen cheeks and grew breathless from eating bananas. We stuffed ourselves with them all round the clock and had not the heart to throw any of them overboard. Rather burst than leave anything over! Bill served up bananas in every form: roast, mashed, as butter, as potatoes, as salad or roasted with other things. There was no limit to his invention.

We got rather blown out, had stomach-aches and slept badly. At last we had to give up. We came to loathe bananas, and those that remained were thrown overboard. After that papaya and pineapple and the other fruits disappeared from the bill of fare, and for our last fortnight at sea we had to live on depressing preserves. Fishing was not much good. Mindful of all our broken lines, we had acquired in the Galapagos a windlass with a thin steel wire on it. It was lashed pretty fast round the mizen-mast and was fitted with strong hooks calculated to take fish of 200 or 300 lbs. The first time we got a bite the hook straightened itself out, and we never saw a sign of a fish. At the second attempt a still stronger hook was torn off the wire. The third time we set two hooks back to back, and fastened them tighter than before. When a bite came it was so violent that the brake of the windlass was smashed, the crankhandle bumped down against the deck and was bent, and the windlass leapt in its lashings. We all jumped to it, but had to content ourselves with saving a line with nothing on it.

The bait, which consisted of a solid metal dummy fish with a bunch of feathers behind it to conceal the hooks, was still there, but both hooks were broken off at the bend, and only the two halves of them remained. Deep, clean grooves in the metal fish showed that some fearful teeth had got hold of it. We never discovered what monster it had been. The probability is that it was a giant shark, which must certainly have had toothache for a few days after.

After one or two further vain attempts we gave up fishing with the windlass and tried again with an ordinary line, but the results were miserable. Fortune had quite deserted us.

In the last fortnight before we reached Tahiti we came into variable weather. We had arrived in regions where it was the rainy season. Squally weather with violent gusts of wind alternated with no wind at all. It was weather that sorely tried our rigging and sails. When there was no wind rigging and sails were chafed in the heavy swell. When the squalls came the wind raged like a fury. We did not escape the usual minor damage: the end of the crosstrees was broken; the luff ropes of the working jib and mainsail snapped, although they were of steel wire; the backstay on the port side snapped; the lamp bracket was broken away; all sheets had to be taken out: foresail, topsail and jib were badly torn, and there were small tears in the rest of the sails. We had, indeed, enough mending to do. Meanwhile time was passing. The nearer we came to our destination the longer the days grew. Our day's runs grew shorter and shorter, and this increased our impatience. On January 12, 1947, we passed Puka-Puka, the first island in the Tuamotu group, which consists of some fifty coral islands (atolls) in a semi-circle round Tahiti and east of that island.

We did not see Puka-Puka, we passed it at night; things worked out so unfortunately that time after time we had to pass islands in the dark. We had an extra look-out on deck on the nights when we were sailing through the swarm of islands. The nights were moonless and the sky overclouded. It rained most of the time. Knud had plenty of work with his instruments; the weather was not favourable for observation, and we had all the time to deviate from the course laid down on account of variable winds and strong, unaccountable currents. The chart was pored over and discussed as never before. Poul was often up in the crosstrees looking out for islands that ought to be there, but he usually saw none. Or he discovered islands which ought not to be there, which caused confusion on board. Bill begged and prayed for a landfall, but in vain.

After several days of peculiar tension we had Faaiti, the last island in the Tuamotu group, astern of us, and we could breathe freely again. We had passed very close to Faaiti to study it, and we noted only one single hut in the shelter of the palm trees on the beach. A fire was lighted there, from which came thick white smoke. As the entrance to the lagoon was just there, the inhabitants naturally thought we were going to land. The smoke signals were without doubt an invitation and intended to mark the channel.

But we conquered our desires. We were in a hurry. We were still 240 miles from Tahiti.

CHAPTER IX

# *South Sea Paradise*

On the last two nights before we reached Tahiti we experienced an electric storm. The lightning flared and glimmered all round the horizon as it had done in the Caribbean—cold tropical lightning without thunder. On the night of Sunday the 19th we did not sleep very much, for next day we should see the earthly paradise—Tahiti. We had reckoned on having it in sight when it grew light on Monday morning—we were only a short thirty miles away—but there was nothing to be seen but a full circle of misty horizon. This was strange. Could there have been an error in our observations?

At last we detected some mountain tops up above the clouds. But we were closer than we had expected, and the beautiful mountain tops and volcanoes of Tahiti gradually appeared out of the mist. The usual preparations for landing were made, and we were ready several hours before it was necessary. While waiting we studied the pretty, smiling, world-famed island. After we had feasted our eyes on the colours and shadows of the mountains we could begin to distinguish houses and trees and churches, and soon we were so close under the island that we could see Papeete, the only port of Tahiti, where white South Sea schooners lay side by side behind the reef, which formed a natural breakwater for the harbour.

When we were near enough to the harbour, we started the engine and took in sail, but then hell broke loose. The light wind suddenly grew strong, and we had the greatest difficulty in taking in sail. The sails beat about and flapped like mad things. The engine, as usual, was not much use when it was blowing, and there were indications that the hull was overgrown with barnacles. We could not get up any speed at all. Close by was a foaming reef. In these conditions, and with the dangerous entrance to Papeete ahead of us—the current there could be as swift as five knots—we found it most advisable to hoist the pilot flag.

The pilot came out at once and brought *Nordkaperen* into a safe berth in harbour through a channel which passed between two reefs and for part of the way close alongside a reef. It proved later that the expression 'a safe berth' was a rather indefinite one.

A Tahitian police officer came on board when we had made fast. He examined our papers very carefully, and when he could find nothing whatever to object to he was very disgusted and thought of something for himself. Was our passport not stamped by a French authority?

We pointed out that it was not necessary. We had special ship's papers which were valid all over the world; moreover, a voyage round the world would take fifteen years if we had to get a separate visa for every port.

'It's unfortunate—hm—yes, extremely serious,' he said. Tahiti had its own laws.

Three packets of Chesterfields now changed hands, and the serious police officer was willing to try to ease matters for us, but at the same time made clear to us the frightfulness of the prospect if his action should fail.

Quite absent-mindedly I gave him three more packets. He thought there was now more hope of his being able to settle the matter satisfactorily for us. When a tin of milk and two more packets of cigarettes had been laid upon the altar, he gave us the impression that he could easily clear up such a trifling matter by his personal influence.

Later, over drinks in the town, we were slapping each other on the back and he was asking most politely if he could buy a few more tins of milk. I said I would think it over. I was rather proud of being able to get round a person in authority in this manner until I found out that it had been quite unnecessary.

Our papers had been good enough all the time.

After the police examination three Customs officials came on board at once. *Nordkaperen* was examined for the first and only time during the whole of our voyage—and what an examination it was!

Had we any cigarettes on board? They waited eagerly for the answer.

'Oh yes,' we assured them, but added: 'Not many, though. Just take a sample!'

They greedily accepted five packets each. After that they did not think that our five or six thousand packets were too many for our own use. Later, at a restaurant, we were offered cigarettes at a stiff black market price that were exactly the same brand and in the same wrappings as those we had given the officials.

Three hours were spent in negotiations with the authorities. Not till the last had gone ashore again had we leisure to study our surroundings.

In the harbour—one long quay with the reef as a breakwater—lay many white South Sea schooners, some motor trading vessels, fishing and pleasure craft. These were ships from all the islands and ports in the South Seas which were seeking shelter in the hurricane season. The waters round Tahiti were visited by one or two hurricanes annually, but on Tahiti itself there had not been a hurricane in living memory. This was one of the reasons why Papeete was a sought-after port in the months of January, February and March—the hurricane season. The crews were using the time of waiting to give the boats an overhaul. *Nordkaperen* lay at anchor, stern on to the quay, and what a quay!

Between the water and the street that ran along the quay there was a strip of grass about ten yards wide, with tall, spreading, shady trees. On the other side of the street also there was grass, and here the trees overshadowed low, brightly painted houses. The central part of Papette was close to this waterside street, which was used by the population for their evening walks.

A large crowd of Tahitians had quickly assembled close to

*Nordkaperen* to study and discuss her. We stole curious glances at them to see if the reports of the beauty of the Polynesian race had been true.

They seemed to be right enough. Nearly all the people were good-looking and well-shaped, not least the girls, each of whom wore a flower in her coal-black hair. We found later that the Tahitians were as friendly as they were handsome. That very first day we were gripped by the magic in the air of Tahiti. Well—we had been thirty days at sea and may have been more receptive than was good for us, but only clods can withstand cheerful smiles, music and dance, the scent of flowers and assurance—and we were no clods. One never forgets Tahiti, but in Tahiti one forgets everything else!

When darkness fell, the native crew of the schooner alongside us began to sing and play. Four men sat on the after-deck and sang Polynesian songs in parts, while at the same time two of them played stringed instruments in masterly fashion. The effect was wonderfully harmonious, and we made ourselves comfortable on deck to listen, silent and enchanted. Common interest in singing and music built a bridge, and soon we got into conversation.

The end of it was that all the singing natives, plus some of their sweethearts and wives, came on board *Nordkaperen* as visitors. The rest of the evening was passed singing and making music, and we were also given an exhibition of Tahitian dancing by both women and men.

On motor trips in the neighbourhood of Papeete we enjoyed the scenery as much as possible, but it is not ideal to rush along and only be able to enjoy it in halves.

The interior of Tahiti consists of mountains and wilderness, and the whole population lives in a narrow strip of coast round the island. I had the idea of bicycling right round it, a trip of about 125 miles. The boys approved the proposal, but when the day came only Poul wanted to start. It was not too easy to get hold of the bicycles. No one was keen to guarantee them, which we very well understood later, but at last we found a man who would put two good bicycles with new rubber tyres at our disposal quite cheaply. For the first forty miles the road was not so bad, but for the next thirty we had in several places to go along roads and over bridges which were under three feet of water. We had to walk up to our knees in water with our cycles on our shoulders, while a tearing current did its best to knock away our legs from under us. We were making the acquaintance of the rainy season. We went along mountain roads on which all the earth had been washed away by the water, so that we had to ride on the bare fragments of stone and rubble. For long stretches close to the sea the road shrank to a narrow path, and here the wheels sank into the sand up to the hub. At many points the sandy paths had been repaired with mussel shells. It was like riding through broken glass. The violent storms we met with on our way seemed to us heaven-sent—which in fact, they were. When we, hot and dirty, were caught in a tropical storm, we enjoyed it to the full.

On the east side, where at many places there was no reef to break the force of the seas, the surf broke violently against the cliffs. Where we stood on the road cut out of the cliff we could see the spray fifty feet high in the air. We gazed long, as though hypnotized, on the frothing, boiling, thundering breakers. Every scrap of earth in Tahiti is covered with green. Now and then the road cut inland through deep ravines and valleys, where the vegetation formed a complete wilderness. Trees and palms closed over our heads. When we had pushed our bicycles up steep mountain roads for half an hour on end and looked forward to fizzing down on the other side, we were as a rule sorely deceived. One does not fizz over broken stones and rubble; one uses the brakes.

We took three days over the trip. We ate and slept among the natives and got a good picture of their habits and customs. Everywhere we were met with smiles, hospitality and kindness in the fullest measure.

The first night we spent with a Dane, Henrik Levinsen, who lived in the Paea district, about fifteen miles from Papeete. His rather tumble-down but pleasant house, with its palm-leaf roof, lay only a stone's throw from the sea on the outskirts of a cocoa plantation. The eternal surf broke over the reef half a mile out, and the rumbling noise, suggesting the noise of passing trains, was always in the air. Levinsen lived alone with his two riding-horses as his sole company. He was not at home when we arrived, but after waiting a little while we saw him coming up from the water with one of his horses behind him. He had been swimming in the lagoon with Little Mare, as he called the horse. We were cordially received and invited to stay at the hut for a week or two. We were obliged to refuse this invitation for the moment, but we promised to come back. He persuaded us, however, to such an extent that we did not go on till two o'clock the next afternoon. Pleasant chat, red wine, and rides delayed our departure. We had little idea at that time that we should spend three unforgettable weeks in that same hut.

And so we cycled on. Levinsen had given us an address at which we could spend the following night. The family was called Mau-u and lived in the Papeari district, about twenty-five miles on. The heads of the Mau-u family had been chiefs of the district.

A journey of twenty-five miles is nothing to speak of for a couple of ordinary cyclists, but it was a hard task for us. We were already sore behind from our rides on Levinsen's horses, and our contact with the hard, narrow bicycle saddles did not make this any better. Grilling sun, hot moist air, rainstorms and rough sandy roads made the trip a torment. We were continually having to stop to ask the way, quench our thirst, and look at the view, a cave or a waterfall. This delayed us so much that it was dark before we arrived. The farther we got from Papeete the more we noticed a change in the inhabitants. All whom we now met smiled and waved and stood still when we passed them.

Jurana, they said, and boys and men took off their hats to us respectfully. If we stopped at a group of houses to ask the way, we were at once surrounded by a smiling, friendly crowd, who made us understand that they wanted to do all they could to help us.

For the last lap of our journey we were escorted by a whole party, all anxious to show us where the far-famed Mau-u family lived. A number of palm huts lay in a fair-sized enclosure and a pretty wooden bungalow rose above them. This was the family estate. The house and huts lay on a slope down to a lagoon, surrounded on three sides by palms, trees and green mountains. In the twilight which was just beginning the still water of the lagoon resembled a giant opal.

A tall, powerfully built young man stood in the doorway of the house. We greeted him and asked if we could be put up for the night. He said he must speak to his mother first, and asked us to wait. He soon came back accompanied by an elderly native lady whose straight back and intelligent face showed clearly that we were confronted with a personality.

She invited us in in a friendly manner and asked if we were hungry. The whole family could speak English.

We thanked her and gave her a message of greeting from Levinsen. If she had been friendly before, she now overflowed with amiability. Levinsen had been her husband's—the late Mau-u's—greatest friend, and if we were friends of his, we were friends of the family.

'You must just say what you want. The house is yours. That is the old chief Mau'u's wish!'

Mau-u's eldest son, who appeared later, was a grand specimen of manhood. He was now chief of the district, and all the members of the family treated him with reverence—the reverence due to a chief.

After we had eaten a good and copious dinner, we assembled outside the house, with the numerous grown-up children and children-in-law. We sat on tree-trunks or on the grass. The tropical night had crept upon us. The moon was almost full; its yellow disc looked down through the palm-leaves and cast a magical light on the lagoon and its surroundings. The air was spicy with turf smoke and the scent of flowers. Cicadas and crickets almost drowned the roar of the distant surf. It was all very pleasant.

Singing and music were soon in full swing, Tahitian songs followed Danish ones; more and more natives arrived, attracted by the sound, and if a heavy shower had not lowered the atmosphere, none of the inhabitants of the district would have gone to bed that night.

The two best beds in the guest-room had been got ready for us, and we were soon fast asleep. We managed, however, to kill a few mosquitoes. After a good meal next morning our haversacks were filled with food and fruit. The family begged us to sail our boat round Tahiti on our departure and anchor in their little lagoon. We promised that we would, but did not keep our promise.

On leaving we were given the address of a man with whom we could stay the following night. He lived forty miles farther on. This was the worst bit of road that lay before us; we had to cover desolate sandy stretches and steep mountain tracks.

When we had got about halfway we tumbled off our bicycles to quench our thirst at a little stream.

A stout native woman beckoned to us from a house in the neighbourhood, and we understood from her gesticulations that she wanted to give us something to drink. We wiped the sweat from our faces, removed the worst dirt and went modestly into —or under—the house, for it stood on posts. We had an extremely pleasant reception; our hostess's four young daughters fell on our necks and kissed us, one by one. We rubbed off more sweat and dirt and wiped our mouths, but the salutation was not repeated. We agreed that it was a curious but really not unpleasant custom. The girls pushed us down into two chairs and laughed and made a fuss of us. I saw Poul close his eyes, and I asked if he felt ill. He opened his eyes again, looked round again and said:

'I thought it was only a dream!'

Then he put on a superior expression and threw himself into his part, reaching out his hand, with a demanding air, for a fresh coconut, with which one of the girls immediately came running up. Half an hour later the master of the house came home. He was the pastor of the Protestant church near by and just as hospitable as the rest of the family. He asked with interest for news from the great world and invited us, as a matter of course, to stay and dine with them. Now there was a rare bustle in the house.

We asked the pastor's charming wife if we could buy one or two bottles of red wine in the neighbourhood. She looked round shyly and was visibly interested, but whispered:

'We never drink wine at home, but ask my husband!'

I asked her husband. His face fell, but he promised to get some bottles from the Chinese shopkeeper. His wife looked after him with a triumphant expression as he went off to satisfy the demands of hospitality.

The chief people in the parish were sent for to see the curiosities. When we sat down as guests of honour at the well-furnished table, there were twenty guests in all. They looked at the red wine with some little surprise, but made no comment, and when the pastor had said a long grace, the performance began. We watched to see how the others ate. They did not care about using cutlery, and we wanted to do as they did. They, on the other hand, watched us in order to eat in the way we were accustomed to. They sat brandishing their knives and forks, and confusion spread. Finally everyone ate on his own account, in his own way, and the atmosphere soon warmed up.

We had a hard job to get away. They were determined to make us stay the night. and when that proved impossible we had almost to swear to return. This was another promise we did not keep. I photographed them all before we rode on. I had only one film left, and that was not enough. Twenty times they posed in graceful positions and groups, and I photographed away without a film in the camera! . . . But they enjoyed themselves, and that was the most important thing!

The district, by the way, had unusually many cases of that terrible disease elephantiasis. Both Poul and I had sat at the pastor's table next to serious cases of the disease, and the idea made us a little uneasy.

It was the poor part of Tahiti through which we were riding, and we saw only wretched palm huts and poorly, thinly-clad inhabitants. But here, as everywhere on the island, there were smart churches one alongside another, and always a Catholic and a Protestant church close together. A ceaseless underground war was waged between the parties. When a Protestant church was half built, the foundation stone of a Catholic church was laid close by—or the other way round. It was certainly not the most fruitful manner of collaboration.

We reached our destination, the village of Papenoo (all place-names in Tahiti begin with P), at dusk. Some natives conducted us to the house we were looking for. The man's name was Teriieroo-a-teriierooiterai. He had been chief of the district for fifty-three years and had received no less than six medals from France for various services. He was also the local wise man and magician.

This man of eighty had quite a young wife—his seventh. She was mother to seven small children. He had no record of all the children whose father he had been in the course of years, but there must be as many as there are letters in his name. Only the master of the house sat at table with us; the rest of the family studied us curiously through cracks in the door and from cover of other kinds. While we were dining outside on the verandah, people were busy in a room indoors. They were arranging sleeping accommodation for us, and when we had thanked our host for our meal we went to bed. We were just falling asleep when the water-jug fell over with a crash. Poul sprang quickly out of bed, and howling and spitting followed—he had trodden on a cat. When the disturber of the peace had been shut out on to the verandah, we discovered that all the children of the house were sleeping there in clumps on the floor. It was their room and their beds we were sleeping in. We were on the point of putting them into their respective beds, but were afraid of disturbing the whole house and annoying the old man. Later in the night I was woken by someone creeping in through the window. It was Poul. He had only been outside and had not dared to wake the children by going through the verandah.

We agreed to have a bit of late supper. We had got a pineapple each to crunch, but when Poul was going to put them on the table only half was left; the ants had eaten the rest and still sat in thick masses on the fruit. Then we wanted to light a cigarette to smoke the mosquitoes out, but neither of us had any matches. It was a bad night.

Early the next morning we took leave of the old chief and his large family to go on to Papeete and so complete our round tour.

On the way we passed a river on which lay a row of white buildings. We got off to have a closer look at them. They were partly hidden behind a white-painted fence, and up on the balconies some people were standing and waving to us. We waved back, but we did not smile; nor did they.

It was the lepers' village, their hospital or prison: for most of them a habitation for life—the short life that was granted them. They were dying by inches, cast out by the community, regarded with loathing. The oppressive feeling of hopelessness which hung over the place depressed us. A young mother lifted a boy of five or six up on to the fence so that he could wave to us.

'Devil take the place!' I said, without looking at Poul. He did not reply, and I began to pedal, while he tossed a packet of cigarettes over the fence.

Paradise had its shady sides. The rest of the way back to *Nordkaperen* was put behind us in silence.

The seamen in the harbour and people with local knowledge advised us to wait till the middle of April before continuing our voyage. The hurricane season could not with certainty be regarded as over till then. We therefore decided not to sail again until April. We had no objection whatever to staying in Tahiti a little longer.

Sunday, February 9, was a day of catastrophe for the island.

After several days of violent rain storms and wind, the bad weather culminated on Sunday in a cloudburst so heavy that all the rivers overflowed their banks and did great damage. Many important bridges were washed away, so that communications between Papeete and the rest of the island were cut. A number of houses were carried away by the floods, and in many areas the water was rushing along three feet deep. The disaster was worst on the north side of the island, where a landslip had blocked the course of a river. A lake was quickly formed there, and when at last it overflowed its banks it spread death and destruction around it. Fortunately only a few human lives were lost in this region.

The rain was accompanied by violent squalls, which caused confusion in the harbour. Several schooners had to be hurriedly moved out to buoys, as their anchors could not hold. Nor could *Nordkaperen's*. Inch by inch we were pressed in against the stone wall of the quay. It was hopeless to tighten up the anchor chain, it kept on dragging, so there was nothing for us to do but hang on to the side of the schooner which was lying close to us. Despite the heavy sea in the harbour we succeeded in rowing our big anchor with 150 ft. of heavy iron chain out in a dinghy. The dinghy was in a sinking condition when we came back, but now *Nordkaperen* was riding safely to two anchors. While we were lying alongside the schooner our boat had got some nasty scratches. The putting out of the big anchor was later *Nordkaperen's* salvation.

The Tahitians quickly forget natural catastrophes. They do not worry, they push disagreeable things into the background, and a few days later no one was talking about the storm any longer.

Levinsen himself came to fetch us one day to be sure that we kept our promise to return. Knud was invited too, but he preferred to remain on board the boat. Bill had moved out to stay with some acquaintances near Levinsen. We all three took a bus, but about ten miles from Papeete we had to stop. The bridge we had to cross had been washed away, and transport to the other side was being effected by a temporary cable railway. A large wooden box which could take four passengers at once was hauled backwards and forwards on a wire by natives. Far below the river rushed by, a mass of whirling eddies. We cast a farewell look at the sky before we went on board the box, but when we saw women and children smilingly taking their turn, we had not the face to hold back.

Another bus was standing on the other side of the river, and this took us to 'our' house.

The stay in the hut did us both good. We enjoyed the cool air, the quiet and the simple, wholesome food. To begin with we cooked, washed and so on for ourselves, but it was only fun so long as it was new. We had not really got into the way of using the open fireplace, catching fish or dealing with the coconuts which we had the laborious task of gathering. Nor did we enjoy tidying or washing up when there was a chance of dropping into a slack chair under a palm—with a view across the lagoon. Something was wanting after all in paradise, but Levinsen, the old fox, had an idea. He regarded it as a point of honour that we should be comfortable.

One afternoon, when I was having a nap on an old sofa in the hut, I was woken by something hitting me in the face. I grabbed at it and caught hold of a big lizard. It had presumably fallen from the beams or from the palm-leaf roof. I threw it out of the window. I was accustomed to that kind of thing; the night before I had been woken by a rat tumbling down into my bed. I did not find it till next morning when I shook out the blanket.

Well, but this was my siesta! I looked up crossly at the roof and went off into a doze again. Then there was another smack, and this time straight into my half-open mouth. I seized the creature, which was exactly identical with the previous disturber of the peace, and hurled it out of the window. For safety's sake I took hold of the collar-beam and shook it violently to have them all down at once. But nothing came down but dirt and muck.

I tried again to get a nap. But only a moment passed before

there was another smack. I sat with the lizard in my hand and was wondering more and more at its astonishing resemblance to its two predecessors, when I heard suppressed tittering outside. I shot furiously out of the door and round behind the house, but stopped short, thunderstruck. Before me stood two pretty Tahitian girls. They were shrieking with laughter—and a moment later I was laughing too. In the background I saw Poul and Levinsen, undoubtedly the authors of the plan. They were enjoying the joke just as much. I flung the lizard away sheepishly. Levensen came up to me, saying that he wanted to speak to me seriously.

These two girls, respectively daughter and niece of a friend of his, were offering to cook and wash for us all in return for his giving them riding lessons, he said. Had I any objections?

I looked doubtedly at Poul, but he turned away. I looked at the girls . . . That was a pretty necklace one of them had on. It was made of little white shells from the seashore and contrasted charmingly with her golden-brown neck. They both had flowers in their hair—snow-white flowers in coal-black hair.

No, it wouldn't do.

'That was a good idea,' I said to Levinsen, 'but you do understand that it'll be all quite proper?'

He opened his eyes wide in a comical gesture and said: 'Of course, what else did you think?'

I was certainly out of my depth. A good thing the girls did not understand Danish.

Elen and Margarit understood from our faces that the matter was settled, and twittered with pleasure.

I was somewhat taken aback when I found that Poul knew Elen already. It looked like a put-up job.

Now our existence became perfectly ideal. Every morning, when we opened our eyes, breakfast was served in a little summer-house with a palm-leaf roof alongside the hut. We thoroughly realized how handy and inventive children of nature can be with small means.

They could make the fire burn at any time, they collected fuel themselves and could climb the palm-trees, sixty or seventy feet high, for coconuts. They could fish much better than we—they could really do everything. Tasks which we clumsy helpless creatures had to abandon they carried out in a twinkling.

It must be said to Levinsen's credit that he taught the girls riding well. It was not long before they could ride to the shop or out to pick fruit, and it was a fantastic sight to see them come racing in under the palms at full gallop with their black hair streaming behind them.

In the afternoon we helped them to search for some particular snails which were to be used for bait. After that we went down to the lagoon to fish with long sticks. Poul and I seldom got a bite and gave it up, but the girls continued and came back later with a whole lot of little fish. Then they cooked a splendid dinner of fish and coconuts and a few other oddments over the fire. As dessert we had bananas or sweet, juicy mango fruit from a tree near by. Now and then a chicken had to be killed, and we could get a little rice from the Chinese. We never grew accustomed to eating with our fingers, as the girls did. We found it practically impossible to pick up the gravy, and it took us a long time to overcome our dislike of eating uncleaned fish with the heads and everything else.

We never had our washing better done on the whole voyage. Elen and Margarit washed the clothes in cold water. It was hard work. To make up for it they had a day off now and then, and on these days we ourselves had to be domestic. It was no fun at all. And we missed their lively childish laughter.

One day we ran out of cigarettes. It was a long way to *Nordkaperen*. The girls disappeared for a while, and when they came back they were radiant and had several packets of cigarettes in their hands.

'Where did you get them from?' we asked.

'From the Chinese; he put them down,' they said.

'In my name?'

'Yes!'

They could see from my face that they had done something wrong. I turned to Margarit, who was presumably the ringleader.

'I'm very much annoyed about it. Take them back!'

Perhaps I spoke rather severely. God bless my soul, if great tears were not pouring down her cheeks!

'I'll pay for them myself,' she sobbed.

I went into the house and asked Poul if he would not keep the girls in order. I gave it up altogether.

We were constant guests in many of the huts along the shore, and the native's greatest pleasure was to get Poul to sing. Many an evening passed quickly in singing and eating little fish or sucking pig roasted between hot stones. Fruits and nuts formed the dessert, and we sometimes stood a bottle of red wine from the Chinese at the festive meal.

At the full moon all the native young people assembled round fires on the beach. It was an unwritten law or instinct centuries old. At first we sat some way off and enjoyed the spectacle and the singing, but soon we were accepted into the community. I certainly need not describe a broiling hot night with a full moon on the edge of a South Seas lagoon, surrounded by palms, with a merry crowd of boys and girls singing round the fire. I need not describe it—it is just as you imagine it.

There had been no hurricanes in Tahiti in living memory, and the incredible happened—we experienced one while we were there. According to the newspapers its force was at least 100 miles an hour. The anemometer was shattered to pieces in recording this. The hurricane came on February 16, 1947, just a week after the previous storm.

But before I say any more I will introduce a friend we made in Tahiti. He played the leading part in the events I am about to describe. His name was Jack Rolly, New Zealander and thoroughgoing adventurer. For several months in the year he worked on one plantation or another; with the money so earned he travelled to other islands and in this way had been on most of them. He had a small farm of his own in New Zealand, which he was always talking about. He had come to Tahiti in a South Seas schooner and had not yet found any job. It was a matter of course that he should be allowed to live and sleep on board *Nordkaperen*, and he was pleasant company for Knud while the rest of us were holiday-making.

Jack was short, but as broad as a dray-horse and incredibly strong. His good-nature was proportionate to his sturdiness and strength. He was red-haired and freckled.

Poul and I were living permanently in Levinsen's hut, and Bill near by. At Paea we had several heavy showers about noon, accompanied by gusts of wind of hurricane force. The water was violently disturbed and spray flew in dense clouds over the surface. Withered palm-leaves, dirt and muck flew through the air, and the coconut palms were bent down till they swayed parallel with the ground. The dull thud of falling coconuts resounded all the time, and it was positively dangerous to stand under the palms.

We rescued some of the out-of-doors domestic utensils and fled into the hut. Here we were soon kept busy repairing the roof, which was nearly lifted off several times. Luckily it was not a sea wind—the course of the hurricane was along the coast—or not much of the hut would have remained.

We reckoned that the wind must be blowing right into Papeete harbour, and consequently were very anxious about *Nordkaperen*. The whole thing happened in half an hour: after that everything was as before, except that all the coconuts were down and the roof of the hut badly damaged. For a hurricane it did not seem to have been very severe, but we certainly only had the edge of it. Unfortunately it was Sunday, and the buses were not running. We could not ride to Papeete because the bridges were still broken, and therefore had to languish in painful ignorance of *Nordkaperen's* fate. The telephone lines were blown down everywhere: we were completely isolated.

The hours that passed before the first bus arrived next morning were very long and full of torment for us. We thanked heaven that Knud had not come with us. His presence on board gave us a feeling of security, for he knew what ought to be done.

The bus crawled along at a snail's pace; the ferrying over the ravine in the box took a long time; the journey seemed endless. Levinsen had come with me while Poul was left in charge at home, and he consoled me as well as he could.

At last the bus stopped. We turned down towards the quay, full of anxiety.

Yes, hurrah! *Nordkaperen* was still afloat. . . but what a sight she was!

The weather service had failed: the hurricane had come without warning—like a thief in the night. Most of the schooners had only two or three men on watch when the first gust of wind came, and they were quickly cut off from any help from land, for along with the storm came a tidal wave which ran high up into the streets of Papeete and cut off all communication with the ships. By the greatest of good fortune Knud and Jack were on board when the first gusts of wind came at about twelve o'clock. They came from the north—due head on to the ships, and all the anchors dragged. Some ships ran stern first into the stone quay. The inadequate watches on the boats round us worked at top speed trying to tighten the anchor chains; they toiled at the capstans like ponies or flung cables from one ship's bow to another. They shouted and yelled to be audible above the noise from wind and water, and sounds of crashing and scrunching were heard all the time. Some craft managed to start their engines and get out into the middle of the harbour and make fast to the buoys. The seas came over the reef, and the water of the harbour was violently disturbed.

Jack and Knud too were busy with *Nordkaperen's* capstan; they succeeded in tightening up the anchor so that the boat avoided touching the quay. They were standing in water up to their waists. The whole forward part of *Nordkaperen* was under water; the long heavy anchor chain hampered the boat's movements.

Tahitian women making copra

PLALE VI

Express train on Viti Levu (Fiji)

Four typical Tahitian girls on board

PLATE VII

Tahiti—charm

In a lagoon on the South Sea Islands
Knud, Calle, Bill, Poul

After half an hour, to the great relief of the ships' watches, there was a sudden calm; for many ships it came at the last minute. Some of the men stopped working when the wind dropped, but others, more sensible than they, went on working at the vessel's moorings.

*Nordkaperen* was all right; both anchors had held, and she had not suffered the slightest damage.

Then back came the hurricane!

It had moved about 45 degrees and now hit all the ships three or four points forward of amidships on the port side. If there had been no panic before, there was now. Most of the anchors began to drag, and the boats drifted into one another. All attention and strength was now concentrated on fending off—the moorings must look after themselves. The scrunching, crashing noises grew louder than ever. In the eastern part of the harbour a small motor vessel got into difficulties; her cables and anchors were carried away, and she ran broadside on into the stone quay. When she had smashed herself against the stone wall once or twice she went to the bottom.

All the ships suffered damage—from collision either with one another or with the stone quay.

On the port side of *Nordkaperen* lay the pretty white South Seas schooner *Tiara Toporo*, a famous craft which had formerly been skippered by the well-known South Seas trader, the Dane Viggo Rasmussen, called by the natives 'Papa Viggo'. *Tiara Toporo* had had trouble with her moorings; she went adrift and bore down on *Nordkaperen*. Knud and Jack sprang to the capstan in a twinkling to slacken the moorings enough to ride free of the schooner, but this they failed to do. The schooner ran into *Nordkaperen's* port side with a horrible crunching noise and crushed some ten feet of the pretty teak bulwarks. The pressure of the schooner was too much for our boat. The stern moorings on the port side were broken, and the schooner took the opportunity to cut our bowsprit off with a crack like a pistol shot. The topmast also threatened to fall. We had two firm anchors out, but they could not hold the heavy weight on them; they began to drag.

The moment for which we had held up *Tiara Toporo* had given her crew an opportunity of getting things under control, but Knud and Jack now had a job which made the greatest demands both on their strength and on their seamanlike ability. Now one of the moments came in which *Nordkaperen's* fate hung on a thread. Her anchors had dragged and were being pulled unresisting along the bottom, and slowly but surely she was drifting in towards the stone wall which was hidden by the water: only fountains of spray many feet high marked its position now and again.

Knud had to keep fending off all the time to save the rest of the bulwarks. Several craft threatened to run into us. He wanted to make the apparently quite inevitable collision with the quay as slight as possible, and this required work on the moorings as well. The hurricane shrieked, the seas were whipped up to a fantastic height, and the noise round Knud and Jack was so fearful that they could not shout to one another.

For what he did at this juncture Jack's name is written in *Nordkaperen's* history in letters of fire. He stood on the fore-deck as though nailed to the capstan with a hand on each crank-handle and his mighty muscles strained to the uttermost. Both his sturdy legs were fixed to the deck like bollards. At one moment the fore part of *Nordkaperen* was swaying high in the air, the next it was deep under water, and Jack was standing in water up to his neck. Inch by inch he pulled the boat free of the stone wall, but again and again she was forced in. Knud also had to take a few swimming strokes now and then, and his attention was fixed on a small motor vessel which was fairly close on the starboard quarter. At the same time he had to let Jack know when *Nordkaperen's* stern was swaying over the edge of the stonework. And Jack's back was bent to his task. He was soaked with water and perspiration and his whole body was trembling with the strain. The anchor chain grew shorter and shorter. It was only a question of time when the anchors would cease to offer any resistance.

When things looked blackest and Knud had already prepared

himself for an unpleasant landing, the storm ceased—just as suddenly as it had begun.

*Nordkaperen* was saved and had perhaps also saved *Tiara Toporo*.

I thanked the boys for what they had done, and Knud could not praise Jack Rolly enough. The honour of having saved *Nordkaperen* was Jack's, he said—but I know Knud's modesty. His own contribution too had been indispensable.

Outside the reef a fishing-boat had gone down with all hands. The gable and roof of the school had been blown off a quarter of an hour after the children had been sent home. Many thousands of coconut palms had been blown down on the other side of the island; whole plantations had been wiped out, and the hurricane had left much devastation of other kinds in its wake. A hurricane had passed Tahiti 500 miles away, and one arm of it had found its way to the island. There was not one ship undamaged in Papeete harbour. *Nordkaperen* had got her share—with her crushed bulwarks and bowsprit broken off, and many other ugly scars she was, taken all round, a lamentable sight.

But she was afloat—afloat—and our voyage round the world could be continued!

## CHAPTER X

# *From Tahiti to Suva Bay*

LEVINSEN and I looked at the damage to *Nordkaperen*, made a few small purchases, and got into a bus to return to Paea. We had five bottles of red wine with us in a basket.

Travelling by bus in Tahiti is a sort of picnic. All the passengers are quickly shaken up into one large family, and the journey is accompanied by laughter, lively talk and song. The coachwork of the bus is as a rule home-made, the seats consisting of a few loose benches knocked together. If the rear entrance is blocked people just crawl in through the windows. They take the same route to get out again—men and women alike.

We had arrived early and had taken possession of the two best places—the outside places at the entrance. It was coolest there, and one need not perform acrobatics to get out again. On the other hand, we had the job of helping elderly people up into the bus and receiving goods. This consisted of such different items as large and small fish, bundles of cloth or live fowls.

I had put the basket containing the bottles under the seat, where they clinked menacingly as the bus bumped along over the holes in the road. The time of departure according to an unofficial time-table was 3.45 p.m., but the driver showed no signs of activity till an hour later. The bus should be full before a start was made.

When at last we were halfway to Paea, the bus was stopped by a crowd of people, half the passengers of a bus which had broken down. There were fifteen of them in all, and they now wanted to come with us. Although all the seats were occupied, room was made for the newcomers as well, though only after a fight. The driver of the broken-down bus crawled out of his vehicle and pursued the fugitives to get his money. He demanded the full fare. A brawl followed, during which some of the Chinese passengers tried to hide to escape paying twice, but the driver dragged them out by the hair, so to speak, and they had to pay up 10 fr. each.

Levinsen and I were busy all the time helping passengers up into the bus and taking in goods, and each of us had a baby planted on him. His was a little Tahitian girl of two, and mine a Chinese baby. I had expected the mother to appear when things had settled down, but no one demanded the dear little boy. The child began to feel comfortable with me; he babbled a little and then fell fast asleep. This did not suit me. I pretended to want to light a cigarette, and with an appealing smile handed the child to my neighbour, a young Tahitian married woman. She realized my difficulty and took the baby from me, laughing; but I never found out who its mother was.

Levinsen was less fortunate with his foster-child, who also was missed by no one. When the child began to whimper, he held her up in his outstretched arms to talk to her, but unfortunately the roof was too low, and she bumped her head against it. A whimper rose to a bellow, and Levinsen got busy with baby talk—to the great amusement of the passengers. At the same time the blow had made the child make water; it could be seen on his trousers. It was a long time before he got rid of his foster-child, wet at both ends.

Our bus was stopped again—this time by a twenty-stone matron who had placed herself in the middle of the road so that it could not get past. My native chivalry made me give up my seat to her, and I installed myself outside on the step, where six were already hanging on. It was difficult to keep one's hold, for the bus set off in kangaroo-like bounds, and shortly afterwards a bundle of live fowls fell on my head. It had been up on the roof, but during the bus's wild career, it had slowly glided aft and finally tipped over the edge and descended on my head, the birds cackling and flapping their wings. I lost my cap in my efforts to free myself from them. Now at last the fowls lay cackling on the road, while a little way farther on lay my cap. We got the driver to stop, and a young Tahitian ran back after the cap and came back with it on his head. It was much too big for him and came down over his ears. He was dragging the bundle of hens behind him in the dust.

The episode created further amusement in the bus, and this was to rise several degrees higher when we got off. We selected our parcels and paid our fares, but just as the bus was about to start, I remembered the red wine. A shout made the driver stop again, but it was none too easy to get hold of the basket containing the precious bottles. It was under the stout lady's seat, and her long skirt, spread wide between a pair of sturdy legs, barred the view and impeded access. I tried to explain to her by gesticulations and mimicry that I had some wine under the seat. I leaned my head back and drank from an imaginary bottle, and then pointed at her flowered skirt. She followed my movements with a smile and nodded gently, but showed no sign of moving an inch. I tried still more vivid mimicry, and went so far as to lift her skirt a little. The whole bus howled with laughter—but I wanted my wine! As the stout lady still failed to understand what I wanted, and as the driver was beginning to finger his self-starter again, I grew more determined than ever. I bent down and lifted enough of the skirt for me to get hold of the basket, but, of course, it was stuck fast. I took a strong grip, and when the basket at last came out, I had nearly torn off the big lady's skirt.

I thought afterwards that the uncontrolled laughter which shook the whole bus was rather out of place, and sent an angry look after the swaying and serpentining vehicle as it bumped away along the roads of Tahiti, but one look at the basket and its contents made me gentle and peaceable again. Levinsen and I went up to the hut, where Poul was grooming horses. The girls were swimming out in the lagoon, their black hair floating on the surface of the water.

A little while before our sailing date Poul and I moved on board *Nordkaperen* again to repair the boat and put her in order. Knud, our trusty caretaker, was already under way, and by energetic hard work we transformed the smashed, scarred boat into a shining new yacht.

Unfortunately we ran short of red-lead and varnish. Such things were not to be found in Tahiti, but a Norwegian vessel, the motor-ship *Thor*, which came into port for three days, removed our difficulties. We were treated royally for the three days she lay at Tahiti. Not only we were our countrymen's guests throughout their stay, but we got loads of cigarettes and the captain gave us nearly 60 lbs. of red-lead and the same quantity of varnish. The goods were cleared in the regulation manner: we had to pay Customs duty and sign an undertaking that they would not be resold. They were transported from the *Thor* to *Nordkaperen* under a strong police escort.

Just as the *Thor* was leaving harbour a message came from the French authorities politely requesting to be allowed to buy some red-lead and varnish. We were short of money and let them buy some, but this time there was to be no Customs duty or clearance papers, and when we pointed to the undertaking not to sell that we had signed, they only laughed and said that that did not mean anything. They were going to use the paint on the buoys in the harbour.

On the whole we were treated well by the French authorities. We were freed from tourist duty—500 frs. a head—and our cigarette, sugar and butter rations were larger than usual.

The day Poul and I returned after a wonderful holiday at Paea we saw that a new yacht had come into the harbour. She also was sailing round the world, and both crew and boat had a good deal in common with us.

Her name was *Alk* and she came from Rotterdam. Her crew consisted of three Dutchmen. She was a new boat, specially built for a voyage round the world, of heavy steel plates. The deck also was of steel. All hatches were of steel throughout, were watertight and fitted with plugging and clamps; she had watertight bulkheads forward and aft, and so was unsinkable. There were four stiffeners in the already strong deck. *Alk* was strong enough to force Niagara. There was thus no striking resemblance to *Nordkaperen* as regards security; but the three men had started the same week as ourselves, were to take two years over the trip and were following the same route as ourselves, The owner, Captain A. van Nieunkopp, was married and had two sons, like myself. This again was the only point of resemblance. I cannot deny that when I went on board the *Alk* I felt depressed; I could not help comparing our chances of getting home with theirs. The Dutchmen, capital fellows, did not parade their fine things and their information to make me envious and lower my spirits. It was sheer pride of possession.

Nieunkopp was a professional captain who had sailed the South Seas for many years. All the expenses of the tour were divided among the three (not a sound plan). There were four sets of new sails (*Nordkaperen* had one set), and a powerful 50 h.p. Diesel engine (*Nordkaperen's* was 18 h.p.). They had also four different barometers, four compasses, the very best chronometers, wireless, several ultra-modern sextants, etc. They had also established provision depots in the ports at which they were to call. They had masses of dollars and strong forces behind them in the shape of newspapers, publishers and sailing clubs. They were sailing sportsmen as we were. The only thing we had behind us was our ability to stick together and a firm resolve to carry out our enterprise.

Finally they showed us five different kinds of photographic cameras and cinecameras, coloured films, microcamera, etc. My old camera, the last, was about to be sold—of sheer necessity. Our last pair of binoculars had been sold, our wrist-watches had gone the same way. Their exhibits had, therefore, a doubly depressing effect on me. Before I went the skipper produced his log-book and showed me how fast *Alk* could sail, and there at last was something in which I could hold my own. *Nordkaperen's* average speed was more than 25 per cent greater than *Alk's*. The log-book was quickly laid aside.

'To judge from my experience,' the captain said, when taking leave of me, 'our chances of sailing round the world are about 90 per cent.' I speculated with anxious foreboding on what *Nordkaperen's* chances might be.

On the way back to *Nordkaperen* I stopped and observed her efforts to assert herself among the rich Americans' pleasure yachts. My visit to *Alk* had rather knocked me endways, but by slow degrees my good humour began to return. I decided that the rich men's boats were like floating pavilions with their high deckhouses and freeboard. All the fittings were painted—certainly practical in the South Seas—but compared with *Nordkaperen's* shining teak they made a poor show.

*Nordkaperen's* slender little hull with its racing lines and strong northern rigging could certainly, for beauty and seamanlike qualities, compete with her larger, newer and more expensive comrades, not least as regards speed. I had recovered my indispensable confidence and when I came on board, I ran my hand along *Nordkaperen's* pretty bulwarks.

'Cheer up, old thing!' I said. 'We won't let them get us down!'

While in Tahiti we increased our collection of stowaways. We had brought from St Thomas a cicada, which had sung to us every night for more than six months, and from the Galapagos some large cockroaches which we hunted unremittingly. Bill declared that they were so large that they could be heard walking about! Now, in addition to some pretty little lizards, a disgusting rat came on board. We hunted it day and night and set traps for it, but it cunningly evaded all our efforts to catch it. Then Jack had the idea that a ship's cat would get rid of it, but a cat being a rare and valued animal in Tahiti, Jack and Knud had to tramp for many miles up into the mountains and get a cat from some people we knew. After a six hours' walk they came back weary and perspiring with a wild spitting cat. It was shut into the forepeak to accustom itself to conditions on board.

Poul came home the same evening, He had no idea that the cat was there, and when in the course of the night he was wakened from his beauty sleep by its mewing and scratching, he thought it was a cat that had come on board uninvited. He leapt out of his bunk, got hold of the cat and flung it ashore. It disappeared like a streak of lightning.

Next morning Jack poured milk into a saucer and called the cat in caressing tones, but no puss came. Jack and Knud searched the whole boat. While they were doing so Poul woke up. He looked at them in astonishment as they poked their heads into every locker and every heap of rope.

'What are you poking about after?'

'A damned cat we've been a whole day fetching,' replied Jack.

'A cat! . . . Why! — Why, I threw it ashore last night!' Poul burst out.

Knud cursed, and the usually mild Jack was furious, and Poul had to jump out of his bunk in a hurry and bolt with his trousers under his arm.

The ship's company underwent a change. Jack, our friend to whom we owed so much, cherished a desire to come westward with us, a desire to which we gladly acceded. Bill, who as usual wanted to see a number of islands at which we could not call for economic reasons, and because our time was short, wished to join an American yacht which was going to some islands to the northward. He would try to join up with us later. Jack, who was a good cook, would take over Bill's job for the time being.

Apart from Jack's liking to be on board *Nordkaperen*, the real reason for his wanting to come with us was that he had an unhappy love affair. A pretty little girl whom he had met in Tahiti would not accompany him to his farm in New Zealand as his wife.

The chances of running into a hurricane were now small, and we decided to sail on March 31. Although Tahiti was the best and most beautiful place we had yet visited, we were impatient to get on. But Tahiti resisted. A few days before our sailing date both Poul and I fell sick. Poul had painful kidney trouble, and I a boil on my neck. This delayed our start by one day, and when we were about to sail next day, we heard at the last moment that a schooner was to arrive on the following day with mail. At 5 p.m. on April 2 we were ready to sail, but just as we were throwing off the mooring ropes a Customs official came running down to tell us that a copy of one list among our papers was missing. The office was shut by then, so again we had to postpone our sailing by one day.

Friends and acquaintances, who had faithfully assembled to take leave of us each time we were to sail, had shrunk in numbers when at last we got off at 11 a.m. on April 3. A violent squall of wind and rain swept over us a short time before we sailed. But we would not be made fools of any longer. We defied the beating rain and the fresh gusts, and bored our way into the thick curtain of rain outside Papeete harbour.

When we were well outside the reef and had got the sails set, we cast a farewell glance back towards Tahiti, but the island, sulky and defiant, had shrouded itself in a veil of rain and clouds.

There was a full moon that night, and we got another glimpse of Tahiti. We could see the distant mountains far astern, their peaks bathed in moonlight. Then a dark cloud glided across like a curtain falling on a scene. Next act—our voyage of about 2,000 miles to the Fiji islands.

It took us three days to get out of the Society Islands waters. In three days and nights we advanced only 150 miles. The miserable wind and the strong current acted well together; it was two steps forward and one back. At last we got free and caught the south-easterly trade wind, but it was not as strong as it should have been, and its direction was variable. Nevertheless we were able to log daily runs of over 100 miles. The squally weather we had on the way to Tahiti would not leave us in peace even now, but it was not so treacherous or so violent.

On the fifth day a great black storm-cloud rose up slowly from our lee side. Finally, it stopped, and we sailed along the edge of it for half a day. It caused a lot of trouble, with the wind going round and blowing first from one quarter and then another—right round the compass. We tried to clear out and run away from it, but it held us fast. There were heavy falls of rain along with the gusts, and we had plenty to do all the time easing and hauling on the sheets, and going about. After five or six hours of this the storm withdrew and left us with a few small rents in our sails plus a smashed crosstrees end.

We felt ourselves that we had gradually sailed the vice out of us and agreed that we should not sail *Nordkaperen* so hard. It was tiresome to be always doing repairs and mending sails, and the chances of getting new sails were small too. So we cut down our canvas, and that—combined with a foul bottom—made our daily runs shorter than we liked. Not many days had passed before our good resolutions began to irritate us. I reckoned that the topsail and the other headsails could easily give us a few knots more if they came up—perhaps 40 or 50 miles more a day, but I did not say anything. I would not have the others calling me a turncoat. Meanwhile Knud and Poul were thinking just the same—those damned agreements! Eyes were cast up to the rigging and heads were shaken; the log was read with deep sighs. One beautiful morning the sun was shining in a cloudless sky, and there was a fresh steady wind from the south-east.

'Hm!' Knud began, 'fine weather to dry sails in.'

'You've got something there,' I said, 'let's have the headsails up on deck.'

This was done with unusual energy and speed. Of course the end of it was that before long *Nordkaperen* had every stitch of canvas set.

It was splendid now to stand at the wheel again. *Nordkaperen* foamed along with seven filled bellying sails, up one swell and down the next. But it was not only the sails and speed that gladdened us. We had cleared Tahiti of all the rope and wire it possessed, and the many new falls, stays and sheets were pleasing to the eye.

When we had been a week at sea Jack gave us some bad news. All our bread was mouldy. We had usually been able to keep it for three weeks. Our flour, our macaroni, most of our rice and various spices had also gone bad. We had certainly had a great quantity of fruit given to us in Tahiti, but we knew from experience that that would not keep long. On the same day we discovered that the rubber boat was perished—burnt up by the sun despite its packing.

We should be on short commons for the last part of the voyage, and it was now necessary to keep the trysails up day and night in all kinds of weather, and to screw the last fraction of a knot out of *Nordkaperen*. After a succession of quiet, unexciting days we had on Saturday, April 12, the freshest weather we had had so far experienced.

In the afternoon the wind began to freshen from the east, rising steadily. It gradually grew to a strong breeze, and with bleeding hearts we had to take the headsails in one by one. They had begun to split at the seams. The jib had to come down too, and we found it necessary to take in the mizen. At sunset it was blowing half a gale, the seas became high rollers, and the foam blew in flakes from the tops of the billows, till the Pacific came to resemble a snow-field.

The mainsail, which was heavy and hand-sewn, was strong enough to be sheeted right out. We had the wind astern, and the jib was bent on to a strong stay. If the wind had come suddenly we should certainly have hove to, but the slowly increasing strength of the wind made us hesitate. In this way we became accustomed to the conditions, and when we found that the rigging and sails could hold, and that the boat behaved well no power on earth could have made us take in more sail or heave to. We did not notice the force of the seas because we were going at more or less the same speed as they. It was a risky piece of sailing, but we had unlimited confidence in *Nordkaperen's* stout rigging. Every time Jack asked if we should not take in sail, we replied: 'Yes—but let's wait half an hour.'

And so we waited, till the whole thing was over.

Towards midnight, when we had grown accustomed to the conditions, the wind began to drop again slowly, and when the sun rose next morning all the headsails were set after a short inspection.

There came another series of uneventful days, when the wind kept steady. The sun shone in a cloudless sky, and really the only thing we noticed was the magnificent display of colour at sunrise and sunset. We passed the time in mending our clothes, patching and washing, and in keeping rigging and sails in order. All fish and bird life in these waters seemed to be dead. When we had had supper we sometimes had a game of chess or cards or sat down comfortably with a good book.

Then a day disappeared for us—vanished into thin air. We crossed the date line on April 20. When I relieved Knud at the wheel after midnight, he said: 'Well, that's the longest watch I've ever had—from Saturday evening till Monday morning!'

We had now sighted the lighthouse on the island of Waitagilala and were heading in through the Nanaku strait, which gave access to waters thickly dotted with small islands and reefs. The approach to Suva, the capital, on the largest of the Fiji islands, Viti Levu, was rather dangerous for navigators without local knowledge, but the weather favoured us, and we were not in doubt as to our position for a single moment, but wound our way between reefs and skerries like experts.

The last afternoon before we landed we caught a big fat tunny —the only one on the whole world voyage—and there was a feast on board. We regarded it as a gift of welcome from Viti Levu —a good omen.

On Tuesday morning, April 22, the mountainous island rose up out of the dawn with a veil of mist over its valleys and low ground. We found the entrance to Suva Bay, between two thundering reefs, and immediately after were able to anchor a little way out from the quay. It was a long time before the British authorities came on board, but when at last they did come the examination was over in a moment.

We had a remarkably kind reception and were at once invited to lie at the Suva Yacht Club's guest buoy.

Our joy at having reached harbour was quenched by a sad piece of news. Flags were flying at half-mast all over the town and on board all ships. We asked a British officer the reason.

It was the King of Denmark, Christian X, who was dead, and our Dannebrog glided slowly down to half-mast.

## CHAPTER XI

# *Fiji*

It had been dinned into our ears from all sides that Suva was the dreariest and dullest place in the world.

And so it was—for anyone just passing through, who had not time to accustom himself to the conditions of life there. But we, who were in contact for two and a half months with both whites and natives all over Viti Levu, had a pleasant time which we shall be slow to forget. The white people, mainly Australians and New Zealanders, took us to their hearts and made much of us, and one could not help liking and respecting the handsome, slender, proud natives of Fiji. More than half the population of Viti Levu were Indians 'imported' by the British, and they threatened to displace the Fijians. The Fiji islands were often spoken of as 'Pacific India'.

The first thing that attracted our attention was the natives' dress and hair. Men's and women's hair grew just alike—in a high curly black bush, and the men wore skirts, so that to begin with we were a little puzzled over the sexes.

Even the police and soldiers had bare legs and skirts. but despite their—to our eyes—comical appearance they were smart, sturdy fellows, whose calm, intelligent faces commanded respect. As on most of the South Sea islands, there were many Chinese business people. We learned to esteem the frugality, energy and orderly ways of the Chinese, and we made many loyal friends among them. There was also a mixed race in Fiji. These so-called half-castes were positively loathed and hated. If there was anything in the least suspicious about their colouring, however slight, they were expelled from all pure-blooded communities and cold-shouldered.

There was a great difference between Tahiti and Fiji in the

relations between white and natives. In Tahiti one could go to a consular reception or to the smartest restaurant with a native lady. One could sit in a Tahitian's company without anyone taking exception to it. In Fiji, on the other hand, it was a most serious offence against etiquette to shake hands with a native or sit at table with him.

The scenery of Viti Levu was pretty and fertile, and the inhabitants' ideas of morality differed a good deal from the Tahitians'. But the lush, luxuriant scenery of Tahiti and the people's carelessness and joy in life were still in our blood, which was really unfair to Viti Levu and its inhabitants. Jack's comparison of the capitals of the two islands was short and to the point: Suva respectable and dull, Papeete dirty and delightful!

We had not been many days in Fiji before a little pink scented letter arrived for Jack. It was from Tahiti. What was in it we never knew, but it delighted him, and a nervous unrest took possession of him. In the evening he asked us hesitatingly if we would release him from his promise to go north with us.

'It isn't because I'm tired of being on board *Nordkaperen*—quite the contrary—but I've something I want to fix up in Tahiti.'

Of course we were sorry to part with our stout friend, but were heartily glad that he should get his little girl in Tahiti. He was lucky enough to obtain a passage the very next day.

A few days later we had a telegram from Bill, who had arrived in Samoa. He begged us to wait for him. And no more than three days later we were hailed from the shore. It was Bill wanting the dinghy. The first thing he did when he came on board was to throw himself down on a cushioned seat, give a sigh of relief and burst out: 'How lovely—home again at last!'

He complained of the other boat's slowness and the crew's lack of humour. But I did not feel that his words on returning could make up for his unfaithfulness to *Nordkaperen*.

Strong wind and rain were inseparable from Suva Bay. We

had one period of ceaseless rain for eleven days and nights, and violent gusts of wind twice caused *Nordkaperen* difficulties. The strong tide made it impossible for the boat to lie at the quay; we had to lie at anchor a little way out in the bay. The strong current, which changed twice a day, sent the boat round in a circle. This caused the anchor chain to twist itself round the stock and one fluke, and the value of the anchor was then its weight and no more.

Bill and I had been out amusing ourselves one evening. It had become pretty late before we thought of going home to *Nordkaperen*. When we had gone ashore earlier in the day the weather had been fine and had invited us to put on our white shore clothes, but when night was approaching it began to blow hard, and the wind was accompanied by heavy rain. We struggled through the rain and storm with our thin clothes clinging to our bodies. It was pitch dark, and when we reached the yacht club's landing stage we discovered to our annoyance that the dinghy had gone. In normal conditions we would have hailed those on board, but we were late, and they would be asleep; moreover, the rain and wind would prevent our hail from being heard.

We stood somewhat at a loss, staring out over the disturbed bay, where we could see *Nordkaperen's* riding lights twinkling feebly through the thick rain. Bill thought we had better go back and get put up by some of our friends, And though it was not pleasant to wade back through the rain, I agreed, with the water washing about in my shoes. We were walking back along the landing-stage again, when Bill caught sight of a skiff drawn up on the shore.

'Can't we use that?' he asked.

A closer examination showed that it would be risky to use it. There were no oars either. We sent a last look out towards *Nordkaperen*—but then I made a discovery!

'Look, Bill, look!' I shouted excitedly. '*Nordkaperen's* drifting, the anchor must have dragged.'

The boat's riding lights had become fainter and had changed their position. *Nordkaperen* was moving out towards the reef. A common instinct made us rush towards the skiff. We dragged her through the mud to the little slip. We tore a couple of planks from a fence near by and jumped on board the boat after having taken turns to haul it down the greasy slip. It was a fine bit of launching, which ended up in the water, whence we got on board the skiff.

'Did you get wet?' Bill asked.

'No, only a little water in my ears,' I replied, And we paddled out towards *Nordkaperen* till splinters flew from the planks. When we had got some way out into the bay, the short sea and strong wind began to hamper us. We drifted away, and at the same time we discovered that the skiff was leaking. I had to bale with my cap. This interfered somewhat with our progress. The worst of it was that *Nordkaperen* was drifting as fast as we were advancing. She was getting nearer and nearer to the reef, the white surf on which we could just make out in the darkness.

Bill sat in the bows, paddling like an Indian. He bent his back while the plank whipped the water into foam. I myself had taken my plank under one arm like a crutch and was paddling with one hand and baling with the other. It was a hopeless task—just as much water was coming in from above as from below. To counteract the drift away we had almost to proceed sideways, and we gradually realized that we could not reach *Nordkaperen*. We tried to hail her, but our shouts were swallowed up in the wind and rain. We made one more desperate sortie against the elements, but we almost marked time. It looked as if *Nordkaperen* was only a few yards from the reef when suddenly a light appeared on board. Knud had been woken by the boat's unaccustomed movements in the rough sea, and quickly realized what had happened. He and Poul had hauled in the anchor and started the engine, and a course was set into safe waters. Bill and I forgot to row for sheer relief, and nearly went on the reef ourselves, but we hailed Poul and Knud and they took us on board.

Twice later did *Nordkaperen* go off on her own. On one occasion, fortunately, we had a big shark hook out on a steel wire, and it caught in a cable at the bottom of the harbour. We were driven broadside on through a crowd of small boats and fetched up only a boat's length from the quay. The second time we were woken by the pilot and his crew. They came swarming on board one morning and asked if we meant to sail now.

'No!' we replied, bewildered.

'Yes! you're bound for Australia now!' said the pilot.

Quite right—*Nordkaperen* was circling round between the two reefs which bounded the entrance to the harbour. We thanked the smart, alert Fijian skipper for his trouble, but he waved us away with a deprecating gesture.

Suva was a wretched anchorage—a muddy bottom sloping steeply down to immense depths, and a very strong, variable current.

The days passed, while we were dragged from one party to another. It was for the most part members of the yacht club who wanted to see us. That meant a good deal, for nearly all the white men were members of the club. At first we were not the only visitors to be enjoying the hospitality of the Suva yachting people. There was another circumnavigator passing through—a small ketch called *Alone*. She came from the USA and her skipper's name was Francis Agnew. He had only one man on board to help him, and they had taken 71 days to cover the same distance which *Nordkaperen* had covered in 31 days. Further, *Alone*, though strongly built, was not an ideal craft for a voyage round the world. She was too broad and too short, and the skipper was a bit casual. Francis was a splendid fellow, always good-humoured and full of cheery wisecracks—and as kind-hearted as the day is long. We spent many jolly hours with him. He had copper stays in his rigging, and we warned him not to continue to use them, but he scouted our warning, saying that he just tautened them when they grew slack.

Poor, rash Francis—he had not had any bad weather yet, though *Alone* had sailed 7,000 miles. The good weather he had had in the Pacific would not hold all the way, and we prophesied to him that that rigging would not see him round the world. But he was full of optimism. We wished and hoped the best for him and his crew when *Alone* sailed for New Zealand on May 2.

But she never reached New Zealand. She was a total loss. Perhaps a lonely reef was her fate, but there is strong reason to believe that she went down in a prolonged gale which at that time was raging north of New Zealand.

The Suva Yacht Club and authorities did all they could to clear up the mystery of her loss. The whole of the south-western Pacific was notified. Military aircraft searched, airliners kept a look-out, all ships were informed; but all in vain.

Bill made our purchases and cooked for us, as a cook should, but one afternoon—on my birthday, as it happened—he said quite unexpectedly:

'I'm not going to cook today, I'm going ashore!'

We stared at him incredulously. This was strange behaviour. If he had said it nicely, perhaps we should have said nothing, but before we had recovered from our astonishment, he added:

'But if you'd like to go ashore at six, I'm giving a dinner at the McDonald Hotel.'

'Ha, ha! Bill, old chap, you won't die a sinner!'

I think we were all three thinking the same: when Bill for once in a way opened his purse there was usually nothing in it.

'Thanks, Bill, you can be sure we'll come.'

When the time approached, we put on our white ducks and got into the dinghy. Bill had disappeared long before. On our way in to the quay we passed through a flock of big sharks, five or six of them, and Poul hit one of them on the head with the oar; it gave a jump and then disappeared, while a fountain of water shot high into the air. We saw more and bigger sharks in Suva Bay than anywhere else in the world. They swarmed round the ship day and night, but despite persevering attempts we never succeeded in catching any. They were apparently more frightened than we.

We arrived, tied up the dinghy and sauntered along to the hotel. On reaching the hotel we had a great surprise. Bill and a number of our friends had arranged a big dinner for us. It had been kept quite secret, and neither solid nor liquid food was lacking.

First the whole party assembled up in a room inhabited by a jolly girl from New Zealand. She was manageress of the local telephone exchange and her name was Denis. In her flat the foundation of the dinner was laid with a sea of cocktails. The room was so crowded that people had to sit on the floor, the back of the sofa and the chest of drawers. Then we swarmed down to a well-furnished table in the dining-room.

After dinner Danish, English and Fijian songs succeeded one another, and there was dancing. An American officer came to me at the piano and asked me to play a tune. He asked for '*I Danmark er födt*'.*

Not till then did I realize that the man spoke Danish. His name was Clemmensen, and he was the last officer of the American forces which had had their base in the Fiji islands during the war. Clemmensen stood us whisky-and-sodas and invited us and *Nordkaperen* to visit a large military camp on the other side of the island, at a town called Lautoka. We thanked him and promised to go.

We were turned out of the hotel several hours after closing time, and there was a strong majority in favour of finishing the evening on board *Nordkaperen* with a cup of coffee. We reached the landing-stage in extended order, but then problems presented themselves. We disposed of two dinghies, but they would not take the whole party. Bill and I would have to remain on shore with four of them, while Poul and Knud each took a dinghy and rowed out to *Nordkaperen* with the rest. While we were waiting, I thought I should enjoy a little swim. Close in to the landing-stage there was no danger from sharks, and the thin tropical clothes I had on would have to be washed anyhow. I asked a young lady to hold my cigarettes and dived into the water. At the same second Bill too shot through the air. We swam a little way along the wharf, but some of our guests misunderstood our action. Three

* 'In Denmark is born . . .'

of them, two men and Denis, jumped into the water too with all their clothes on, and, what was worse, they swam as hard as they could out towards *Nordkaperen*, which was lying two or three hundred yards out. Bill and I shouted and yelled, but they did not hear us. So we swam fast after them, shouting warnings all the time, but they were just enjoying themselves and talking loudly to one another. At last we made contact, swam with them in a group and urged them to make all the noise they could, beat and splash in the water and, generally speaking, get out to *Nordkaperen* as quickly as possible.

They had not given a thought to the sharks, and one can safely say that they had gone pretty mad. We got on board safe and sound. A little farther out a couple of shark fins glided through the moonlit water as a justification of our forebodings. Although Denis had suffered a slight nervous shock, the festive atmosphere was not destroyed, and it was not till the eastern sky was reddened by the rising sun that we rowed the guests ashore.

The McDonald Hotel became our social centre. We gradually came to know all the guests, and the proprietor or his wife often asked us to dinner—a kind of reward for our having so often cheered up their guests by our singing and playing. One evening we met there a New Zealander who had been living in the South Sea islands for a generation and was a bit of an eccentric. When the hotel closed, and we had begun to go down the street to return to *Nordkaperen*, he overtook us and said he wanted to show us something interesting. He would take us to a native kava-kava feast, if we would like to come? Of course we would.

We left the smart quarters of the town by empty streets, where we met only bare-footed native policemen, and we noticed that they gave our guide a comradely greeting. He told us that he felt more at home among the coloured people than among the whites, and was particularly fond of Polynesians and Melanesians. He worked himself up as he talked and finally emphasized his loathing for civilization by flinging out a 'damn it!' and spitting on the pavement.

Policeman in Suva (Fiji) with skirts and bare legs

View in Fiji

All sail set to catch every breath of wind

PLATE IX

Washing-day in the Pacific 2,000 miles from land

'He's got bats in the belfry,' said Knud to me in Danish, and I felt there was something in it.

We had gradually made our way into the coloured quarter. We turned down a narrow alley, passed a row of neat little huts and stopped by a high wall. Our new friend looked carefully all round to make sure that no one saw us, and then he drew us in with him through a door in the wall. After creeping across a dark yard we came to a sinister-looking, darkened house. Our friend knocked at the door—a definite signal—and a pure-blooded Fijian opened it. He looked frightened on seeing Knud and me, but our friend whispered a few pacifying words in his ear, and we were welcomed in. It was a quite illegal affair at that time of night, but we were reassured that two officials were of the party.

We had entered an oblong room in which two tables stood. On each table was a bowl filled with a greenish liquid. This was kava-kava. Room was made for us despite the crush, and soon we were sitting flanked by Fijians, men and women. If only our English friends had known!

There was only one drinking cup on each table—half a coconut shell. A woman was occupied in filling it with kava-kava and passing it from mouth to mouth. Before the cup was raised to the drinker's lips the members of the party clapped their hands twice, and when it was empty they clapped again. It had to be emptied at one draught.

'Well, Knud, old chap,' I thought, 'now for a test of your self-control!'

The man who had to drink before Knud was chewing betel and dribbling copiously, but Knud made the sign of the cross and drank bravely. The woman handed the shell to me. Her fore-finger had almost disappeared into the kava-kava. All eyes were turned on me, and I looked down into the unappetising green liquid, while the exhorting hand-claps sounded in my ears. Then I shut my eyes and drained the cup.

Why good God, it was just soapy water!

I was on the point of spitting it all out, but overcame the urge to do so and handed the shell back with a sickly smile. It was washed out and refilled for the next person.

'Now you mustn't disappoint them by saying you don't like it,' our friend said. 'When one gets accustomed to it it tastes very good!'

We promised to do what we could. The cup returned, once, twice, thrice, four times: at last we lost count of the number of times and just drank automatically when a dusky hand passed the coconut shell to us.

They seemed to be making a dead set at us, and it was with great difficulty that we managed to swallow the soapy water each time.

'It's been a delightful evening and night,' we told our friend, 'but now we must get down to the boat.'

He received special thanks for having taken us to the kava-kava feast. Then we tumbled out into the fresh air, but our legs seemed to have become independent units, with their own views as to direction and time. It seemed to me that large and small soap-bubbles surged out of our mouths when we spoke to one another. They gleamed like opals and vanished up into the starry sky, but Knud could not see them, although I pointed them out. He must have been quite drunk!

The day dawned when we had to fulfil our promise to Clemme to visit the military camp at Lautoka. It was a sail of 130 miles outside and inside reefs. Clemme had promised us proper beds to sleep in, shower-baths several times a day, and as much food and drink as we could consume, so it was with great expectations that we started one Friday about noon.

We could save ourselves a detour of 40 miles by sailing through a little passage, about ten miles long and a mile broad, between Viti Levu and the small island of Mbennga. People with local knowledge had most certainly advised us against going through if the weather was not fairly good. The channel was not marked. On the Viti Levu side there was a long reef, but the surf made it visible. On the Mbennga side, to port, there were thousands of rocks, some of which projected above water. The narrow strait twisted like an S, and there was a strong current. We naturally remembered our mishap in the strait in the Galapagos, but here we would have a chance of a general rehearsal; we were soon going to pass through waters of the same kind in the Torres Strait.

The weather was not so bad, so we decided to force the strait. We were at the entrance as early as 2 p.m., and all promised well. The log was streamed, and Knud set about getting bearings on different points. An hour later heavy clouds rolled up from the south-east. They looked as if they had water in them. At the same time we noticed that the current had become fierce. We were not getting anywhere. The engine was started, for we had to get out before it grew dark. Not long after the rain was on us, accompanied by variable but heavy gusts. The thick rain made visibility nil, and we had to steer blind. One hour after another passed, and darkness began to creep on. We were still three or four miles from the entrance.

At 6.30 p.m. it was pitch dark, the rain was streaming down, and the racing wind had raised a sea with white horses on it. We had not had a sight of anything at all for several hours; we were sailing by the log only and had to guess our position. At last we could stand no more of it. It was like walking on the edge of a precipice with shut eyes. Knud proposed to go in towards the reef to get a sight of it. The proposal suited me all right. Although it was a dangerous joke, it was better than uncertainty, and by keeping a sharp look-out we should be able to see the surf on the reef in time to be able to go about.

So we turned a little to starboard. Poul was at the wheel, Knud crawled up into the shrouds to starboard and I to port. It came suddenly—before we had expected it.

'Look out—reef!' Knud yelled, 'port—more—more still!'

Poul reacted instantaneously and turned the boat almost up into the eye of the wind.

I saw the reef just as Knud shouted his warning. It ran almost at right angles to *Nordkaperen's* course, but what I noticed in particular was the rollers, the tentacles of the reef. There had not been much water under our keel. It would be a good while before we got free again. The reef stretched far out into the water like a tongue, but now we knew where we were, and it did not take Knud long to set a safe course out into open water. Moreover, Knud's guess at our position had been correct to a hundred yards.

The night passed without trouble. At 9 a.m. next day we were in behind the reefs, and at 3.15 p.m. we anchored off Lautoka.

We spent a delightful week in the camp, in the jovial and pleasant company of Clemme and his British officer friends. On our last evening in the camp a festivity on a large scale was arranged, at which native women and men sang and danced to us in the light of a great fire. It was very interesting, but the Fijians lacked some of the Tahitians' charm. About noon next day we weighed anchor and set our course back to Suva. Bill was not with us this time. For some reason he wanted to stay at Lautoka a few days longer and come to Suva later by bus, but we had three passengers instead—Captain Clemmensen, a lady from Suva and a boy of twelve. In return for their free passage they had a trip they will never forget!

It began with fine weather and a faint breeze, but towards night we got the wind dead against us, and it began to blow. At about 8 p.m. we had to take in the topsail, and at the same time it began to rain hard. At 10 p.m. the jib had to be taken in. We now had a really strong breeze. About midnight we took in the mizen. *Nordkaperen* was pitching a lot and her fore-deck was continually under water, but she pushed along through the seas well and steadily. It was a long time since she had sailed close-hauled, and she liked it.

Our passengers, on the other hand, did not. They had been given the after cabin, and they lay there rolling about in their bunks, sleepless and seasick. When the rest of us were having meals and drinking coffee, they demanded that the doors into the cabin should be shut, for the sight and smell of food made them sick. Sometimes they called to us feebly—to open the skylight. A moment afterwards *Nordkaperen* was buried by a heavy sea, and cascades of water poured down into the cabin. They called to us and asked to have the skylight shut again. We were kept busy all night opening and shutting the skylight and carrying buckets, medicine, and so on.

At daylight we went about and steered for the Mbennga passage, which we made in broad daylight and without any excitement. At dusk we could make out the lights of Suva, and at 8 p.m. *Nordkaperen* was again lying at her moorings in the bay—to the great surprise of the people at the yacht club. They had not expected us in such bad weather.

One of the reasons for our staying so long at Fiji was that we had to wait more than six weeks to get the boat up on to a slip. There was normally a delay of over three months, but the intervention of the yacht club saved us a longer wait. There was only one slip at Suva, and that belonged to the Government, but its leading men were all members of the yacht club. They looked after us in all kinds of ways. We had eight men placed at our disposal, we got material and good service of other kinds, and the bill presented us—for the sake of appearances—was ridiculously small.

*Nordkaperen* was smartened up again, and we gradually began to think about starting for Australia. Twice we announced our departure, and twice the club arranged a farewell party for us, but we were continually detained. I was awaiting a most important postal packet on a definite date, but it did not arrive, and so we had to postpone our start. Not till July 5 were we ready to sail. The members of the club had the third farewell party ready for us that evening; but it had to be held without us; we resisted all persuasions.

*Nordkaperen* lay alongside the quay to take on board water, petrol and other goods. Among the farewell presents was a small kitten, which was a great source of amusement to us later. It was given us by the harbour-master and was christened Isa Lei. That is a Fijian farewell greeting addressed to a person departing whom one does not expect to see again.

We promised to go two hundred or so miles off our course, when approaching Australia, to look for *Alone* on some of the isolated reefs. We should have done it even if we had not been asked to do so, and even if the chances of finding *Alone* were one in a thousand.

Among the things we shipped was a brand-new rubber boat to hold seven persons, which we obtained in exchange for our old worn-out boat (military service) to hold five, and all for nothing.

At last we slipped away from the wharf, and at the same time an aircraft appeared over the mountains. It descended over our heads in spirals and circled round dangerously close to *Nordkaperen's* masts—several times close enough to give us a bit of a shock. Our friends in the military camp had come to say good-bye to us.

The sails were set one by one, and we were soon outside the reef. Two motor-boats came shooting after us, crowded with people who wanted to accompany us, but *Nordkaperen* was already going at a good speed. They could not reach us without coming along with us outside the reef in the big seas, and that they obviously did not want to do. They had to wave us good-bye at long range.

Viti Levu disappeared into the darkness. Now life was following its daily round there; people were dining, going to the cinema, playing cards or passing the time in other ways just as when we were there. But we were back again in our narrow, lonely little world on the vast heaving sea. We pulled ourselves together and looked ahead. We had nearly 2,000 miles ahead of us. Our destination was Cairns in Australia.

We obtained at the last moment a pilot's chart of the waters behind the Australian barrier and the Torres Strait, through which we were to pass. The information the chart gave us made us green with chagrin, for our route appeared to be packed with drifting mines. And we had thought we had done with that kind of foolishness!

CHAPTER XII

# *Through the Barrier Reef*

NEXT morning Isa Lei had disappeared, and a thorough investigation was started. Every corner of the boat was searched, but without result. Not till Poul wanted to wash the deck did the kitten come to light. She had been sleeping peacefully in one of his rubber boots. This was not the last time Isa Lei performed the disappearing trick.

Sometimes she slipped into a drawer or a locker without anyone noticing, and half a day might pass before we found her. For the first three days we had a light easterly breeze, which took *Nordkaperen* along nicely, but when we came near the southernmost islands of the New Hebrides the light breeze and cloudless sky were replaced by thunder-squalls and overcast skies. Although the rain and thunder were violent, there was not wind enough to fill an old hat, and we were becalmed for several days.

Every reef or small island we passed was closely examined. We were looking for the wreck of *Alone*. At night we carried a special light so that if her crew were there they could see and hail us, and we studied the horizon attentively. We knew they had signal rockets on board, but the chances of finding them alive were small, and if they were alive they might be thousands of miles from us. Our field of visibility was limited to ten miles, and it was almost looking for a needle in a bundle of hay. The crew of *Alone* and their fate filled our minds by day and by night, and this naturally set its imprint on life on board. Our spirits were not what they usually were.

On the third day we caught a 30 lb. tunny. Before it was dead Isa Lei rushed at it and began to gnaw off its tail. The tunny in its convulsions lashed out with its tail and Isa Lei was sent flying, but she dashed in again like a fury and was sent hurtling through the air several times before the tunny gave up the struggle. Isa Lei was not slow to learn that the fishing-line provided delicious food. When the line was hung out, she stood on her hind-legs with her 'elbows' on the bulwarks. She watched the line closely and executed a war dance as soon as the catch was being hauled in. The moment the fish touched the deck Isa Lei flung herself on to it and caught hold of its tail.

When it grew light on the morning of the fourth day, we discovered that *Nordkaperen* had come in between two islands. The most northerly was called Tanna and had a volcano from which smoke and flames were pouring. Bill began to worry; he wanted to go ashore and have a closer look at the volcano. I did not require much persuasion in the quiet weather we were having. It looked really exciting, and with such a calm sea we should not take much time or lose much distance by going there. Poul did not need much persuasion either, but Knud was rather sceptical. The chart of Tanna and its coast was pretty old and not very detailed. However, after a thorough study of the chart we decided on a landing-place. To go ashore we should have to start the engine, and to get it going the magneto must spark—but it just would not. The magneto upset our plans and turned *Nordkaperen* into a madhouse for the next few days. We had decided to land on Tanna, so temptingly situated about five miles away, and no magneto on earth should prevent us from doing so. Every time the magneto was taken off the engine the sparks flew gaily, but immediately it was screwed on again not a spark was to be seen. All hands eagerly watched this process which was repeated some twenty times, and the hours passed. It had grown dark, the volcano flamed and lit up its immediate surroundings, while impatience devoured us. The magneto was taken to pieces and it appeared that an insulating ring was damaged. Knud and I promised one another that we would not sleep till the engine was in order; not because of Tanna, but because we were going through the Australian barrier by the Grafton Passage, extremely difficult waters in which the help of the engine would be necessary.

We could not have finer conditions for repair work. It was dead calm, and if we took too long over it the consequences might be unpleasant. We spent the whole night experimenting with different materials with which to make a new insulating ring, and to keep the fire of enthusiasm alight we enlisted the help of a bottle of whisky. All the ebonite, galalite and other 'ites' we had on board were raided: razor-boxes, soap-boxes, and things from the wireless. The new ring was carefully adapted so as to be the right shape and size, but the sparks jumped past it all the same.

In the morning Poul came in to us. He had taken a serious decision. He took a deep breath, produced a gramophone disc and said:

'If you can use that, saw it in pieces if you like.'

It was a great sacrifice. Poul had got the disc from the Suva wireless station as a mark of gratitude for his Danish songs, and it was his own rich tenor that resounded from it.

There was not much likelihood of the disc being of use to us, and we thought he had better keep it, for, as Knud said, 'the engine will only get hot when your melting voice comes near it'.

No, we must find something else. The smashed insulating ring was examined, and it appeared that it could be put together with a soldering iron. We set about collecting the mosaic, and meanwhile Bill kept a sharp eye on our distance from Tanna, which grew longer and longer. He was beginning to fear that we should not land on the thrilling volcano.

About midday, when we were all occupied with the fate of the magneto, we heard a faint whistling noise from the sea. The noise gradually rose to a loud roaring and seething, and Poul ran up on deck to see what it was. He called to us excitedly and all hands were quickly on deck—the cat first. A strange sight met our eyes. The surface of the sea as far as the eye could reach was covered with little jets of water, a foot or two in height and a few inches apart. We thought at first that millions of fish were jumping, but a test with the net showed that there were no fish under the jets. The sea, just now so shining and calm, was now sputtering and bubbling as if the water was aboil. Were we on top of a submarine volcano? Hardly: there was no sulphurous vapour or smoke, and the water was no warmer than it had been all the time. But we noted small eddies running aimlessly round one another. There was no doubt that we had come upon a collision of currents of an unusual kind. Isa Lei was most interested in the jets of water. She thought they were fish, and called our attention to the possibilities by loud mewing.

The curious spectacle held our attention for a whole hour. Then the undecided water disappeared southward, and we dived down to the engine again. Next forenoon—two days after we had started on the repairs—the engine was working. The mountains of Tanna were now faint silhouettes. Bill was the only one of us who still wanted to go ashore there. The rest of us thought only of sleep, and as a fresh south-easterly breeze sprang up at the same time, no attention was paid to Bill. We thought no more about Tanna and set our course for Australia. Bill went on grumbling. I pointed out to him that the considerations there had been in favour of landing no longer existed; we were thirty-five to forty miles from Tanna, and now had a fresh favourable wind, which should be used to take us to Australia and not to tack laboriously back to Tanna. The question led to unfriendliness between Bill and myself.

The fresh wind held steadily, and *Nordkaperen* bowled along under all the sail she could carry.

On the sixth day our run was 191 miles, and on the ninth day we worked it up to 209 miles. We were obviously out to beat our own record of 222 miles, but we had not the great rollers with us as we had then. For a few hours on end we could log about 12 knots, but the wind nearly always dropped for a time, especially about sunset, and this destroyed the possibility of a record. Our farewell to Tanna and the volcano brought us into the last lap of our crossing of the great Pacific, the part which is called the Coral

Sea. We had sailed geographically halfway round the world and so had Denmark no longer behind us, but ahead—a thing we found stimulating to our morale. We realized that we had been covering the easiest part of our route with an almost constant trade wind. Now the difficulties would come with variable weather and a lot of tacking, which would impose a great strain on the gear.

On the first day in the Coral Sea, towards evening, I noticed that Knud was having trouble with his calculations. He calculated and wrote, tore up his paper and began again.

This happened several times, and his face became one large angry question mark.

'What's the trouble, mate?' I asked, interrupting his monologue of oaths and curses.

'Damn it all,' he fumed, 'I've worked it out time after time, and it all comes out exactly right.'

'Then what is there to be annoyed about?'

'We're sailing right on to an island in the New Hebrides!'

'Never mind,' I consoled him, 'that'll suit us very well.'

'May be I'm going potty. Just go through the figures for yourself,' said Knud.

There was nothing wrong: the calculations were correct. If the observations were right too, which Knud guaranteed they were, the mistake must be found somewhere else, and it was.

The chronometer had lost about twenty minutes, the wireless control showed. It had never happened before. It was usually a matter of a few seconds. On the same day our ordinarily so reliable watch clock stopped, and our compass got out of order. Courses on which we had previously had a deviation of from nil to one degree now had a deviation of from 7 to 10 degrees. It looked queer, but it must have been a combination of coincidences. We were quite unable to find any rational explanation of it.

For some reason *Nordkaperen* could no longer steer herself. We had certainly messed about with the rigging too much when we were at Suva. So we always had to have a man at the wheel. Of course it was difficult to make a boat steer herself with the wind on her quarter, but *Nordkaperen* had done it before.

A man on watch at night might well find the time long; he had to be at the wheel all the time. As a rule he wished he was lying in his bunk like the rest, and when one is longing for something the time goes terribly slowly.

It was almost full moon—the friendly round moon that has kept men on night watches company for long solitary hours. It seemed almost like a live person—the first thing one looked for when one tumbled up on deck to take over. If it was not there, one felt twice as solitary.

The stars were unusually bright; they twinkled more than usual. It almost looked as if it was the fresh trade wind that made them flicker. The trade wind clouds raced over the sky, and the moon had great fun playing hide-and-seek among them. It disappeared behind a cloud and carried the moonshine on the water with it, to emerge again a moment later. First it ran a little way along the edge of the cloud with just its eyes over, peering cautiously around. Then it leapt forth in all its brilliance, roguish and laughing, and again flooded the whole sea with prismatic hues and crystal. I often caught myself sending a smile to my friend the moon.

The bright cone from the ship's light fell on the watch clock; it was 1 a.m.—an hour had gone, and it was cigarette time. At the end of each hour I smoked a cigarette. They tasted best when they were rationed.

The shapes of the clouds that night were fantastic. One was like a horse with no hind-legs. Then something appeared which resembled hind-legs, but at the same time the head vanished. The horse gradually became a turtle, and sounds of hard breathing and grunting were heard. These did not come from the clouds, but from a school of whales desirous of examining *Nordkaperen* more closely. They moved round and under the boat for some time.

Hallo! there came a cloud—like a man's head! Ought I not to know that profile? It was Hitler to the life! He raced along with open mouth, made straight for the moon and ate it. He should not have done that, for now he became an indeterminate mass.

The moon sprang out again and smiled more coquettishly than usual. Wider gaps were formed between the clouds, and—

'Hell!' I was just on the point of jibing. It was not easy to look at the sky and the compass at the same time. I got into a regular sweat.

Then Hitler became a shirt hung out to dry, and my observations of the sky were interrupted when I glanced at the compass. A large cockroach was sitting on the glass of the binnacle. I hit at it with my souwester, which was lying beside me, missed the cockroach, and made a star-shaped crack in the glass . . . The cursed brutes!

We had got a few on board in Tahiti and the Galapagos, but those on the wharf at Suva must have been particularly keen to travel. We got thousands of stowaways on board and did not realize how serious it was till we got to sea. They were cunning enough not to show themselves before. On the previous evening we had had a great battle with them, but they employed elastic methods of warfare.

The beginning of it was that Knud and I, all unsuspecting, were lying asleep in our bunks. Bill was messing about in the galley, and on opening a locker discovered a whole army of cockroaches, ready for their deeds of darkness. We had on board a little container of poison gas intended for the extermination of mosquitoes. Bill got this out and turned its jets on the cockroaches, which were overwhelmed in the first round. Some lay on their backs in surrender at once, but the greater number fled—straight into Knud's bunk and mine.

The cat slept with me, and when I felt something touching my ear I thought it was she. I passed my hand drowsily over my ear, but got hold of a sprawling cockroach. I turned on the light and found that my bunk was swarming with cockroaches of all sizes. I flung the big one out to Bill and abused him for having chased the brutes into our cabin through the thin bulkhead.

'I *am* sorry—I *am* sorry!' Bill kept on repeating, but a smile played in the corner of his eyes.

We went into the after cabin to look at the swarm, and Knud was now awake too. His bunk also had become alive with them, and he was now sitting in its farthest corner slogging about wildly with a rubber shoe in his hand.

'I *am* sorry. I *am* sorry,' Bill repeated, 'so sorry!'

'Can't you keep your damned beasts for yourself?' Knud hissed, hurling his shoe at the cockroaches so that a shower of them flew into the air.

While Poul sat at the wheel, we three others opened the battle against the cockroaches that night and killed perhaps ten thousand in different ways. Isa Lei was as keen as any of us, but she wanted to play with them first, so that her offensive took rather longer. Half a bucket full were swept up on the deck, and we thought the enemy's ranks were now well thinned. We discovered later that there must be at least as many left.

The sky by degrees had become cloudless. Sky, sea, moon and I were alone again.

What was the time? The devil—five past two.

I called Knud in a low voice. It was his watch now. And I took the last cigarette of the night.

'Very practical,' Knud said, when he saw the star-shaped crack in the glass of the binnacle, 'now one can look at the stars and the compass at the same time!'

As we gradually drew near Australia, the wind grew fresh and shifted to the south. We had wind force 5 and 6. It continued to shift and ended up in the south-west. The headsails had to be taken in one by one, and at last we were carrying only mainsail and foresail. The seas became high and irregular, and we had many of them on board. It was too hot to keep hatches and skylight shut, so when the boat filled, as she did now and then, the water poured down into the cabins.

On the morning of Sunday, July 20, Knud began to be uneasy. He did not like our not being able to see anything of the Australian barrier. We had imagined that it consisted of small islands and reefs, but there was nothing to be seen. I found this queer too, especially as we could faintly see the distant mountain-tops of Australia on the western horizon. The barrier was supposed to reach out into the water for about thirty miles. The chart showed visible reefs, but no surf was to be seen anywhere. There were a few islands lying close to the shore, but they blended with the mainland, so they were no help to us. On account of thick weather we had had to sail on dead reckoning for two days. At last we had no idea where we were, but by the greatest luck the sun came out for a moment. Knud managed to shoot it before it disappeared again. His misgivings proved to be justified. We were sailing right *on* the Australian barrier. The mainsail was struck, and we crawled out into safer waters. We found out later that off Cairns the barrier consisted of submarine reefs from two to six feet under water—some, however, visible at low water. We looked for the Grafton Passage. We had come rather far south, but agreed to put off going on until it was dark. We could then get a safe bearing on the powerful lighthouse on the mainland.

Our decision was changed, however, when we thought of the many mines which were reported to be adrift in the passage. We would wait till 4 a.m. before we went in. Then we could set our course by the lighthouse and at the same time keep a look out for mines in the growing daylight. It sounded very nice, but was not so easy. It was a fearful night, on which every kind of ill-luck pursued us.

We had set the mainsail again when our troubles began at about 10 p.m. We had taken our bearing on the lighthouse, had got into position for entering, and were preparing to lie and wait in peace and comfort till 4 a.m. An innocent little gust of wind sprang up from the east. It was followed by a bigger squall with more wind, and we had difficulty in keeping our position. It was an onshore wind, and had shifted from south-west to east.

An hour later earth and sky were all one. The wind came howling in strong gusts, and the sea rose violently. High rollers came raging on at a fearful speed, with the whole Pacific behind them. The mainsail had to be taken in. It was a hard job. We ran the boat into the wind, the sails thrashed and beat about. All in a minute, the peak halyard had got fouled, the topping-lift was caught up in the crosstrees, the topsail sheet twisted itself round the gaff and the main sheet broke free. The water poured in over us time after time. When we had overcome one hindrance a new one arose at once, and a few ends had to be cut through before we had the mainsail under control. We tried to keep *Nordkaperen* hove to under the small sails, but were only buried in one sea after another. When we had had the boat full of water several times, we agreed to keep in through the Grafton Passage despite the mines. The boat was turned about and the engine started, after which we steered straight towards the lighthouse. The sea was high and violent, but the wind disappeared after half an hour. It all went very well till we were about five sea-miles into the invisible channel. Then it began to blow again from the south-west, and the seas became white-crested again. We could keep our position with mizen and foresail, and one engine going, but without the engine we could not—and it stopped.

There was silence on board when the pleasant, comforting noise ceased. Now we heard only the roaring of the sea. It was the worst thing that could have happened. Knud flew down to the engine to find out the cause, while we prepared to set the mainsail again. It appeared that our provisional repairs of the magneto had not been lasting. We could, therefore, no longer count on the engine for a help in an emergency.

If the mainsail had had a game with us when it was to come down, it did so no less when it was to go up again. We hauled on the throat halyard with all our might, but the mast-hoops had got fouled with some loose ends, and they were pinched against the mast. The halyards were in continual disorder, and we could not stand on deck with the boat rolling so heavily. Knud and I were standing side by side, each hauling on his sheet, when he suddenly vanished into the night. He was dangling three or four yards out over the ship's side, when the boat started a new roll and came rushing back again.

'Where the hell have you been?' I asked in astonishment, but never got an answer. The deck disappeared from under my feet, and it was my turn to get my feet wet. I tumbled in against the mast with a crash and did not come out of it as gracefully as Knud, which he too noticed:

'Hi there—more beef into it—more beef to the throat halyard!'

And we all four hauled at once. The sail went up, but the three upper mast-hoops and half the gaff lacing were torn off. While we were busy setting the mainsail, we made an unpleasant discovery; we were no longer heading for the light!

Instead of the usual four short flashes, the lighthouse was showing one long and two short. We were in the danger zone!

If we had had a light list, the disaster would not have been so great; but the light was fairly new and our knowledge of it was limited. We knew that it ought to show four short flashes when we were on our right course, but not what it showed when we were south or north of the channel. We tried to get a bearing, but the sea was too broken and high. On account of our leeway we had held the wind, and the uncertain current could have taken us south, but the deviation caused by the wind could also have carried us north. The choppy sea might mean that the current was running against the wind. So we had a fifty per cent chance of making the right choice. It would be an exciting life and death experiment.

Knud proposed that we should go out of the passage again, but I protested vigorously against this. It might be all the same whether we went out or in, when we were no longer head on to the light.

The lighthouse was showing one long flash and two short ones, but when we were sailing up towards the entrance from the south, I thought that I caught a glimpse in the dusk of two short flashes and one long one. I was not quite sure, but the chance of backing the right horse was greater if we went in southward.

*Nordkaperen* came up into the wind, and we held on southward.

Then came the minutes none of us will forget. The rubber boat was got ready and the ship's papers collected. Poul sat at the wheel, Knud had Isa Lei in his arms, and Bill and I stood on the fore-deck. Soundings were no good, for the water was bottomless right up to the reefs.

We had a sick feeling when *Nordkaperen* plunged far down into the trough of a wave. What would the next sea bring?

We stared at the light: no one said a word. One minute after another passed at a snail's pace—still one long flash and two short ones. It was too dark to look out for surf. Only when the boat was flung up unusually high and rushed down again into the trough of the sea did we look ahead for a moment. Otherwise we all gazed at the light as though hypnotized. The long flash began to be slightly obscure in the middle of its period, and hope was kindled in us.

A moment later we saw four short bright flashes!

What a relief it was to know that we had water under our keel again! Poul offered to take the wheel for the rest of the night, and Bill offered to station himself on the fore-deck and warn Poul if the light changed. It was all we could do to keep our position, but thanks to Poul's care we did not have to go about, and when I came on deck next morning the mountains of Australia were close ahead.

We were off the entrance to Cairns early in the forenoon but we did not get ashore that day. The sailing channel into the harbour is a dug canal, five miles long and about 45 yards wide. We tried to tack in, but when we had got halfway the wind became uncertain and variable in direction. It was the fault of the mountains. Accordingly *Nordkaperen* was put about, and we went out again. If we had known the harbour conditions we should perhaps have gone on—even with the incalculable down-draught, but the boat wanted tidying up, and we needed sleep. A new continent demanded an entry in style.

The anchor was dropped out in the bay; we had a substantial breakfast and then fell down and slept.

Next morning Knud patched the magneto up yet again, so that we could get ourselves into harbour by our own efforts.

At three o'clock on July 22 we were able to set foot on Australian soil.

## CHAPTER XIII

# *The Passage of the Torres Strait*

WE could not see much of the town of Cairns from the sea side, as it was hidden by warehouses and trees. The harbour was pleasant, and suggested a harbour in a Danish provincial town. Schooners, motor vessels, fishing boats and other small craft lay there in idyllic disorder. High green mountains flanked the deep bay or fjord on one shore of which the town and port had grown up. On the opposite side of the fjord thick mangrove scrub grew right to the foot of the mountains.

Now and again we heard the barking of the packs of wild dogs from across the water. Great birds of prey sailed over the marsh, peering down and hovering, in search of a meal.

The harbour-master allotted us a place alongside a small motorship, and we thus escaped having to change our moorings several times in every twenty-four hours on account of the tide. As we glided in alongside the *Rooding*, as the ship was called, a voice called down to us in real Danish:

'You can take this line, and I'll help you tie up.'

The voice belonged to a seaman on board who later introduced himself as Erik Jacobsen. He and the rest of the crew, twelve hands in all, became our first friends in Australia. They at once insisted on showing us Cairns through the bottom of a glass of beer, and thus our first impression of the town and its citizens was that an unquenchable thirst prevailed and that there was a bar in every house.

I will not say that the authorities were unfriendly to us, but the Australian laws about visitors and ships in general exceeded anything we had to submit to either before or since. Papers, papers, more papers—I had to sign something like sixty different forms and declarations. The ship's cat Isa Lei was the subject of hours of acrimonious discussion, but at last we agreed to the following conditions:

If the cat left the ship or disappeared in any other way, a fine of £50 sterling should be paid.

The cat should be examined by a veterinary surgeon—two men came to do it!

Once a day—sometimes twice—a couple of men came to establish Isa Lei's continued presence on board.

According to law we should have deposited £50, but we escaped that.

Isa Lei was now kept under extremely close guard. She was carefully locked up when we went into the town, and if she took to performing antics on the bulwarks or out on the bowsprit, our hearts were in our mouths. The official who had dictated the conditions to us became a frequent guest on board, and it was not long before he offered us another cat if Isa Lei should run away.

We were astonished to hear what high wages the *Rooding's* crew received. The ship had put into Cairns with a broken shaft and was going on to Singapore when the repairs had been completed. The sailors had no less than £126 paid out to them every fourth Saturday.

We asked why such high wages were being paid. It appeared that the *Rooding* was to have a big lighter in tow, so that her speed would be reduced to two or three knots, and she and her tow would have to go through the Torres Strait with its strong current and many reefs. But the chief reason for the high wages was the danger from mines. The waters behind the Australian barrier and in the Torres Strait were full of mines. We, by the way, were to sail by the same route!

The newness of Cairns was plainly visible from its soulless, barbarous architecture. It was a new settlers' town. It had no traditions as yet, and a couple of cinemas and a mass of bars were its temples of culture.

A black soft hat on the back of the head, no jacket, so that the obligatory braces were visible, a home-rolled cigarette dangling between lips which never stopped talking about racing—this was the typical male inhabitant of Cairns.

Four or five straight main streets with long, low, white business premises, and in the outer quarters wooden houses on posts with galvanized iron roofs—there we have Cairns. Galvanized iron abounded everywhere in Australia. No doubt practical, but ugly.

But Cairns had its good points as well, and its inhabitants were friendly and hospitable. We got to know the neighbourhood on our expeditions and visited among other places a small town called Kuranda, about fifty miles from Cairns. We were told it was situated at the most beautiful spot in Australia, and we did not doubt it. It was close to the famous waterfall Barron Falls, which is 1,075 ft. high and provides a great part of Northern Queensland with light and power. Kuranda's fascinating little railway station is worthy of mention. On one side the top of a high mountain, on the other a deep gorge with the river roaring at the bottom. Mountains, forests and flowers on all sides.

Blossoms of all colours on the roof of the little building, wonderful blossoms hanging in rows of pots under the eaves. Along the platform, along the walls—everywhere, indeed, where they could not impede traffic—hung flowers with brilliantly coloured birds flitting among the tendrils.

But still through the scent of flowers another smell was perceptible—the smell of beer from the cool, shady station bar!

While we were in Cairns a huge fair was held. Thousands of people came to it from all over Northern Australia. The show, which lasted for several days, was a combination of cattle show, exhibition, sports and menagerie with all the usual buffoonery and racket. The noise and dust were quite indescribable.

The visitors were mostly farmers, who had been travelling by train for several days to take part in the festivities. What attracted these many thousands was not so much the exhibition of different kinds of produce, cattle and machinery, or the sideshows, as an attempt to break the jumping record. For some unexplained reason horses always jumped higher at Cairns than anywhere else, and for the last ten years the world's record had been broken there.

The last year's record was 8 ft. 6 in. We refused to believe it, but our own eyes convinced us. After a quite short run-up the horses leapt over wooden fences on a level with the rider's face. The day we were present 'only' 7 ft. 9 in. was achieved. Apart from the jumping it was a dreadful day—racket, crying children, heat, sweat, soft hats and braces, shoving and pushing. Farmers' families dragged themselves aimlessly through the dust and the burning sun, from which only the clouds of dust afforded a little shade. It was the long awaited, great day!

We got to know a young married couple in Cairns, Tom and Ella. Ella was of Danish descent and spoke good Danish. Her vivacity appealed to us. She had an uncle near Rockhampton, Hermann Svendsen. He had a big farm, and we got an invitation from him through Ella. The farm was in Emu Park, about 900 miles from Cairns. It was a thirty-five hours' train journey, but we did not hesitate long before accepting.

Before we set off there was a matter I was anxious to settle. Bill had gradually become a problem to me. His ironical remarks in season and out of season, because my plans did not accord with his wishes, had begun to put a strain on our comradeship. The solidarity of Knud, Poul and myself was being endangered, because he was trying to split us in different ways—and not always by the nicest methods. Then, when I learnt from friends and acquaintances that he could not control himself behind my back either, the limit was reached. God knows, Bill was a real man; he had never shown a sign of fear or hesitation even in the most critical situations, and it is understandable that a young man wants to see as much of the world as possible, but I was restricted by limited means and time, and also—unfortunately for him—the boat was mine.

One evening after supper I asked him to come up on deck with me and have a talk. I could see by his face that he expected what was coming.

'You're certainly just as good a man as I am, if not better, but we can't work in harness together, Bill; I don't want to lose Poul's and Knud's friendship for the sake of your company. There's more in this for us than just seeing the world. We are absolutely determined—and it is our real object—to sail round the world as sportsmen and we've done a year's work preparing for it. The least thing that can damage or undermine our plan is cut out right away, and so you must leave *Nordkaperen* now.'

Man that he was, he understood me and took it as I had expected. Perhaps there was a little bitterness in his voice as he said:

'Next time I sail round the world I'll stipulate that it shall take at least five years!'

Immediately afterwards I went to Rockhampton with Poul, Tom and Ella. Knud did not feel well and cried off at the last moment. Uncle Hermann proved to be a pleasant, hospitable Dane, and Aunt Martha was his no less hospitable wife.

A great surprise awaited me when I went on board on our return. Bill was still there. I had counted on his having gone long ago. He came up to me on the deck.

'Calle,' he said, 'it's impossible for me to get a passage or a ship at Cairns. If I behave myself, may I come with you to Singapore?'

He was hard to resist.

'Yes,' I said, 'but not a mile farther!'

'O.K.,' he replied, and nothing more was said about it.

Bill kept his word. He behaved irreproachably and did not grumble any more. We were on a friendly footing till he left us later.

There was a general survey of *Nordkaperen's* rigging and engine. We took precautions against further trouble with the magneto, and we also got ourselves a skiff. This was the only kind of boat to be got in Cairns, where dinghies were not used; but under any circumstances the skiff was better than nothing.

A short time before we sailed, Tom and Ella asked if they might come north with us—for the present as far as Thursday Island. We had become particularly good friends with Tom and Ella, had bunks enough and had no objection to having them with us, but we advised them not to come. We should pass through the Torres Strait, with its many drifting mines, and at the same time we made them aware of the many possible hardships and sleepless nights they might expect. They stuck to it, however, and they got their own way. Of course they had to sign a statement that they came with us on their own responsibility, and it was pointed out to them that they must give a hand where necessary, and pay for their own food.

It was with a sigh of relief that we put out from Cairns on August 21. It was not that we had not been well treated—on the contrary—but we had for a long time been rather nervous about the passage through the Torres Strait, which could be dangerous enough even without the mines. We had discussed this part of our voyage and attached more importance to it than to the crossing of the Atlantic. We had had plenty of warnings, but it had become a point of honour with us to carry out our intention. We *would* get through.

We had been told that sailing behind the barrier would be a delightful experience. We should pass through green islands, and so on, but those who said it cannot have been spoilt as regards beauty. The islands along the north-east coast of Australia we saw just as grey lumps of rock with burnt-up dry vegetation. Only a single island with palms here and there—and they could not compare with the South Sea islands we had just come from. As we got farther out, the green coastal mountains of Australia were transformed into gigantic heaps of rubble—a dreary desert of stone without the smallest speck of green.

We saw no drifting mines, but often heard distant reports, when they exploded against reefs or were disposed of by minesweepers.

On one single day we counted eight explosions, but they were so far away that we could not locate them.

Towards evening on the first day Tom was allowed to take the wheel for a moment. We were running before a steady breeze abaft the starboard beam. Two of us were standing on the fore-deck looking for drifting mines and at the same time discussing the possibility of finding an anchorage for the night. We were sailing in waters where forty mines had been observed in the previous month; we found no reason, therefore, to tempt fate by sailing in the dark when there was no necessity to do so. Suddenly we noticed that *Nordkaperen* was shooting off her course to leeward.

'Tom, for God's sake—starboard—starboard, or we'll jibe!'

Tom came to life at once. He had mistaken eight points on the compass and was now turning the wheel like a madman.

'Stop, that's the wrong way—the other way—hurry up, do you hear?'

It was too late. The wind caught the mainsail and the boom came over with a groan, struck the starboard backstay and snapped with a crack.

On account of the many changes of course in zigzag channels we had no brace on. We were too lazy to change it so often, and we had to pay for it now.

We sailed on with two filled headsails and mizen, and at the same time we started the engine. Tom was much upset at his misfortune, but we consoled him by saying that the boom had had a weak point after being cracked before. It was going to be taken out anyhow.

We found a good anchorage the first night under the lee of a small island, Low Islets. The boom was taken down and the mainsail rolled up. Before we turned in we missed Isa Lei. She had completely disappeared. At first we did not worry about her, expecting that she had hidden in some crazy place, as was her habit, but gradually as time passed without her paying any attention to our calls, and every hiding-place had been searched, we grew anxious. Had she fallen overboard?

Spearing fish at night—more idyllic than practical

PLATE X

Crew and ship's cat Isa Lei

On an Australian farm (no wonder the cat would not come out when called!)

Isa Lei in her summerhouse

PLATE XI

Isa Lei on deck

Suddenly Knud's face lightened.

'By Jove, I believe I know where she is!'

He rushed up on deck and we after him. The mainsail was unrolled again, and right in the middle of the bundle lay Isa Lei asleep. She stretched herself luxuriously when she was unpacked, arched her back lazily, and behaved as if it was the most natural thing in the world to sleep rolled up in a mainsail. For that matter, it was not the last time she played this trick. Early next morning we weighed anchor and stood northwards again.

We caught a big fish. The engine hummed like a sewing-machine, the weather was fine—fresh breeze and blue sky—and our spirits high. It looked like being a good trip in spite of the cracked boom.

In the afternoon, however, the compass began to be uncertain. It was not reliable to six or seven degrees. So instead we had to be ceaselessly looking out for islands, reefs and seamarks. Unfortunately the sea was too rough for us to rectify the compass by swinging the boat. There are magnetic fields on some of the islands in the Australian barrier, and they may perhaps have affected the compass. That evening we failed to reach an anchorage which had been recommended to us, and we therefore decided to anchor behind a reef which we certainly could not see, but which we knew ought to be there. We crept in towards it. Poul took soundings, and I climbed up to the crosstrees. Though we were sailing very slowly indeed, the coral bottom rose up so quickly that we were only just able to back away from it. At last we found a place with eighteen or twenty feet of water and dropped anchor. We were well sheltered if the night should bring a strong on-shore wind with a high sea. The reef, which lay a few feet below the surface, would protect us against the worst.

Next morning the wind had gone, and the sea was like a mirror. This was fortunate for us, for, although we were sailing back from the reef on exactly the opposite course, we put *Nordkaperen* aground. We worked like horses to get the boat off again. As we had done on previous groundings, we laid out anchors with ropes to the masthead. We swung out the boom with a heavy weight on it. We backed and went ahead with the engine as hard as we could, but *Nordkaperen* did not move an inch.

A closer examination of the sea bottom showed us that we had sailed right into a lagoon with a narrow entrance, which we failed to hit when we wanted to get out again.

Now we could only wait for the high tide, which would come about midday, and hope that it would be high enough to lift us clear. We spent the time of waiting in peering down through the crystal-clear water at the life and colours of the coral bottom. Bill, Poul, Ella and Tom got into the ship's boat and rowed in to the reef to have a closer look. It was queer to see them wading knee-deep in the water about twenty miles out to sea.

Knud and I stayed behind as watch-keepers and closely observed the depth of the water. Soon after midday *Nordkaperen* began to bump gently on the bottom, and we called the truants back by firing three shots, but the water rose so rapidly that Knud and I had got the boat out of danger before the others returned.

We went on zigzagging northward. We slipped between reefs and islands and had become the richer by one experience: we would never again anchor in the neighbourhood of reefs. We had unusually good fishing that day. The line had only just been cast when a big 20 lb. kingfish bit on it. We got it on board with some difficulty, but the line had become twisted in the struggle. I flung it overboard to straighten it out, but not five yards from the ship another kingfish, equally large, bit on the hook. We got that one on board too. This was more fish than we could eat in several days, I tied a big bunch of cotton-waste round the hook when I threw it out again to straighten out the line.

In a few seconds the line was torn out of my hands, and an unusually large fish disappeared with hook, spinner, cotton-waste and half the line. It was a great day for Isa Lei. Before evening she was so blown out that she could hardly touch the ground with her feet.

The result of the delay on the reef was that we did not reach any anchorage that evening, and we therefore went on sailing by night, keeping a specially sharp look-out. Tom and Ella, who before we left Cairns had stoutly declared that they were good sailors, began to have symptoms of sea-sickness. They refused to eat and lay in their bunks all day. They said they could not understand it—it must be food poisoning.

The compass had by degrees become quite impossible, and we had to concentrate more and more on the look-out. Things were not improved when the morning after our night sail brought with it a strong east wind. In the course of the day it began to blow hard. Even with her small sails *Nordkaperen* was doing seven or eight knots, so the calculations had to be done very quickly. We had to be continually changing course. The current was strong and variable and there was some hard work for Knud. The sea rose gradually and tended to be lively. Demands for buckets came from Tom's and Ella's bunks down below! A high mountainous island with good anchorage and shelter for the night interested us very much although it lay five miles off our course. Stanley Island was its name. It was necessary to correct our compass, and to judge from the chart there should be a little bay there sheltered by high cliffs. We therefore, changed course, using the lead. We cast anchor close in to land. Under the lee of the cliffs we could hear only faintly the duet of sea and wind.

Stanley Island looked thrilling in the light of the full moon. The white strip of sand shone in the darkness, and up among the trees on the mountain-side we caught glimpses of houses which looked extremely desolate. There were no lights anywhere. Poul, Tom and Bill wanted to go ashore to investigate, and Poul took a rifle over his shoulder. 'One can never know,' he said. As they were pushing the ship's boat off, Isa Lei jumped on board. She was curious too.

A couple of hours later they returned. They had solved the riddle of the silent island. It was a former military base, but now it was quite uninhabited, and the empty hutments stood among stunted trees waiting till they should rot. The party had seen nothing else of interest.

Next morning there was an opportunity of correcting the compass in calm water, and in the course of an hour we had swung the boat and could continue our voyage with the assurance that the compass was all right. This was the last night we anchored before Thursday Island. There were no more decent anchorages.

As we approached the narrow part of the Torres Strait, the current became stronger. The chart showed that the speed of the current could be up to seven knots; we never had this, but a good four knots was quite enough for us—especially when there was no regularity in the turn of the tide. It turned at the queerest times. The log was almost worthless. It showed twelve miles when we had sailed three, or the reverse.

The evening before we were to land on Thursday Island we approached the dangerous part of the Torres Strait—the part which is called the 'ships' cemetery'. We arrived there too soon. None of us wanted to make the passage in darkness. It could be difficult enough anyhow. Accordingly the engine was stopped, we slackened off on the sheets so that the sails did not draw, but so that we could just keep steerage way on the boat.

A short time before dusk a fresh easterly wind sprang up which slowly increased in strength. The sea became high, with long rollers, and *Nordkaperen*, which was almost stationary, had to take what came her way. In our optimism we had taken the ship's boat in tow instead of on deck. A particularly impudent sea gave her a blow which severed the painter, and she went adrift. At the same time it tore off the fitting on the outrigger which held the mizen sheet and the sail began to thrash and beat about like mad. We recovered the ship's boat and repaired the sheet, but it cost us work and wet jerseys.

About 8 p.m. the wind had become strong, and the seas were hammering mercilessly on *Nordkaperen's* broadside. They rushed on furiously, short and deep, and filled the boat time after time. It was hell to be on deck. We considered heaving to, but one look at the chart made us change our minds. The channel was narrow, and the nearest reefs on our lee side were not far off. Also we had to maintain a check on our position, and although *Nordkaperen* moved forward slowly, we kept on our course.

We waited for an hour, but when shortly afterwards two particularly heavy seas buried the whole boat, so that literally only the masts were above water, we had to take a decision. Poul, Knud and I held a little council of war.

As we could not heave to, and likewise could not go on as we were without danger of losing our rigging or running on to a reef, there was no choice but either to go through the Torres Strait in the dark or to put back. The latter did not appeal to us, and we knew that if we were only in the narrow part of the strait we should get smooth water. We had no difficulty in agreeing to increase our speed and go ahead. Bill was told: he had no objection, nor had we expected that he would. Tom and Ella were utterly indifferent. They did not think death by drowning could be any worse than the torments of sea-sickness which they were undergoing at the moment.

The sheets were hauled taut and the engine started again, and being on deck immediately became more comfortable. *Nordkaperen* worked up a good speed and shook off many seas. We three stayed on deck all night. We were soaked to the skin despite our oilskins. Incredible as it may sound, Isa Lei stayed up with us. She always wanted to be there when anything was happening, and had a marvellous capacity for avoiding the seas. Although she was in the cockpit making love to the man at the wheel, she could get under cover in the cockpit for the time it took the sea to hit the deck after first breaking against the ship's side. When the water had run off the deck again Isa Lei came creeping out. Perhaps she was infected by the excitement with which the air was loaded. Our zigzag courses reached their height that night—outside one reef, inside another or right between the two next. The log was read again and again. We had to estimate the force of the current for ourselves. Knud hung continuously over the azimuth dial and took a bearing on every point which could be made out in the darkness. He compared every seamark with the chart. Our position was plotted on the chart every half-hour—not for one single moment did we lose track of our position. Knud produced his masterpiece as a navigator that night.

Poul and I took turns to take the wheel and keep a look-out from the fore-deck or shrouds and give Knud a hand with the bearings.

The sea had become calmer when we came in among the islands and reefs, but the wind still whined in the rigging.

*Nordkaperen* passed close to a little rocky island, whose dark silhouette was visible against the night sky. The seas foamed with wrath at its resistance, the spray hung eighteen or twenty feet above the stone mass of the island. The white foam shone with a ghostlike glimmer through the darkness.

We had just lost sight of a light which had been a great help to us.

'There's trouble coming soon,' Knud shouted.

We knew to what he alluded. About a mile and a half ahead a submarine reef lay in wait for us in the middle of the strait.

We were to alter course—from due north to due west—when we were right on top of this reef. Then we were to keep a westerly course for barely a mile till a seamark or the breakers from some reef appeared in the darkness.

We should sail along the reef for two miles—twenty-seven minutes—after which we should be free of the central reef and could make our way back to the original course.

The whole thing was a calculation of probabilities. The current might play us a trick. We must keep a sharp look-out, for visibility was not more than fifty yards. We had the good luck to detect the seamarks on both reefs.

The very moment Poul shouted: 'seamark to starboard close ahead!' I put the helm hard-a-port, altered course eight points, and chanced our jibing. We were only carrying mizen and two headsails, so it would not be such a great disaster if we did.

The next seamark and the reef put a strain on our nerves. They were a long time in appearing. According to our calculations it should be about twelve minutes' sail down to it, but fifteen minutes passed, and then sixteen, without our observing anything. We trembled when *Nordkaperen* put her nose into the sea. We feared every moment that she would run aground with a crash, but at last the vague outline of a seamark rose up out of the darkness, and we saw the faint glimmer of a white fringe of foam. The moment I shouted the warning Poul turned the boat away. It was his turn at the wheel.

The current had robbed us of several minutes. Knud was all the time busy with his instruments.

An old skipper had said to me in a bar at Cairns: 'With a little luck you'll get through the Torres Strait all right—if you don't hit a mine—but if you lose track of your position, I wouldn't give much for your chances!'

We did not lose track of our position, nor did we run against any mine. We were lucky too—but our luck was that we had a skilful navigator on board. We spent the night tacking among reefs and islands. One single lighted barrel, which was not marked on the chart, was the only thing that gave us a bit of trouble. When a sea poured on to the deck, no one took any notice of it. Only once were we a little anxious. This was when several tons of water were washed on board and nearly carried away the chart, which was lying on a sliding table in the hatchway. It would have been a catastrophe for us if it had disappeared, and Knud cursed vigorously as he tried to dry it.

We had been handicapped by darkness and half a gale, but we had got through the Torres Strait; a passage that had been planned for three years and constantly discussed had been successfully achieved.

At last the east began to grow light: how long that night had been! The wind dropped a little. The new day revealed to us a far from pleasant sight. Ahead of us lay the rusty wreck of a steamer, half capsized on a reef. Beside her lay the wrecks of two smaller ships. To starboard we saw the ribs of two small sailing vessels close in to the coast of a little island. When we rounded a point to turn towards Thursday Island, there was the forepart of an old clipper ship projecting from the water. The bowsprit and figure-head were pointing almost straight up towards the sky. Half a mile away a wreck lay on dry land. And there were still more. Since Torres discovered the strait it has been the scene of many tragedies.

For the last five miles before Thursday Island we were met by a very strong current. Normally, with the engine at full power, we could sail at more than five knots, but now it took us more than six hours to cover the distance. Sometimes we stood quite still—even drifted astern—while the engine toiled till the boat shook all over. But at long last we rounded the last point, and the little town of Port Kennedy came into sight. It was the only town on the island, and the houses were very scattered. The place looked dry and windswept, and the tumble-down wooden buildings gave the landscape a poor and depressing aspect. Twenty or thirty ketch-rigged craft of *Nordkaperen's* size lay at anchor in the bay or tied up to a wharf. They were pearling luggers. At a distance they looked like pleasure craft. They had graceful lines and were nearly all painted white, but when we came nearer they proved to be dirty and in bad condition.

At last we worked our way in, and at 2 p.m. on August 27 we cast anchor among the pearling boats. *Nordkaperen's* graceful white hull and well-kept fittings, and her ship-shape rigging, made her look like a clean pretty girl among a crowd of ragged negresses.

We had gone short of sleep for the past three days and nights, and we fell down straightway and slept. We shut our eyes with a feeling of incredible relief. Indeed, we were almost off the ground! A load that had long oppressed us had been removed. It was delightful to be able to go to bed in dry clothes and conscious of a task performed—life was splendid now.

Getting ashore proved to be something of a task. The strong current made it quite impossible to row the ship's boat ashore at certain times of the day, but luckily we met a man called McDonald. He had bought the wharf from the military, and we enjoyed the honour of a berth alongside—and all for nothing. It was not surprising that many of the pearl fishers were envious, for there was a shortage of berths at Port Kennedy.

Soon we lay alongside the pearling luggers, which swarmed with coloured people. Most of the crews were negroes, but there were also Malays, Polynesians, Japanese and Indonesians—indeed, I think that races from the whole of the southern half of the globe were represented.

The wages system in the pearling luggers was simple. The crew received a third of the profit for distribution among them, and the skipper took the rest. As soon as the take was turned into money, the majority of the crew bought masses of cheap spirits and lived royally for three days.

Of the people who lived on Thursday Island, about a thousand in number, two hundred were white, and they all lived directly or indirectly from the pearl fishing. The only public amusement on the island was an open-air cinema; there were also fourth or fifth class hotels with bars. Fortune-seekers from all the countries in the world, hard-boiled adventurers or people with pasts, made their way to Thursday Island. Some did well out of it; others remained hanging about on the island till they ended their days as drink-sodden wrecks. Money, poker and whisky were in circulation all the twenty-four hours. Easy come, easy go.

We met a Dane during our stay at Thursday Island. He was fifty—let us call him Hans—and was a constant visitor on board. He was always worrying us to take him with us to Singapore. We were opposed to it, for Tom and Ella also wanted to come, and after all there were limits to our space on board *Nordkaperen*. Hans had taken root on the island and had neither the means nor the energy to escape the prison it had become for him.

However, things turned out favourably for him. Tom and Ella could not get their papers in order in less than four months, and we others could not wait that time. The great possibilities of earning money on the island of adventure tempted Bill, and as at the same time he became engaged to a pretty little girl, he thought he could just as well leave the boat there as at Singapore. (We heard later that Bill had married the girl and that they were doing well.) So we no longer had any reason for refusing Hans, and it was positively touching to see his joy when we told him that he certainly might come with us. He should have the post of cook.

'I've been to sea before, and I'll be all right,' he said. He hitched up his trousers and spat over the lee bulwarks.

The coloured seamen gave us presents in the shape of turtle flesh, sea-cow flesh and turtles' eggs. They gave us pearl shells and caught fish for Isa Lei, who had the run of all the ships and was much petted. It was not for the sake of our *beaux yeux* that we received so many presents. We sometimes gave cigarettes—a rarity on the island—in return.

It proved impossible to get hold of a piece of timber long enough for a new boom. We had, therefore, to splice the old boom and shorten it by three feet. That meant that we also had to take three feet off the after-leech of the mainsail. The wharf was a sailmaker's workshop for several days, but it was hard work sitting and sewing in the burning sun.

We secured various advantages by shortening the boom. The worn part was removed from the sail, and it became handier. We had practically seen the last of the trade wind and would soon be going through waters with variable wind and weather conditions, so a reduction of our sail was welcome. Also, we now had room for a staysail on the mizen-mast, so that besides the mainsail we could carry four small sails: jib, foresail, mizen staysail and mizen —a good thing in very rough weather. The cockroaches were gassed by a specialist, but a month later the ship was again swarming with the little parasites.

On Sunday, September 14, an Australian corvette struck a mine and sank immediately. Three men were killed and twenty-six injured. Another corvette which was in company with her hurried to her help and saved the rest of the crew. The disaster happened about twenty miles from Thursday Island.

On Monday, September 15, several drifting mines were observed just off Port Kennedy.

The war had quite upset the administrative routine on Thursday Island. The young officials had no idea how a foreign ship should be treated. It was their first experience of the kind, and there were no forms for health clearance, etc., We ourselves had to help them as well as we could to get our ship's papers in order. There was only one doctor on the island, aged twenty-five; he did not know how a health clearance certificate should be made out, and he did not want to have anything to do with it. At last, however, we taught him the art.

If they could not make head or tail of our ship's papers, they were agreed that we should pay £4 duty for petrol we had obtained at Suva. We protested vigorously, but this gave us an insight into the peculiar laws of Australia.

A couple of days before our sailing I was walking along the beach and looking at the different kinds of stranded goods. Among empty drums, rusty landing craft, boxes and lumber I saw a rowing boat lying bottom upwards. The stern was almost torn off on one side, and she was badly damaged. She had a familiar look about her, and a closer inspection showed that she was our own ship's boat. How long had she been lying there?

We had tied the boat up to the wharf close to *Nordkaperen* and had not noticed that the rope was broken—probably due to the strong current. We had not missed the boat and had no idea that she had drifted across the bay. She had turned bottom upwards on the way and bore clear marks of having been dashed against the stones on the shore. She could not possibly float as she was, and I therefore went back to *Nordkaperen* to fetch some tools and oars. I thought that she could probably be taken back after provisional repairs had been carried out.

And I really managed to get the wreck screwed together so that it would be possible to row her back to *Nordkaperen*, a distance of about half a mile. Unfortunately it was low water, so I had to drag her for about fifty yards before she would float. I had to use all my strength to get the waterlogged boat to move a few inches.

A young man came walking along and looked with interest at the boat and me. He stood as still as a statue without uttering a word—a strange man.

'Pouf—this is a hard job,' said I, to open a conversation.

He did not seem to hear me.

'Is that going into the water?' he asked a long time afterwards.

'It almost looks like it,' I replied acidly and went on toiling.

'What is it?'

I looked at him in astonishment. Did he mean what type of boat or was he pulling my leg?

I was on the point of asking if he thought it was a wheelbarrow, but refrained. I could not remember the English word, and perhaps I might still make some use of the eccentric man. I asked him if he would give me a hand.

Without replying he sauntered to the other side of the boat, took hold of the thwart and began to pull, while I heaved on the bulwarks. It could not be denied that he put all his strength into it. At the same time I discovered how rottenly the boat was built. She was sewn together like a packing-case.

The thwart flew off, and the solemn man did not recover his balance till he had run about ten yards like a billygoat with his head down between his knees. He came back with the thwart under his arm and laid it carefully in the bottom of the boat without moving a muscle. The gravity of his countenance froze my apologetic smile off my face. He took hold of the fore-deck; several long minutes passed, and we advanced at least ten yards. Then it was my turn to pull, and I came back with half the knee with three ribs on it. I consigned the wretched packing-case to perdition and expected to get a grain of sympathy from the stone man, but was confronted with a totally expressionless face. It was becoming uncanny. I began to feel awkward and on my way to developing inferiority complexes. Once more we brought our weight to bear, and this time we got the boat out into two inches of water.

Then the planking of the fore-deck gave way. Unfortunately the board which the stone man was holding on to! This time he lost his balance and sat down in the water, still holding the board in his hand. He remained in a sitting position for a moment, carefully examining the board and its two seams.

I apologized as well as I could, but the statue did not honour me with a look. He rose with dignity, carefully laid the board alongside the rest of the stranded goods, took hold of the remains of the rope which hung at the stem, and pulled like a horse, while I pushed. The water was dripping from a large heart-shaped wet patch on the seat of his trousers.

When the boat was afloat, I thanked him for helping me, but I might just as well have thanked the Nelson Column.

I hurriedly got the oars into position, and I went out through the light surf with long, vigorous strokes. But I did not get very far.

I had put all my strength into it to show how well and stylishly I could row a boat, when a clamp of the port rowlock fell off. Next moment I was lying at the bottom of the boat with the rest of the stranded goods and studying the silhouette of my toes against the decorative background of the blue sky.

Hang it all, now he *must* smile, I thought, as I laboriously hauled myself up again; but no! He was standing quite motionless on the beach: he did not so much as shake his head.

On the other hand, three negroes had arrived. They stood with their legs crossed, holding on to one another in order not to collapse with laughing. Then I gave it up, dragged the boat as high up on shore as I could, took the tools and oars on my shoulders and walked off to *Nordkaperen* without saying good-bye. Later in the day we borrowed a dinghy and towed the skiff to her proper place.

On the voyage from Thursday Island to Timor *Nordkaperen's* after-deck was turned into a boat-building yard. We took the skiff to pieces, assembled her again with screws, put in strengthenings and new thwarts and painted her. So when we approached Timor we had a new ship's boat again. This time she was strong and solid.

At last the day dawned when we were to sail for Timor—it was September 19. The merchant from whom we had obtained our stock of provisions emphasized his affection for us by sending three bottles of Scotch whisky on board as a parting gift. The young but senior official, who had become an excellent friend of ours, came on a farewell visit of several hours and took almost one of the bottles of whisky ashore with him in his hardened stomach.

We weighed anchor at 10.15 a.m., passed through the little Normanby Sound and stood out through the Torres Strait. A racing current took us ahead quickly. We waved good-bye to Bill, Tom and Ella, who were standing on the shore under some windblown palms, with friends and acquaintances from the island.

On a mountain slope the scrub and weeds were being burnt off, and the smoke from this drifted down over the tumble-down sheds of the scattered little town and mingled with the clouds of dust. We were sorry in our hearts for those whom we were leaving behind. Farewell, Thursday Island, but not *au revoir!*

Although Hans had declared that he had been at sea for many years, this did not prevent him from being sea-sick. For the first four or five days he sat continuously on deck on the lee side with his head over the bulwarks, gazing despairingly at the foam as it flew past. Now and then he gave us a pained look in which all the world's sorrows were mirrored. Thus, for the first part of the trip he was of no use to us as cook. On the other hand, he made us laugh.

Just before we were to sail he had got new teeth, and he could never find them. His teeth were being eternally searched for and were found in the most unlikely places. Whenever he was going to try to eat, or be sick, he took them out and could never remember where he had put them. There was a continual refrain of:

'Hasn't anyone seen my teeth?'

At long last he overcame his sea-sickness and proved to be a very good cook.

Pancakes were his speciality: he could make very good pancakes of flour and water, whether it was blowing hard or not. Later Poul often tried to bake from the same recipe, but the result was always wretched.

Hans had a few pecularities. Among other things, we were convinced that he put a third ingredient into his pancakes besides flour and water, but he never let us into the secret.

He was very proud of being a member of the secret Rosicrucian world organization. He proved his brotherhood by letters and mysterious documents, and declared that he had been born again. Rosicrucianism had saved him, and he proved this by producing two photographs. One had been taken immediately before his rebirth, the other directly after. The first showed an unshaved, ravaged criminal's face, the second a well-groomed countenance with eyes gleaming with energy and intelligence. We asked him what one should do to be born again.

'It is a inward cleansing process,' he said. 'I have been greatly strengthened by hypnotism.'

The few books he had all dealt with supernatural, mystical forces. We began to be seriously afraid of his hypnotising us, but there was a comic streak in all his ceremonial seriousness.

He had not invented powder, as the saying goes, and was very easily offended.

'If everyone had been like you there'd have been no war,' I said to him one day. Unfortunately he thought I meant it seriously and began to expound his ideas about world peace.

'I didn't mean it like that,' I interrupted.

'What did you mean then?'

'I meant that powder wouldn't have been invented!' I regretted my words when I saw how hurt he was. 'Come now, Hans!'

But he did not speak to us for two days.

CHAPTER XIV

# *The Timor Sea*

Our passage from Thursday Island to Koepang in Timor was ideal. The distance of 1,168 miles was covered in exactly nine days, an average speed of 5.4 knots. We had a fresh breeze varying from south-east to north-east behind us all the way.

We had plenty of fresh fruit on board. We caught fish and gorged ourselves with hot fillets. Only for a couple days did we notice the notorious devilry of the Timor Sea, and that was not enough to destroy the impression of general excellence. For the first six days the seas were regular and gentle. By day the sun shone from a cloudless sky: by night the waxing moon made the water glitter and shimmer and gave *Nordkaperen* the aspect of a phantom ship. A moonlight night like this, with a steady breeze and smooth sea, could set the helmsman's imagination working and send him on a long voyage into a delicious dream world.

I caught myself whistling or humming a waltz in time with the pitching of the boat. Soon I had the impression that *Nordkaperen* was a living creature capable of keeping time. What she liked best was a slow, soft Viennese waltz. Sometimes she was a trifle slow in turning, so that I had to dwell on the note, and now and again she tried to put in a few bold variations, such as putting in a couple of short steps between the normal ones, but she generally went wrong over it and a moment might pass before contact was restored and we were waltzing on through the moonlight.

Isa Lei could be relied on to keep the man at the wheel company at night. She lay in front of me in the light from the binnacle. I could not look at her without her catching my eye. She had got a weakness for Hans. She studied him—used to jump up on to a shelf or table near him, sit down and look at him intently for hours at a time.

At first it made Hans feel queer. 'Why the hell is the damned cat always staring at me? Take it away!' he said furiously. Yes, we got a lot of fun out of Hans and Isa Lei.

It was not to entertain the man at the wheel that Isa Lei was on deck. No—she was waiting, waiting for the flying fish which gleamed in the moonlight and now and then fell on to the deck. Isa Lei was on them in a twinkling. But when the flying fish realized that their last hour was near, they fought and struggled for several minutes. There was a regular fight for life on one side and supper on the other. It was a strange sight in the moonshine. At last the flying fish had to give up, and ten minutes after not a scale of them was left. Isa Lei did her work with care and thoroughness.

When she had had a good wash she crept under my cardigan—there was one place where a button was missing—made herself comfortable just as she liked, rolled over and poked her head out again. It could be pretty cold at night, but Isa Lei always found a warm place. She purred contentedly while waiting for new flying fish. Two was the usual number. When I looked down to see if she was asleep, I met a pair of grave, unfathomable eyes. Am I talking too much about an ordinary Fiji cat? Try living with it in the same conditions as we did!

Several times a day we were visited by dolphins which accompanied us for a little way. They came in schools and played snorting round the ship. Pleasant beasts—especially at night. One might well feel a trifle lonely and forsaken when they disappeared again.

On the seventh and eighth days we saw the Timor Sea at its most contrary. The wind was not particularly strong, but still the sea was rough and very uneven. We had experienced this twice before, but not so badly as now. Seas came from the lee side, the weather side, from astern—sometimes all at once. Keeping *Nordkaperen* steady and dry was a sort of crossword puzzle business, for logic and calculations did not apply. When a steep sea had caught the boat up and played with her for a moment, it tired of the game and flung its plaything indifferently away, so that *Nordkaperen* fell with a splash on her belly—down into the bottom of the trough of a wave. Before the boat had recovered from her confusion, another sea came from the other side and the joke was repeated.

Records for broken crockery on board were established. The weather was hard too on our rigging and sails. On the first evening in these difficult conditions Hans was to have his first two hours on watch in the dark. We kept an eye on him so as to be able to come to his help quickly if things became critical. I stood at the top of the cabin stair to watch him. It was really an interesting sight. The upper part of his body and face were faintly illuminated by the light from the binnacle. As usual his hair stood straight up in the air, his spectacles gleamed, and his wide-open eyes were glued to the needle of the compass. He was turning the wheel like a madman—first one way and then the other. He never noticed when a big sea came which might capsize the boat, never noticed whether *Nordkaperen* was afloat or sinking, He had grown on to the compass—the course should be held, the devil it should! When I asked him how things were going, he was so blown that he could hardly reply.

On the eighth day we sighted the mountains of Timor on the northern horizon, and we prepared to approach the land. It had been our intention to go through the Roti Strait, a narrow channel between western Timor and Semou Island, but as usual *Nordkaperen* reached it too early. We could not make landfall in the dark, and therefore decided to sail outside Semou Island. When we were due to change course according to our reckoning, we found that the contours of the land did not tally. We sighted shadowy mountains which according to the chart should not have been there. There could be only one reason, namely currents, and on a comparison being made with the charts it appeared that we had been sent twenty miles west of where we should have been, right in a bay, Telok Pepea Bay. We therefore hauled our sheets taut and tried to get clear of the northern point, which ran far out into the sea. We could see the surf from the reefs. After an hour's sailing it was clear that here too the current was so strong that we could not clear the point. Normally in such circumstances one goes about and steers out to sea again, but the sea was heavy, and we had recourse to the other way out, to start the engine: and with the help of this we just got clear of the reefs. We followed the west coast of Semou Island the whole night, and at daybreak we were able to enter the Roti Strait from the north, instead of from the south, as we had originally reckoned on doing. Now the wind died away completely, and when we turned into the little bay at the end of which the town of Koepang lies, it was dead calm. We took in the sails and set the engine at dead slow. *Nordkaperen* glided gently and almost noiselessly over the glittering water.

From a little island to port the joyous twittering of small birds reached our ears. The sun blazed in a cloudless sky. A real Sunday morning atmosphere hung over Koepang: it was September 28. We could gradually make out the buildings on the shore—and was that not church bells we could hear? At least we heard the noise of cocks crowing. These sounds floated lightly out to us through the sea of sun. A few spots on the beach were the natives, bathing or fishing. We crept nearer and nearer—and the nearer we came the more clearly we saw that the town, whose white buildings had looked so pleasant at a distance, was only a heap of ruins, a pile of shattered masonry.

The Japanese had been there, and they had done their work well. Not one house in the town was intact. The Sunday atmosphere was spoilt.

Koepang had no harbour. We had to sail as close to the shore as possible, using the lead, and then cast anchor.

But although there was no harbour, there was a harbour-master, who came out to us at once in a boat rowed by natives. He was a young Dutchman in a smart uniform. He gave us a hearty welcome and invited us to his house, the only one in the town with a roof on it. This cost us a bottle of gin.

While we were at the harbour-master's an invitation came from the Resident, the commander-in-chief of a long string of islands, of course including Timor: would we not honour his house by coming to supper?

Thank heaven, the harbour-master answered our discreet questions about dress with:

'Oh, yes—democratic man—white tropical suits!'

We breathed a sigh of relief and sent our thanks for the invitation.

We were fetched at dusk in a gigantic luxury car with a footman and chauffeur and driven to the Resident's house, formerly Japanese officers' quarters, which lay a short way outside the town. This was a provisional dwelling-place pending the restoration of his own palace.

It was a lively, pleasant evening, and the Resident set the tone. He was a wonderful help to us later.

All shades of the Indonesian race were represented in Timor. In Koepang there were surprisingly few white people, about eighty. Among the Indonesians were natives of a small island called Kisa. These Kisarese occupied a special position in the community. They were hardly as dark-skinned as the kindred races. Some had blue eyes and light hair, and they claimed the same social rights as whites. This is the reason:

Many years ago a company of Dutch soldiers was sent to Kisa. For some reason they were completely forgotten by headquarters, and the little band waited in vain for orders to return: but life must be lived: and the soldiers married and had children by the native women and so brought confusion into the racial pattern of the little island. To this very day this 'forgetting' can be traced in the Kisarese, and they always claim—and get—equal rights with the whites.

The natives in Koepang were friendly, clever little people, unbelievably dirty and ragged. Only the Chinese looked fairly well-groomed. They were a sort of native upper class. Every time we went ashore we had a string of natives after us. They followed us like shadows and kept a close eye on the cigarette stumps we threw away.

It was heart-breaking to see the many fine stone buildings of Koepang in ruins. We saw temples of which only the pillars remained. Gables bearing the stamp of Eastern architecture towered up out of heaps of rubble. At one place the remains of a gallery, a beautifully wrought piece of lattice-work, could be seen, hanging between the gables. At another place, in front of a rich man's house, two lions guarded the ruins. They were carved in beautiful mosaics and sat one on each side of their master's portal. Curiously enough they were whole and intact.

On the other hand, it did not appear that the terrors and devastation of the war had set their mark upon the population. They had the patience and ability to forget characteristic of primitive peoples. They found our distress at the devastation most amusing. They themselves lived among the ruins with a bit of galvanized iron or a couple of sacks for roof, and a closer examination disclosed a teeming life among the debris: in a cellar here, in a washhouse there, behind a straw mat, in a corner with fragments of masonry piled in front of it, lived the fertile, frugal native families.

Poul and I wanted to have a meal in one of the provisional eating-houses, not because they looked inviting—on the contrary—but from curiosity. We finally arrived at an eating-house through limestone dust and rubble, walking over natives as we went. We had already seen natives sitting delousing one another like monkeys at the Zoo. Both parties were enjoying it, one blissfully passive with closed eyes, one lost to the outside world, poking about in the other's hair with the rapt expression one sees on a hunter's face.

At last we arrived at the ruin, undoubtedly a former stable, where an old board announced a 'restaurant'. We took our places at tables fixed in the earth on similar chairs, and the proprietor, a fat Chinese, was visibly astonished at the appearance of white men in his kingdom. He hastened to turn his apron, which concealed a Buddha-like stomach, and shuffled bowing over to us.

A moment after we had given our order four Chinese in turn brought food and drink. Fifteen or twenty natives had assembled in front of the open side of the restaurant and followed the procession and the procedure with eager attention.

The food was rather indefinite—a mixture of stringy cabbage, rice and macaroni. A whole heap of little lumps turned out to be meat. A few cockroaches may have got into it, but, of course, they too were a kind of meat. With our meal we drank tea, served in cut-down beer bottles, and also a bottle of home-made wine. On the label, an ordinary scrap of packing paper, was written in pencil: PI SANG SANANC HATI ANC I KIONG NAIKOTEN.

The last word strongly suggested nicotine, and we raised our glasses to our lips with uneasy foreboding—especially when we met the gaze of twenty pairs of eager eyes. We survived the first glass and agreed not to tempt fate any more. The food also slipped down our throats, and we paid and left. The proprietor was astonished at our not wanting to take our wine with us. It had been paid for.

'Those whites are crazy.'

I could read his thoughts.

On the way to the post office, which was about three miles from Koepang, we passed through scenery which was attractive and picturesque. The country was up and down and rose steadily towards the mountains. Oases in the shape of little palm groves brightened the landscape, and on the slopes we saw the native huts, made of palm leaves, which blended with the rather faded and dry scrub. By the watercourses native women sat doing their washing. Their naked golden chests and shoulders contrasted effectively with the white cloth. The sun irradiated the whole scene and penetrated the shade-giving leafage of the palm-tops.

On the paths and roads a ceaseless procession of men and women came and went. They had either heavy loads on their heads, or a yoke over their shoulders from which hung baskets filled with we knew not what. Patient and dignified they stepped through the dust. We were on the threshold of the East now!

I was suddenly taken back many years, home to my grandmother's sitting-room. On the wall over the sofa hung a tapestry, a Gobelin, depicting a rather unusual subject. It was the same that I saw here: colours, brooks, trees, men and women with loads on their heads, goats grazing on the slopes and the mountains in the background, There was the same evening light with long shadows.

If I had seen that tapestry now, I should hardly have paid any attention to it, but it was wonderful to me in my boyhood. I could sit looking at it for hours, and my boyish imagination called the picture to life. Men, women and animals moved, and I could hear the rippling of the brook. My dreams may have carried me far afield in those days, and now they were making the return journey. I had not given that tapestry a thought for thirty years, and now I remembered it so clearly. Possibly the subject was taken from India, possibly from South America, but for a moment I was back in my grandmother's sitting-room.

Timor invited a stay of some length, but time was short. We must go on while the weather was fairly settled. The rainy season was close at hand. Our stay in Timor was, therefore, no longer than two days and six hours. The Dutch had given us an extremely good reception. There were no limits to their hospitality. I had ordered fruit, provisions, water, petrol, etc. and it was brought on board by a gang of natives. When I asked for the bill no one would take the money. We learned to our astonishment that it was to be regarded as a gift from the Dutch in Koepang. One of the reasons for Danes being so popular was that we had been kind to the Dutch children after the war. We thus came to cash in on the nation's behalf.

The military authorities gave us directions as to minefields, which lights were extinguished in the waters through which we should pass, etc. They warned us against pirates, who abounded at that time. We were to sail with lights out, and if we wanted to have arms—machine-guns—we could borrow them and hand them over again at the last place we called at in the Dutch East Indies.

A senior officer advised us not to take arms with us.

'They won't help you anyway,' he said; 'the pirates or rebels come in armed speedboats which the Japanese left behind. You've a better chance of saving your lives if you show your flag and let the pirates, if you meet any, search the boat. Don't give any provocation.'

We took his advice, but only after long reflection. The Resident informed the authorities in Batavia by telegram. If we had not arrived there by October 15, a search was to be made for us. We were almost wrapped in cotton-wool. The Resident was married to a Danish lady. She wept when she saw *Nordkaperen*. She had not seen the Danish flag for twelve years, so we had to reconcile ourselves to being made a fuss of in Timor.

CHAPTER XV

# *The Java Sea*

ON the afternoon of Tuesday, September 30, we weighed anchor and set our course for Batavia in Java. We had a voyage of about 1,200 miles ahead of us, and were in the Timor Sea again. For the first two days the weather was promising: moonlight and cloudless skies, but the wind was decreasing. On the third day there was very little of it, and on the fourth day it died away altogether. After waiting for it in vain for a day, we started the engine.

The heat gradually became diabolical; the sun blazed right overhead, the air round us seethed and simmered with invisible flames. We were drained of all energy and lost our appetites. The water, or liquid, we drank was exuded through our skins at once.

We examined the horizon with care many times in the course of the day: the Dutch had made us a little nervous about pirates: but we did not see one ship.

When darkness fell, our spirits rose a little. The darkness was our ally.

The engine worked steadily, and each day saw us a good hundred miles nearer our destination.

Unfortunately the heat grew worse every day: the thermometer was soon showing over 104 degrees in the shade, and there was never the faintest suggestion of a breath of cooling wind.

When we had been at sea for a week, I noticed Poul's and Knud's appearance. I sneaked into the after-cabin to see if I looked as awful as they. I did.

Fat Hans did fairly well: he was accustomed to the heat, and moreover he had the rare capacity to sleep all round the clock. We three others looked like characters in a film about ship-wrecked men in their third week on a wooden raft.

Our only clothes, our trousers, were neither whole nor clean. The sweat poured down our faces, chests and backs. Our eyes were hollow and bloodshot from the glare of the sun and irregular sleep, and our skin was stretched tight over our bones. From the week-old bristly stubble of beard on our faces home-rolled cigarettes projected. Our hair was ragged and tangled.

If one of us accidentally trod on the deck with bare feet or touched a metal fitting, there was an outburst of strong language.

On Sunday, October 5, we changed course from west to north and turned into the seething eddies of the Lombok Strait. The water became black and angry; the white crests came at us like surf, boiling and snarling, but pretty harmless. The current was able to tame them. There were wide smooth spaces in which the water was shining and flat; the current milled around in circles, and when the waves reached these places they slipped or fell down and could not rise again.

In the course of the day we passed Bali. It had been our definite intention to visit this renowned island, but for various reasons we changed our plans. For one thing we were behind time if we wanted to have fairly settled weather all the way to Batavia, for another there were minefields round Bali, the location of some of which were still unknown. Accordingly we contented ourselves with passing Bali and enjoyed the spectacle of the high green mountains whose cone-shaped peaks towered up to the sky.

We were sailing for the most part through waters not used by traffic, so it was quite enlivening sometimes to meet a few junks, which could maintain a good speed with their large and incredibly patched sails.

On the Monday about midnight we had a mysterious experience—not so mysterious, perhaps, to scientists and deep sea research workers, but at any rate to us.

Hans and Poul were asleep on deck and Knud in his bunk. Isa Lei and I were at the wheel. All was calm and peaceful, and the waning moon had not yet risen. I perceived to my astonishment the reflection of flashes of light on the mainsail and turned round to see what they came from. There was no light—only the black night. But the flashes still appeared on the sails in regular series, and they were fairly strong. I turned round again to find the cause, but still there was only the black night. Feeling rather uncomfortable I rose in my seat—and then the mystery was explained. The flashes came from the water close by *Nordkaperen*, or from the depths below. Regular flashes—about two in a second—were thrown up to the surface of the water. They came from six or seven places at once.

That a flat space of about two square yards should be illuminated as by phosphorus was not in itself astonishing. We had seen it before, and it was possible that it might be strong enough to throw a reflection on the sails, but what astonished me was its flashing like a lighthouse.

I woke Poul and Knud to have witnesses of the phenomenon, but when they had rubbed the sleep out of their eyes, the flashes had stopped. They advised me to see a doctor about it.

This annoyed me, but it occurred to me to flash a strong light down into the water, and the whole sea began to flash delightedly.

We made many guesses—not all equally serious—at the causes. Poul thought we were sailing on the edge of a minefield, and that the Japanese had put flashing lights on the mines. Knud's guess was a sunken town whose illuminated advertisements still showed signs of life. I ventured the suggestion that it might be mermaids shooting at us. The flashes disappeared again and returned when we showed our light. Perhaps they were colonies of minute creatures with the power of giving light, but if so how well they kept time!

A little later, when the moon appeared, the ghostly display ceased. Next day we had a visit from a school of dolphins, who played round us merrily. Knud went on to the fore-deck and got the harpoon ready. Poul and I smiled rather sceptically. The harpoon had been got ready so often, and Knud had often tried his luck with no result. Dolphins are as quick as lightning and difficult to harpoon, and Poul and I did not pay much attention to Knud's attempt. But everything must have a beginning, and an impudent dolphin became Knud's trophy!

'I've got him,' Knud said quite calmly, 'come and give me a hand.'

Poul joined him and they held the fish with difficulty till I brought a rifle and gave it the *coup de grâce*.

We had fresh animal food that day, grilled liver for lunch and steak for supper. We agreed never to harpoon a dolphin again. Only Isa Lei liked the taste. Her weight increased by two lbs. that day. The rest of the bloody meat we put on to the shark hook to follow up our stroke of luck. But when we had delicious shark bait we never saw a shark, and when we had no bait but ourselves they were our faithful followers.

The days passed, and the fine weather held. We sighed for rain and a little coolness. We flung buckets of sea-water over ourselves, but the result was small. A minute afterwards we were as dry as sticks and were covered with a white layer of salt.

On Wednesday, the 8th, just after breakfast, Hans, dripping with perspiration, announced that the fresh water pump was out of order. This did not frighten us; it had happened before. First Poul tried to repair the pump, but gave it up. Then I tried, also in vain. Knud fared no better. We could not squeeze out a drop of water.

Surely the tank could not be empty? Hideous thoughts began to creep into our minds. Impossible: it had been filled at Koepang only nine days before; and normally a full tank gave us water for sixty days.

We watched eagerly while Knud unscrewed the cover of the tank to carry out a test. A stick was pushed down to the bottom of the tank, and when it came up the whole length of it was as dry as a bone.

We slowly realized the gravity of the situation, but we encouraged one another by making light of what had happened.

Could some mistake have been made when it was filled? Had Hans, our temporary cook, been extravagant with water or forgotten to turn off the cock? Or might the tank be leaky? But no—a new, big tank!

No one knew, and no one ever will know.

As was right and proper, we did not discuss the cause, but concentrated on repairing the damage. We studied the chart, and it appeared that the nearest harbour of refuge would be our destination, Batavia. Certainly other points on the coast were nearer, but there were thick minefields between us and the coast. We reckoned that in the most favourable conditions it would be three days' sailing and that with the engine going all the time. There was no wind, and none came.

We collected the rest of the fresh water that was on board. Our reserve supplies included a bottle of distilled water for the accumulator, and by screwing a cap off the bottom of the tank Knud brought to light nearly a quart of dirty water. All in all we had two and a half pints of water, three cups of coffee and two tins of pineapple. Four men and a cat were to live on this for at least three days. There was no danger, but the idea was unpleasant.

Of course we felt thirsty at once, but the rations were hidden as long as possible and served out drop by drop. All in all each of us got two cups of liquid and the cat one. Hans was told to cook light food with no spices, and—if it was at all possible—to cook without water. The first day we were optimistic. Rain would come, or we should meet a ship that would help us. Our fear of pirates had receded into the background.

But as the days passed that hope disappeared. We fervently hoped that the trusty little engine would not fail. When it missed once or twice it gave us a severe shock.

We stopped eating the very first day; it increased our thirst too much. Our only food for three days was a two-pound tin of apple jam. The acid taste reduced our thirst.

We filled the ship's boat, which stood on the after-deck, with water, and we took it in turns to lie in this bath for hours on end.

The water the body consumed relieved the dryness of our throats. When we took a small mouthful of water, we kept it in our mouths for a long time before swallowing it. No one was allowed to work or move unnecessarily. The sky was studied as never before. If only a rain-storm would come, but unfortunately the few clouds that passed lazily overhead were only white wisps.

Hans was the first to finish his water ration, and he nosed about in pots and saucepans to find forgotten water. I caught him wringing out the coffee-bag. Then he routed about in the store of preserves. He thought there might be a little something there with water in it. So there was. He got hold of some tins of green peas, but the liquid in them was saltier than the sea-water.

The rest of us were more careful, and each put away half a cup of water as a last reserve. The consciousness that there was still a little water kept away the fear of thirst and had a stimulating effect morally. But it was no easy matter.

Nevertheless we kept our spirits up, made pretence to each other and outdid one another in stories about iced Pilsner. Hans declared that one could squeeze blood out of fish and drink it. This we knew well, but we had had lines out for several days without result. So if we were to live on blood, we might as well lie down to die there and then.

Curiously enough Isa Lei did not touch her water for the first two days, and Hans grumbled about this.

'The stinking cat,' he muttered, looking at the bowl of water out of the corner of his eye.

On Friday evening, the day before we landed, a black storm cloud came up from the north. We were sure it would pass over us and made preparations for collecting rain water.

It gave us a miss. It passed so close to us that we could see the falling rain, but not a drop came on board *Nordkaperen*.

At 3 a.m. on Saturday, October 10, we sighted the Edam Island light which marks the approach to Batavia.

We celebrated this by drinking what remained of the water. The sight of the coast was like the sight of an oasis in the Sahara.

I had hidden my half-cup of water in my locker, but when about to drink it enthusiastically I discovered that a loathsome great cockroach was floating about in it. The water was not clean to begin with, and this carrion did not make it any more appetizing.

I measured the distance to land: then I fished out the cockroach and gave Hans the half-cup with an air of noble self-sacrifice. He emptied the cup at a draught and licked the inside of it afterwards.

Otherwise Hans showed no sign of having suffered from thirst. He always looked just as well-nourished as before, but it was by no means so with the rest of us. If we had not looked bad before, we did now. Our deep-set eyes had a feverish shine in them, and our lips were as dry as parchment. As we had been unable to shave for lack of water, we did not look particularly well-groomed either.

We had evidently been expected, for a motor-boat with a representative of the Royal Batavia Yacht Club on board came out to meet us. He introduced himself as Captain Haag and gave us a hearty welcome. We were piloted to a berth close to the yacht club's large and handsome headquarters. We were to be their guests. We protested against mooring before the authorities had been on board. We had hoisted the quarantine flag, but the captain brushed our protest aside, saying that he would arrange the matter.

We had fresh proof that we were expected when we saw a native waiter standing on the wooden float at which we tied up. He had four cool-looking bottles of beer in his hands. Several painful minutes passed, for the sake of good manners, before we could attack the Pilsners. They were drunk, spirited away, in a twinkling!

When we stopped drinking, quite out of breath, and were regretfully contemplating the empty bottles, believe it or not, there stood the waiter again, this time with eight beers!

A quarter of an hour after we had tied up it was pouring with rain. It was almost too much of a good thing.

'There will be lunch at the club-house at one o'clock,' said Captain Haag. At the same time he ordered our tank to be filled with water. This was done by half a dozen Javanese who ran to and fro with buckets. When we had shaved our beards off, and had got into our shore clothes, we looked at each other in astonishment. Was it really we?

We arrived at Batavia at the hottest and most unpleasant season, just before the rains; nor did we escape some irritating but harmless tropical ailments such as prickly heat, boils, scurf, etc. We had no energy at all for a couple of weeks. The continual changes of climate and diet always caused us trouble. When we entered a new port it was always a little while before we were acclimatized.

A Danish doctor we met, Dr Wedel, patched us up, and we were soon fit again.

*Nordkaperen* can never have lain in prettier surroundings than she did in Batavia. Her berth was at the mouth of a little canal whose banks were lined with tall trees and palms. The yacht club's handsome club-house was visible between the trees less than a hundred yards away. It was in a small park with the most delightful white bathing beach on the sea side of it. There was a tall flagstaff in front of the club-house, and from it the Danish flag flew side by side with the Dutch for the time that we were guests of the club.

## CHAPTER XVI

# *Batavia and the China Sea*

THERE were always crowds of club members on the terrace or under the shady trees of the park, but our life there had its disadvantages. The heat was unbearable both day and night. We had millions of malaria mosquitoes to fight against and the canal water was not of the cleanest. The canal was an outlet from the harbour town of Tanjung-Priok, and the water was sometimes full of filth.

Moreover, the good people of the yacht club were calculated to interfere somewhat with our 'home life'. We always had visitors, and they had a habit of asking exactly the same questions.

*Nordkaperen* was not in urgent need of having her bottom scraped, but when Dutch Government officials (who were also members of the yacht club) offered us a dry dock for nothing, we accepted immediately. We first pointed out that we had no paint, but it appeared that this was included in the offer. We got into dock and were preparing to work, but there stood 25 coolies! We might not lift a finger. Nor were we now much inclined to. The little Javanese ran about round our feet for five days on end, and *Nordkaperen* had a fine clean bottom again.

The first day we were at Batavia we had a visit from the Danish Consul, Mr Kamarling. We were put into his smart car and told that we were going to see something interesting. And we did. We were put out in front of a large hotel, Hotel des Indes, and soon we were sitting on the terraces, where a large orchestra was playing. Birds were flying about freely in the great hall, the roof of which was supported by huge pillars. Then came the surprise—the Consul had ordered a rice dinner. Eighteen servants wearing white uniforms and straw hats came marching in in a long procession. Each carried a large silver dish, and on each dish half a dozen different kinds of food were arranged; the contents of all the dishes were different. There were sticklebacks, legs of chicken, birds' liver, prawns, sea slugs, cuttlefish, etc., etc. Most of the dishes it was certainly impossible to identify. The consul gave us good advice as to which dishes we should eat, how much or how little we should take, and when the parade was over each of us had two platefuls, and very full ones, besides various pastries on the cloth.

What I remember best was some green jelly which looked delicious and inviting. When I took a spoonful I lost my breath completely. It scorched and burned my throat as if I had drunk hydrochloric acid, and the tears streamed down my cheeks. When I hastened to swallow a glass of beer I heard a hissing noise as if a fire was being put out. This was certainly a dish for a more practised hand.

When we had finished the huge meal we could not twitch our ears. Somnolence overcame us, and the Consul drove us swiftly back to *Nordkaperen*, where we fell down and slept.

There was a great deal of military activity in Batavia. By day and night motor vehicles of every kind, full of Dutch soldiers, raced through the streets. The war against the rebels was noticeable in other ways. Thus, no one might go out after midnight, and we were warned against walking alone on country roads after dark. Now and again a white man was found stabbed in the back.

But the whole picture was not military. Rickshaws were also a characteristic feature. They were on the streets in hundreds. A rickshaw man might follow us for half an hour on end with his importunate offers of service in the hope of earning a gulden. We had expected to find rickshaws drawn by a coolie running in front, but they had disappeared altogether and had given place to tricycles, on which the driver sat behind the passenger.

Several canals, whose yellowish water came from the mountains, ran right through the town. These were the natives' paradise. Children, women and men bathed naked and unashamed in the muddy water. They washed their clothes in the same water; they cleaned their teeth with a forefinger rubbed in the earth, and rinsed their mouths in the same water. They obeyed the calls of nature, great and small, side by side with the bathers, washers and teeth-cleaners, and apparently paid no attention to the dead rats that came floating down the stream.

If we were early in the morning, we could meet tens of thousands of coolies in large parties on the roads round Tanjung-Priok. They came from the camps and were going to their day's work. It would be hard to find a collection of more deplorable-looking individuals. All ages were represented, from twelve upwards. Incredibly dirty little people, mere bags of bones, many of them covered with large, hideous, suppurating sores. A miserable crowd to look at!

Batavia is about ten miles from the actual harbour; the road connecting them runs through marshy country. The little town of Tanjung-Priok has sprung up round the harbour. Its houses are nothing more than wooden sheds. The town lives mainly on seamen, and it is the women who keep the little community going. In the main street the bars stand side by side, and in the side-streets are long rows of windowless sheds. This is where the girls live.

The sewage system of Tanjung-Priok was very simple. Along the houses, a foot or two away, ran narrow gutters. Their contents stank indescribably. When we were shown round by the Dutchmen in their cars, they carefully avoided the neighbourhood of the town on the marsh. The town certainly had a bad reputation among nice people, but we sometimes met people there who, despite the loathing they expressed for the place, enjoyed themselves there.

We too, came there, and I do not mind saying that we spent many pleasant hours in Tanjung-Priok. Seamen from all the countries in the world met there, from ship's boys to captains. There was plenty of drink to be had at a tolerable price, there was life and music, it was agreeable and interesting, and there were little

Javanese, Chinese and Japanese girls. They fluttered about in their sarongs or many-coloured trousers, always clean and neat.

They were not importunate—or at any rate only in a childlike charming manner—and they felt no shame over the way of life to which they had been brought up.

When, tired, thirsty, and hot, we sank down on a chair in a restaurant, beer was poured out by the prettiest, best groomed little hands imaginable. We were fanned to cool us, the sweat was dried from our foreheads, cigarettes were placed between our lips, and the girls lit them. Generally speaking they anticipated our smallest wishes. Even the most hardened and roughest seaman assumed a new and gentler manner when these ethereal little beings, with their unfathomable slanting eyes, came to wait on him.

If you were asked today: 'What place did you most enjoy?' Poul and I would reply 'Tahiti', but Knud 'Java!' Knud's judgment was influenced by an enchanting little sarong-clad Javanese fifteen-year-old, who was madly in love with him. And Knud himself? . . . Oh, that road to Mandalay!

It was worse for Hans, who had not our sense of duty. He fell desperately in love with one girl after another, and the little spare cash he had, or which he obtained by selling his few chattels, disappeared slowly but surely on daily visits to Tanjung-Priok. Finally he ceased to pay visits; he lived there, and had quite forgotten that he had been born again.

Hans had come near causing us a lot of unpleasantness, and only the tactful intervention of the Danish Consul saved us.

We had found out through the girls that Hans had talked of deserting from *Nordkaperen*, and when at the same time he began to remove his belongings and bedclothes from the boat piecemeal, our suspicions were strengthened. Hans would have been no loss, but we should have a lot of trouble if he deserted. According to the law the captain of the ship had in such circumstances to pay a fine or give security for an approximately fixed large sum. Otherwise the authorities could detain the ship till the matter was cleared up.

Twenty-five Javanese coolies at work on *Nordkaperen* at Batavia

PLATE XII

Knud brings a fish on board in style

Don Jacobs (from Ceylon to Dover) as a tiger trainer

Twelve noon

PLATE XIII

Coast scenery in Southern India

For the last three days before *Nordkaperen's* announced sailing date Hans went underground. We hoped to the last that he would change his mind and return before we put to sea, but he did not appear. We were to sail on Sunday, November 2. Hans was not there. He had defied the warnings which had been sent him through his accomplices, the girls.

The Danish Consul had asked us if he might come with us to Singapore. We had not the slightest objection—and that was what saved us. The Consul waited for Hans too and was soon even more furious than we were. He also would have unpleasantness in his capacity of Consul if Hans deserted.

I decided to make a last attempt to persuade Hans, and took a rickshaw into Tanjung-Priok. We had yet another strong reason for wanting to find him. He had taken a large bundle of washing from *Nordkaperen* to some place or another in the town, and we did not at all want to lose that. We had inquired at every laundry in Tanjung-Priok the day before, but without result.

I decided to visit the places where Hans was a regular customer. The people there might know something of his whereabouts. The girls were sitting and sunning themselves, and several of them were busy with needlework when I came up into the room. They were friendly and pleasant, but when Hans was spoken of they became completely mum. I searched one tavern after another, but no one had seen or heard anything of Hans. At last I came to one where I knew Hans was well known. The place was owned by a Chinese woman who was called Mama. She had a large flock of girls in her pay.

First I brought up my heavy artillery and told them that Hans would be searched for, arrested, put in prison, and so on—which was true. Of course they did not care in the least. I borrowed writing-paper and an envelope from Mama, wrote a few words to Hans and shut up the envelope. I made a few thin strokes over the flap, so that if the question arose I should be able to see if the letter had been opened.

'Even if you don't know where Hans is,' I said to the girls, 'perhaps one of you could try to find him and give him this letter. There are five gulden to be earned!' (Twenty gulden were paid for a dollar on the black market.)

Two of them offered themselves, having obtained leave by imperceptible nods from Mama.

While they were gone I began to have an idea why they were keeping guard over Hans. I gathered from the girls' talk that they thought Hans rich and a man of some standing. Perhaps his hypnotic powers had had some effect.

When the girls came back, as they soon did, they said they had not been able to find Hans, and so they did not want any payment for their trouble. It was clear that the letter had been opened; the girl's demeanour told me that too.

Then I tried other methods and stood all the girls a glass of lemonade and cigarettes, while I gave Mama five gulden on the sly. I loudly lamented my own position, spoke of the troubles that awaited me, and so on, and I saw that I was beginning to make converts. Soon afterwards I exploded a little bomb with great effect.

'I think it's hard luck on his wife. She's sitting on board *Nordkaperen* waiting for him, and they've a dear little boy . . .'

It was like being in a poultry-run. The girls divided themselves into two camps—those who believed me and the sceptics. Mama joined my side. She told me with shining eyes where Hans was staying. Unfortunately I allowed myself too much time; he was warned before I got there, and the cage was empty. It was a consolation, however, that one of the girls, in her anger at Hans' unfaithfulness, blurted out that it was her mother who washed for him. And indeed, I found the wash, half done, with an elderly woman in a squalid cabin. She had washed for Hans all the time that *Nordkaperen* had been lying at Batavia, and he had only paid her half the sum he had demanded of us. Born again? Well, well!

I got into a rickshaw with the bundle under my arm to return to *Nordkaperen*. I abandoned Hans to his fate. When I turned the corner, all the little gaily-coloured, trousered Eastern beauties were standing there waving me good-bye.

Even if I had seen him on my way back to the boat I should have done nothing about it. His taking of commissions made me angry.

The Consul cursed Hans and consigned him to perdition when I reported on the result of my trip. Then he took a quick decision, rang up the various authorities and made himself responsible for Hans' desertion. Now we could sail without any trouble arising.

Here, as in Timor, the authorities offered us weapons for our defence against freebooters and pirates, but we refused the offer with thanks. Instead, the naval authorities at Singapore were informed of the approximate date of our arrival.

A hundred members of the yacht club had assembled to wish us a good voyage. We waved a good-bye landward, dipped our ensign and then turned our attention to what lay ahead of us. A fresh breeze carried us out quickly through the swept channel, and in two hours we were out of sight of the coast. The first twenty-four hours were fine as regards both weather and distance. The Consul found his feet quickly, and Poul had to take over the post of cook again instead of Hans.

On the evening of the second day we reached the Caspar Strait, the entrance to the China Sea. We sailed through in the dark, and next morning we were in the China Sea itself. And that was the end of the good sailing weather. We had hard, treacherous squalls to contend with. They came sweeping in from Sumatra. Till now we had had a steady easterly wind, but now we had contrary and variable weather, so that we had to be at work on the sails day and night.

Time after time Sumatra attacked us during the four days in the China Sea, and two of the attacks were particularly bad. Our first meeting with the treacherous weather was on the Tuesday morning. A storm-cloud rose up in the south-west. It was as black as the grave and continuous with the sea. Several times it looked like disappearing again, and once for a short time we really thought we should escape it. But then it quickened its pace and hurled itself on us.

When the first gust struck *Nordkaperen*, she was thrown or forced down on her beam ends, so that the deck on the starboard side was under water. Then she increased her speed and rushed along over the water; the sea had still not got up. There was an ominous groaning in the rigging.

Then the rain came! It came like a wall—we could hear it a long way off. Cascades of water were poured over us—ice-cold rain that made our teeth chatter. We agreed not to take in sail, as the wind was abaft the beam and we knew from experience that *Nordkaperen* could stand a lot from that direction.

The fishing line and the log line, which were trailing astern of us, had fouled each other and we hauled them in to clear them. While we were at work on this the jib halyard snapped, and the jib had to be taken in in a hurry if we wanted to keep it. We had only just finished this when the luff-rope of the foresail snapped, and the foresail was in danger of being torn to pieces. This sail too was hurriedly taken in.

We proceeded with only the mainsail and mizen, and they held out against the storm for three hours. In this time we had sailed thirty miles, but the whole distance was lost again in the high sea which had got up. And then the wind dropped.

The Consul and I had made a bet. He declared that he could not be sea-sick; I affirmed the opposite. The stakes were a case of Carlsberg at Singapore. Unfortunately for me we had not defined sea-sickness, and he maintained that if a man did not vomit he was not sick. He had all the other symptoms, and I shadowed him day and night. But his strength of will helped him—he was a real sailor. At last we agreed that we had lost half a case each.

A heavy, leaden-grey sky hung over our heads day after day, and when for once in a way the sun showed itself, it was behind a veil.

When the grey sky began to assume a blue-black colour in the quarter from which the wind was coming, we knew what we had to expect. The black sky and the water seemed to have blended into one. The horizon disappeared, the dripping rain turned into cascades of water and the fresh breeze to a lashing wind. Many hours might pass before the horizon lightened again, but seldom did many pass before a fresh squall was on the way. At night the thunder roared, and the lightning sprang quivering from the clouds and lit up the desolate sea.

On our third day at sea, about midnight, I had an unusual experience. It was just after a lesser squall—the water was still dripping heavily from sails and rigging. The others were asleep. It was very dark, and we carried no lights on account of the danger from pirates. The horizon was only very faintly visible. If a specially dark and threatening squall was approaching, the boys should be woken—and that in good time. I peered round the horizon, and my eyes rested on a curious cloud formation right ahead. The cloud was queerly shaped and was coming up from the horizon at a disquieting speed. I leant out over the bulwarks to observe the phenomenon better and discovered to my alarm that the cloud was the silhouette of a large schooner. She was heading straight for us and was not two ship's lengths from *Nordkaperen*. I was at the wheel in one bound and put the helm hard-a-starboard. At the same time I heard loud shouts from the schooner.

I had expected a fearful crash, but *Nordkaperen* answered her helm quickly, and the schooner's swung-out boom merely touched our mizen stay. A light was turned on me, and I could see a whole crowd of Chinese milling about in confusion on the schooner's deck and all yelling at once. The noise had brought Poul on deck. He turned a powerful projector on the strange vessel, and we saw the Chinese calling and waving to us, repeatedly shouting something we did not understand. We did not want to heave to, but we still heard their shouts long after they were out of range of the cone of light. The schooner, like us, carried no lights, and the first confusion of the Chinese may have been caused by their taking us for pirates. Perhaps their calling to us had been a trap, but we thought it most likely that they had meant to warn us, for a few hours later we ran into the worst weather we had so far been in in the open sea.

At daybreak the 'Sumatra' showed itself at its worst and most alarming. It began as a blue-black stripe on the western horizon. It spread rapidly, and before we had properly rubbed the sleepiness out of our eyes the storm was upon us.

The first gust of wind came upon us as suddenly as a cannon shot. *Nordkaperen* was forced down with her starboard side in the water, so that the bulwarks disappeared completely. Everything which could slide was hurled down on to the lee side. Clattering and crashing sounds were heard from the cabins below, and masts and sails groaned and creaked. Knud, who was at the wheel, tried to run the boat cautiously into the wind, but the sails thrashed and beat about till the whole hull quivered. He therefore let *Nordkaperen* fall off again, and we now had to try to get the mainsail down with the pressure of the wind on it. The Consul took the wheel while the rest of us set to work to take in the sail. It was a hard job. It was all we could do to hold on tight with our clothes nearly blown off us and masses of foam driving at us and lashing our faces painfully. The mainsail would not come down—at any rate not more than halfway. We discovered in the course of this manoeuvre that a new peak halyard had swollen to twice its thickness and fouled the blocks. The sea had gradually risen, and it was becoming more and more difficult to hold on on board *Nordkaperen*. Perhaps a little pressure on the gaff might help, and the peak halyard could be hauled over the blocks at the same time, but for this a man aloft was wanted. Poul volunteered for the job. He climbed the mast and crawled out along the swaying gaff. Knud and I held on to the after-leech with all our might, and soon we had the mainsail tied up securely. We managed for half an hour with foresail and mizen, but then the hurricane-like gusts increased in force, and the raging seas swept *Nordkaperen* from end to end. The foresail had to be taken in. We were sometimes standing in water up to our waists as we hauled in the thrashing sail.

It was impossible to keep the boat hove to, for the wind came in gusts and from different quarters. The Consul had gradually become anxious. He proposed that we should put in somewhere. We reassured him as well as we could, but when we had to take in the mizen a moment later to prevent its being lashed to ribbons, he positively demanded that we should put into port. Again we talked him out of the crazy idea. We had started the engine when we took in the mizen, and by juggling with the throttle and revving the engine we kept the boat hove to.

The wind shifted ceaselessly from west to north and back again. This sometimes happened suddenly, and the man at the wheel could not always follow, so that *Nordkaperen* was sometimes broadside on to the wind. The seas broke and crossed, coming sometimes from north, sometimes from west. When the Consul saw how well we were going he recovered completely, but at the same time he swore he would never again sail in the China Sea in a small boat.

About midday we were able to resist the wind. We were no longer drifting, and at about 2 p.m. we began to go ahead slowly. It was a heavy sea to sail in, but forward we went! Although the engine had been going at full speed, we had drifted back about twenty miles, and we quickly agreed that a Sumatra gale was really something out of the way.

When the worst of the gale had abated, *Nordkaperen* was invaded by a multitude of birds. They were mostly swallows and sea-birds, all nearly dead from exhaustion. Many had presumably been carried away from Sumatra by the gale, literally blown out over the sea. They were so tired that they were not particular where they settled—the Consul was especially popular. Once for a moment or two he had a swallow on his head, shoulder and hand. We could scratch the breasts of the birds on the deck without their moving. It was all a great surprise to Isa Lei; she was quite dumbfounded. It was a long time before she recovered her balance—so many birds all at once!

We watched her, exhorted her and explained the laws of hospitality to her. But all the same it was very hard for her to restrain herself—especially when a swallow tried to settle on her back. In an unguarded moment she got hold of a fair-sized sea-bird, which was saved by Knud's speedy intervention. Isa Lei had a severe lecture, after which she slunk down below and attacked her tinned meat.

## CHAPTER XVII

# *Across the Bay of Bengal*

WE crossed the Equator for the second time without paying any particular attention to it, although we were now in our 'own' half of the world again. We soon had squalls and high winds to contend with, not so violent as before, but strong enough for the mainsheet to snap twice and finally have to be replaced by a new one. The mizen halyards snapped too, and by degrees there was not a sail or bit of rope that had not suffered from the weather.

For the last two days before we came into port we had a steady wind. That meant sailing close-hauled. While doing so we discovered a new technique, which saved us several squalls. When we saw the notorious blue-black colours on the horizon, we steered straight for the squall, and by going about we often managed to escape it. At any rate we only got a pinch of it; we seldom met its whole force. We escaped quite a number of squalls like this, but now and again we were surrounded and trapped.

On Thursday we discovered that the wireless was out of order. Luckily the chronometer had been set by the time signal a short time before, but we had to go without evening concerts and the news—to the Consul's great annoyance.

On Friday night we lit our lights again. We were now close to traffic routes.

At midnight we altered course, went westward and steered for the Singapore Strait, and about 1 a.m. we could make out the gleam of the Pedro Branca lighthouse on our port bow. We were where we ought to be. At 2 a.m. we could see the light clearly. That last night we had calm weather with good visibility, the best weather one could want for making a landfall.

When we approached Singapore harbour on the morning of Saturday, November 8, we saw no fewer than two Danish ships lying in the roads—the East Asiatic Company's pretty boats *Selandia* and *Manchuria*. It was a year since we had seen a Danish ship, and we demonstrated our joy by sailing round them both and dipping our ensign. A Norwegian ship got a salute at the same time.

We crept into the harbour amid the hundreds of craft at anchor. There were swarms of busy motor-boats and sampans, the harbour taxis. To our surprise and pleasure we found the Dutch circumnavigator *Alk* with our three friends on board at anchor close to the quay. We laid *Nordkaperen* alongside *Alk* and made her fast. We were delighted to meet again—we had not met since we parted at Tahiti. It was a strange meeting. They had only put into Singapore because *Alk's* chronometer had been broken. They were now getting it repaired here. Since we parted they had had a bad time with illnesses—especially malaria. They were lean and emaciated and looked ten years older.

*Alk* had gone through the northern part of the Torres Strait and had not been to Fiji or Australia, but we found that they were to follow almost the same route as ourselves to Gibraltar, calling at the same ports at the same time. After that they were going north, while we were going south again to Madeira.

The traffic in Singapore harbour was lively. Small boats dashed to and fro among the many vessels at anchor. Tugs, lighters and water-boats glided past us in a ceaseless stream. The biggest ships lay at anchor in the roads, outside the breakwater. There was a shortage of quay space in the busy port. On the land side the harbour was flanked by fine, high, palatial buildings round which a press of traffic swarmed, cars, buses and pedestrians in a steady stream all day long.

*Nordkaperen* was lying a stone's throw from Clifford's Pier, a covered-in landing-stage at which liners' passengers were put ashore. A forest of sailing ships' masts which rose out of the southern part of the harbour showed that scores of schooners had their special berths there.

We were lying in a crowd of anchored vessels of the most diverse kind. There were crazy old wooden ships, modern motorships, converted craft, tugs and water-boats. Nearly all the ships had Eastern names. Through the few openings in the crowd we could descry through the mist the ocean giants and warships out in the roads. Now and then a big junk slid past us, blocking out our view with her great, tattered, bat-like canvas or bast sail.

We were dropping the ship's boat into the water to go ashore, but the Dutchmen advised us not to. We should do better to hire one of the many sampans which were swarming round us: if we did not, our skiff would not be long-lived. We saw the stupidity of getting on the wrong side of the harbour gangsters. Better sacrifice a small sum when we wanted to go ashore or come on board again.

The smiling Malay who ferried us in became disagreeable when we bargained over the cost, but after a violent row and much haggling we came to some kind of agreement about the payment. We knew that the important thing was to get oneself respected at once. So we were in (and on) Singapore. The first thing we did was to visit the Danish Consulate in the East Asiatic Company's building. The company's staff, headed by the Consul-General, Mr Strandberg, and his second-in-command, Mr Lommer, gave us a splendid reception. After bidding a cordial farewell—which lasted a day and a night—to the Consul from Batavia, we accompanied him to the aircraft and then embarked on a closer inspection of Singapore.

It was a pleasant, lively city—a commercial city. Almost everyone lived by trade. There was bustle everywhere, from the gigantic buildings of the great business firms to the stalls of the ragged street traders. A huge advertisement, which was painted on the whole upper story of a house, almost took our breath away. 'Carlsberg Beer', it said—delicious Danish beer. Nor was it long before we found a Chinese who sold Danish beer. We allayed—if we did not quench—our thirst and climbed into rickshaws to penetrate the noise and stench of the Chinese quarter. As in Batavia, the old-style rickshaw had been transformed into a tricycle, but the drivers were as importunate as ever.

'What do you think of that?' cried Poul from the foremost rickshaw, pointing to a brilliant neon sign forming the word 'cabaret'. By this time it had become dark.

'What do you think?' I asked Knud, who was sitting beside me, but before he could reply the driver halted the rickshaw in front of the dance-hall—that settled the matter.

At the box-office we were asked the curious question: 'Do you want the ladies "inside" or "outside"?' In the first case we should get four coupons for one Singapore dollar, in the second we should pay ten dollars an hour. We did not really understand the point of the question, so we said we did not want either. The lady in the box-office did not want to let us in, but a Chinese waiter came rushing out and dragged us inside. We ordered a drink and something to eat and got a really good, cheap meal.

We discreetly asked the waiter what ladies 'outside' and 'inside' meant.

He pointed through the long room at the opposite end of which a band was blaring away, made a sweeping gesture with his hand to include all the girls who sat inside the footlights round the dancing floor, and pointed out Chinese, Malay, Indian and white beauties, with others of mixed descent.

'If you want to dance, it costs one coupon, which is to be handed over to the girl. You can choose whom you like. If you want a girl at 10 dollars, she may come outside and talk to you at your table for an hour. In any case the girl is completely at your disposal for an hour.'

Quite good wages per hour!

The men on the dancing floor were mainly Chinese, Indians and half-breeds. A few half-intoxicated white men in crumpled shirts, wet with perspiration, were also dancing with the coloured beauties, who showed no great signs of delight at having such an agreeable job.

The Chinese waiter asked if he might not get us coupons, but we replied 'no, thanks' in chorus.

It was pleasant to get out again, and we sauntered on, farther into Singapore.

We turned down a side street. It was now nearly 2 a.m., and along the kerb-stones and on the pavements stood a row of stalls and shops, all with strong lights which illuminated the narrow alley as if it was broad daylight. Tables and chairs were placed in the street, and crowds of people sat there enjoying queer little Chinese dishes and quenching their thirst in, among other things, Carlsberg. In the narrow space between the tables, taxis and rickshaws wound their way through with a great deal of noise. The street traders often had difficulty in finding room for their stalls, which contained many curious delicacies. They sounded rattles, rang bells, and yelled and shouted to drown the others' voices.

We spent some interesting hours in the alley. Some white men we met taught us how to eat the various dishes—we, too, ate with chopsticks.

Two young men from the East Asiatic Company drove us up north to one of the company's plantations. From Singapore Island we went over a long bridge with Customs stations on each side, and were now in the Sultanate of Johore Bahru. After a long walk along the winding and uneven paths of the immense plantation we came to a fine large bungalow which was inhabited by a young planter, Ib Andersen, a grandson of H. N. Andersen, the Company's founder.

He lived alone in the bungalow with a Chinese servant, who looked after the housekeeping.

When we drove up to the house, Ib and one of his friends were just starting out in a jeep. They were going tiger-hunting. The coolies had been complaining for a long time that there was a tiger in the neighbourhood, and a few minutes before we arrived a coolie had come running up, quite blown, and had reported that the tiger was now quite close to the house.

Of course we got into the jeep. Who would refuse to go on a tiger-hunt? The jeep wound and bumped along among the dark shadows of the rubber trees, and we were soon at the place in the plantation which the coolie had indicated. Here there was dense undergrowth and scrub.

To tell the truth we were not taking the tiger-hunting very seriously. Only Poul and Ib's friend, who had made himself responsible for the guns, had the air of really keen hunters. Ib, Knud and I got away from the others. We pushed our way into the scrub to get a glimpse of the tiger, talking about rubber trees all the time. Ib was a skilful, vivid narrator, fully qualified to widen what knowledge of rubber we possessed.

But suddenly he stopped. Something was moving in the scrub a little way off.

'How about the guns?' Ib asked, stroking his chin. We had obviously never considered that guns were really part of a tiger-hunt. I showed him my camera and shrugged my shoulders. That was the only thing we could do any shooting with!

Probably it was one of the hunters who was moving about in the scrub, but all the same we decided to go back to the car. We walked back with a calm, controlled gait, but with hurried little backward glances over our shoulders. Soon afterwards the hunters proper also returned without having fired a shot. There was no skin from that tiger!

Later we were sitting in the bungalow round a bottle of whisky. Distant drumming could be heard from the natives' huts. The stringed music of the cicadas resounded through the tropical night. We were fascinated by the peace and stillness of the great forests, and I expressed myself on the subject so fluently that Ib could not avoid asking me to stay at the house for a week. The invitation was cordial and genuine all the same. I was coddled for a whole week by the Chinese servant, who fussed round me and ministered to my comfort while I was writing. Every evening, when Ib came home from the plantation, we went for a drive in the jeep before dinner. We looked out for the tiger or a stray wild pig, but we had no luck at all as sportsmen. I think our tiger will die of old age.

*Alk* was to call at Sabang as we were—Sabang is a small island off the northern point of Sumatra—but they sailed ten days before we did. They were to wait for us at Sabang.

When they had sailed we moved *Nordkaperen* over to the domain of the Royal Singapore Yacht Club, to which we had been invited a long time before. This nearly cost Isa Lei her life.

We had several times chased Malay boys away from the boat. They used to come creeping up in their little canoes and showed a great interest in us and Isa Lei in particular. One evening, when we returned to *Nordkaperen* after a few delightful hours with the Danish families Prutz Rasmussen and Norregaard, we missed the cat, which usually met us mewing when we stepped on board. We called her and searched the boat from end to end, but without result. But then we heard sounds of lamentation a long way off. We all jumped into the ship's boat as one man and rowed in the direction of the sound. A few hundred yards from the boat, on the lower part of a pontoon, we found the cat.

But, good heavens, was this Isa Lei? . . . What a sight! The cat resembled anything rather than a cat. The water about the landing stage of which the pontoon was a part was covered with a sheet of oil an inch or two thick—filthy greasy old oil, and the cat may have been swimming about in this for hours on end before she found the ledge of the pontoon, which was fairly high above the water. Isa Lei's fur was stuck fast to her body by the black grease, her eyes were blind and shut, and she was completely exhausted. When she realized that we were coming she stopped mewing. We rescued her with great difficulty, for she was sitting underneath the landing-stage, and our white clothes were ruined by oil.

Those little devils of Malay boys had stolen the cat, but she had got away from them and fallen into the water—or could they have thrown her into the water? We heard one or two things later on, but who had done it we never found out.

When we got back to *Nordkaperen*, we began to wash Isa Lei in petroleum and hot water with soap in it, but the result was deplorable. We spent the whole night cleaning the cat, which was almost unconscious. Unfortunately she had been poisoned by the oil as well, and she may have been suffering pain of some other kind. Malays are cruel to animals.

For over a week she drank no water and ate no food, and when we forcibly fed her she threw the food up again. She lay like a corpse and was finally as flat as a cloth.

We agreed that we must shoot Isa Lei, but when we had got to do it in earnest, we found that we could wait next day. We could not agree as to who should shoot her. So just one day more . . . She was only a cat, but she was also a comrade who had been with us through thick and thin. She had amused us on lonely nights and had always brought us relief, and lightened an atmosphere of depression, by making us laugh at her pranks. She had indeed helped to keep us together.

Next day the rifle was raised to shoot her. Isa Lei turned her head painfully with a long mew. Her eyes were eloquent. The rifle was unloaded again, and we waited one more day. It was lucky that we did.

Knud and I became the cat's doctors. We filled her with American oil at both ends. At first we thought we had killed her, but our cure turned out to be a miraculous cure. The very next day she began to drink water, and two days after that she was eating solid food.

A fortnight later she had almost recovered from the consequences of her swim. But there was still a certain amount of Diesel oil in her fur.

We had intended to sail on Monday, November 24, but we did not get away till the day after. The provisioning of the ship was somewhat delayed by the natives' philosophy of life—if not today, perhaps tomorrow.

Another cause of our delay was the wireless. We had left it

for repairs with a firm which had been recommended to us. It was owned by three brothers, smart fellows, who promised with one voice to have it ready at the agreed time.

'It's nothing serious. It won't cost you a penny,' and so on, and so on. We believed them.

When I went up to fetch it, an hour before we were to sail, only one of the brothers was in the shop. He stood well protected behind a solid writing-table expressing his regrets, while his head disappeared entirely into his collar, that unfortunately they could do nothing to the wireless. He would have let us know before, but he did not know where we were (!). 'Three bulbs were burnt out' (!): they could not be obtained at present, as they had to be ordered from America.

What I said to the nervous wreck has nothing to do with this story, but in no circumstances would I return to *Nordkaperen* with a useless wireless under my arm. We had got into a serious difficulty. We could not do without wireless—our old chronometer had to be corrected fairly often, for it had begun to be unreliable.

We cudgelled our brains. Then we searched drawers and lockers and took a fond farewell of various things. We did a deal with a Chinese, and the cost of a new small wireless was acquired by magic. It was not as good as our American set had been, but it was usable.

On Tuesday, November 25, we weighed anchor, bound for Sabang. We were soon clear of the Singapore Strait and proceeding northward through the Strait of Malacca. The rainy season set its mark on the voyage. We had many storms, often accompanied by thunder and lightning. In the course of the afternoon of our first day at sea we passed a curious light, Sultan lighthouse, built like a little palace with columns, galleries and towers in Eastern style and colours. From its appearance it could very well have been a harem or maidens' bower, well isolated from the world around it. It was planted on posts in the middle of the Strait of Malacca.

A little way past Sultan lighthouse we sighted two Chinese junks, which were sailing ahead of us on the same course.

We tried to get up alongside them by setting the jib, but they realized our intention and replied by setting studding-sails here and there. Our competition became by degrees a regular race. Nothing was given away. When a fresh breath of wind came, we gained on them, but when it died away they had the advantage again.

The wind was blowing from the Malacca peninsula, and the sea was smooth. Over the mountains inland a thunderstorm was coming up; its blue-black surface was ceaselessly torn and crisscrossed by many-forked lightning. The thunder came rolling from the mountains.

Our rivals the junks had suddenly begun to sail close-hauled. They had got a pretty good start and pitched violently in the fresh gusts of wind. We still had the wind on our starboard beam, but made ready to tack. In a few minutes we were running hard close-hauled. The rain drummed, and the lightning had begun to play round us. *Nordkaperen* raced over the smooth water, and we were soon level with the junks. We felt ourselves victors already, but the grinning Chinese had a surprise up their sleeves. We all three went about at the same time and headed in towards the coast. We came nearer and nearer to the treacherous coast with countless islets and reefs, and at last we dared go on no longer. We turned and stood out to sea again. The junks, whose men knew those waters, went right on close under the coast, tacked among reefs and skerries, and avoided the current in which we were. At the same time the wind was freer close in to the shore, so we had to confess with shame that the Chinese sailed faster than we did. The clumsy great craft with their tattered sails cut through the water at a fantastic speed, and at last we lost sight of them. They disappeared in the rain-haze and the gathering darkness. But we stayed where we were in the middle of the strait, and were not to be drawn on to slippery ice.

Next morning a large motor-ship appeared on the horizon astern of us. She altered course and made for us.

The ship, a Dutchman, followed us hesitatingly for a short time, then increased speed and came up alongside us. She hoisted a string of signal flags, blew repeated short blasts on her siren and dipped her ensign. Poul, who was at the wheel, had to hoist our own flag in a hurry and dip it.

We tried to make out the signal with the help of the signal-book, but without success. The Dutchman was certainly using a code we did not know. Those on board her waved us a final greeting before the big ship turned away again. They probably thought that *Nordkaperen* was their countryman *Alk*: they found out their mistake but elected to give us a greeting all the same.

Since we crossed the Atlantic we on board had never been the original trio. Now we were, and we had become the richer for many experiences. We had acquired the skipper's instinct: we could tell by the look of the weather what was coming. We were no longer turned out at night because the boat was going about. The man at the wheel did the whole job alone. He could shift head-sail and backstay without help—indeed, change the brace and even take in all the headsail if a squall was approaching.

It was a good thing we had cut down the mainsail at Thursday Island. *Nordkaperen* could now carry foresail and full mainsail in anything up to half a gale.

On the morning of the third day a little black dot bore down on us from astern. When it came nearer it proved to be a motor-boat. She remained about a mile away from us all day. We thought this curious, and began to think of pirates again. There were other ships in sight at the time, so possibly the motor-boat was waiting for a favourable moment when there would no longer be witnesses. She was not much to look at, and we were not very nervous, but nevertheless we decided to alter course to see if she would continue to pursue us. *Nordkaperen* fell off four points, and a quarter of an hour later we noticed that the motor-boat was still following us. An hour later we came up again by eight points, with the same result. We were reassured: a pirate would hardly show his intentions so plainly.

The mystery was, indeed, cleared up. When darkness was about to fall a faint gleam was sighted from a lighthouse to eastward. Simultaneously our 'pursuer' turned away and steered straight for the light. No doubt they had not a compass on board, and we had just been acting as a pilot for them all day.

Before we reached Sabang we had to pass through one thunderstorm after another. The full moon which had been delighting us was wrapped in a thick layer of clouds.

Towards evening on the last day before we landed we sighted a fleet of fishing-boats ahead. Here, perhaps, was a chance of getting a fish for the cat, which had had a slight relapse and would eat nothing else. We therefore, steered towards the boats, but as if on a word of command they hoisted sail and fled in terror in all directions. The fear of pirates was evidently very widespread in the waters round the Dutch East Indies.

We had no harbour chart of Sabang and therefore hoped to arrive in daylight, but that did not suit *Nordkaperen*. She arrived at about 11 p.m. on November 30.

We could have waited outside the harbour for about seven hours, but the idea did not appeal to us. We therefore steered for what we took to be the entrance to the harbour, a narrow passage between two mountains. It was now pitch dark.

There should have been a deep bay or lagoon between the mountains on Sabang. When we had got into this, the harbour should have been to port of us in another deep bay. This was always knowledge that might have been of use to us, but the darkness made it hard to judge distances. The silhouettes of the mountains, which could be faintly descried against the night sky, could just as well have been five hundred yards as ten miles away.

When we had come close in under the island, we began to take in the sails. While we were busy with this a few tidal waves came rolling in. They were high seas with foaming white crests, whose roaring could be heard far off. The whole thing lasted for three or four minutes, and then the noise died away again in the distance. But they managed to fill *Nordkaperen*. Knud, who was standing on the weather side, was soaked to the skin and had to go below and change.

With the engine at half speed we crept in between the dark, silent mountains and began our search. The water was quiet inside the bay, and *Nordkaperen* glided slowly forward through the darkness, while we kept a look-out on all sides. We came too close to the southernmost point and nearly came into collision with a row of posts which stood in the water. So we made our way out again. At long last we discovered—or guessed the presence of—a little bay to port, and at the same time we caught sight of a faint red light from a buoy floating on the water. It must be the buoy that marked the entrance, and we made for it. Gradually more lights appeared, and we were now fairly sure that we had found the right place, Sabang harbour. Warehouses and ships at anchor now appeared out of the darkness, but we could nowhere see *Alk*, which was to have waited for us. We were right at the innermost end of the bay. Every mast which stood out against the night sky, and every white patch that showed up in the darkness, was carefully examined, but there seemed to be no *Alk*.

Could they really not have waited for us?

Poul proposed that we should have another look, and so we did. This time we went farther in towards the end of the bay. The skiff was dropped into the water, and Poul rowed shoreward to examine the ships. All at once we discovered *Alk*. She was lying moored to a little landing-stage, which we had at first overlooked.

We laid *Nordkaperen* alongside *Alk* as quietly as possible, but nevertheless our friends woke up and came on deck. We were all glad to meet again, and they made coffee for us. Isa Lei got a big bit of fish, and this made the idyll complete. *Alk* had covered the distance of about 600 miles in eight days: we had taken scarcely five, but they turned the tables later.

One of the first things we did at Sabang was to go to the military doctor and be inoculated against various diseases. There were inoculations against cholera, typhus, paratyphus, small-pox and dysentery. We had the incisions and injections in two series with an interval of four days between them. When we had got over the pain and the fever we felt easier in our minds at once.

The variable weather of the rainy season had been hard on *Nordkaperen's* sails, and we therefore set about a general overhaul. There proved to be three times as much to do as we had expected.

Now we sewed for days on end. One of our friends from *Alk*, William, helped us, and the more we sewed the clearer it became how badly we needed new sails. The foresail and mizen were on their last legs. Time was short, the problems new.

There was hardly anything to be bought in poverty-stricken Sabang. And what there was was appallingly dear. There was no beer or spirits in the island—at any rate not at prices we could afford. All the shops in Sabang, which were owned by Chinese, were in two long rows of sheds. This was the main street. Meat, sugar and milk it was impossible to obtain, and a pound of onions cost five crowns (about four-and-six), a small egg 60 öre, etc.

The natives fared best—they lived on roots and other queer things.

Fortunately we were well supplied with provisions and cigarettes, but we could have done very well with material of different kinds for repairing the boat, and this was not to be had.

Sabang had its beauties as well: wild scenery with high green mountains and jungle. But a great deal of rain fell. I myself had a little proof of what pushing one's way through the jungle in the rainy season is like.

We talked a lot about lightening *Nordkaperen's* rig by using bamboos as topsail spars. We had also thought of getting ourselves some fishing rods. There were bamboos only at one place in Sabang, a little community somewhere up in the mountains.

One day William and I drove up the steep mountain roads to the jungle in a powerful Army truck. When this could go no farther on account of the vegetation and marshy ground, we jumped off and worked our way farther on foot. We had enlisted two natives, who went before us with big knives. The moist heat made the sweat drip from us, and the long grass hid the marsh out of which the jungle rose. Often we were in water up to our knees; sometimes we plunged down into a water-hole or ditch. At the same time we had to contend with myriads of mosquitoes and ceaselessly pick spiders' webs off our faces. If at last we found a dry spot to rest in, we were immediately covered with an embroidery of gigantic red ants which bit horribly. Now and again we came upon huts built on posts—wretched habitations in which it was impossible to stand upright. There was only one opening—a little hole through which the inhabitants could creep in and out. In the gloom of the huts we perceived large and small heads, all eager to see the white men who were walking outside in the everlasting rain. It was fantastic that people could live in that marsh.

We splashed about for over an hour before the natives found the place where the bamboos were. We were wet through with rain and perspiration. As soon as I had chosen the sticks which could be used for *Nordkaperen* the natives set to work to cut and clean them. William could not make up his mind. He sorted and selected with great care and made hard work for the natives. When they began to grumble, he promised them an extra shilling. While the work was thus being protracted, I waged bitter warfare against the insects, but William was completely absorbed in his eagerness to get his sticks, and paid no attention to my oaths and curses. He ordered about and bullied the two natives, rushed up and down, slipped into water-holes, brushed off ants mechanically, and, if my impatience had not finally stopped him, the natives would certainly have left us in the lurch.

At last we could go back to the truck. We thought that this would mean toiling through the jungle for an hour. But in fact the truck was only 200 yards away. So we had been walking in a circle for an hour. I gave our dusky guides a suspicious look, but they pretended not to notice anything. Their rascally faces bore an innocent and naïve expression. We were soon rattling down to the harbour with our booty on the back of the truck. When it came to the point *Alk's* skipper would not become the owner of the bamboo sticks which William had chosen with so much care, or have them on board at all. I was much annoyed with William myself, for his slowness had caused me a large collection of ant-bites, but I felt sorry for him all the same. He had meant it to be a pleasant surprise.

On one of our last days at Sabang a police sergeant came on board to tell us that four prisoners had been brought to the station that morning. One of them was a Dane, and if we wished to talk to him, we had the permission of the police. We were naturally curious and went to the station to see our countryman in trouble. The four men were apparently not regarded as prisoners. They were sitting outside on a bench, basking in the sun. They were two Dutchmen, a Belgian and a Dane, who was only eighteen. His thin, undeveloped limbs and body showed that he was still only a boy. The Dutch were taciturn, while the Belgian had a friendly, winning manner. He was broad-shouldered and muscular.

'Why are you here?' we asked.

'We're deserters,' answered the Dane—'fugitives from the Foreign Legion.'

'Did you sail here?'

'No, we swam!'

We asked the Dane to tell his story from the beginning. He looked at his comrades as if seeking their permission. They nodded assent.

'I'd shipped as boy in a Danish ship,' he said, 'but I felt myself badly treated on board. When we called at a French port I deserted. I'd heard and read so much about the Foreign Legion, and the first thing I did was to go to the recruiting office. I wanted to be a hero. When they saw my papers they shook their heads: I was too young, only seventeen. But they advised me to go to another office near by—perhaps there was some way out.

'At the other office they kept my papers, except my passport, and when I got it back I found that I had become eighteen. I went back to the first office with the passport, and became a Legionary. I had honestly believed that I should be performing heroic actions right away, but I was sent off to Africa with a crowd of other beginners.'

The Dane told us in great detail about the terrible conditions in which they had lived, and the inhuman tortures and sufferings they had had to undergo. The three others confirmed what he said: according to them the soldiers of the Foreign Legion were a lot of crushed, bullied, passive wrecks—just a herd of animals.

(We talked later with Legionaries in Algiers, who were quite happy in Africa.)

The Dane continued:

'After our training in Africa we were sent on board a transport which was going to French Indo-China; there we were to receive our baptism of fire. Our job was to suppress the rebel army.

'The conditions on board the overcrowded ship were indescribable. We were crowded together with negroes and Arabs. Bad food, stink, heat and bullying made us sick of it all, and the Belgian and I decided to desert. We were going to jump overboard one dark night when we were passing an island or were near the coast.

'Here—last night—the opportunity arrived. We saw an island to port. We had no idea what it was called and only hoped it was not British, for the British were bound to hand over deserters. The Belgian woke me about one this morning and told me the time had come. We crept up on to the after-deck, put on life-belts and got ready to jump. At the decisive moment my courage failed me. Remember, I could hardly swim at all! The Belgian tried to persuade me several times, then he lost patience, said goodbye and jumped into the water.

'Just then the overseer—a negro—came along. He had become suspicious. That decided the matter—I went overboard too. When I came up to the surface again I saw the ship disappearing, but I couldn't see my friend—'

'Tell me,' I interrupted, 'don't you know the sea here is full of sharks?'

'No, we never thought about it.'

'And didn't the ship stop to pick you up? I presume the overseer gave the alarm.'

'No, he didn't,' said the Dane, 'and there may have been reasons for it. The negro may have been on our side and not given the alarm for that reason, or he may have thought it wasn't worth the trouble to stop the ship and fish us out. They may have thought we'd been eaten by sharks or drowned. We'd be shot anyway.

'As I said, I couldn't see the Belgian, but I shouted to him, and luckily he heard me. He came back, put my life-belt right (it had slipped up over my head) and began to pull me along. I could hardly move through the water by myself, and I hadn't a notion in which direction to swim.

'When we had been swimming for an hour, I couldn't go on. I was exhausted and didn't care whether I was drowned or not. The Belgian threatened me and tried to persuade me in turn. He was as fresh as a daisy and had kept me going by singing all the time. One of the songs he sang began like this: "This is a jolly way to spend an evening."

'When he discovered that neither prayers nor threats were any use—I was completely exhausted—he took me firmly by the collar and swam off with me. We had calculated the distance to the island all wrong. We had thought it was much nearer than it was. Three hours after we had jumped overboard we found that we could not reach the island—a strong current was driving us north. The Belgian might have coped with it if he had let me go and swum alone, but he carried on. By great good luck a little rocky island appeared out of the darkness farther out to sea. We just managed to reach it. We got a few bumps and scratches when we were flung up on to the stones, but we dragged ourselves up into safety with the last strength we possessed. Just then the sun rose, so that we had been in the water for five hours.

'I am not ashamed to say that we cried like children—a natural reaction after the strain. The Belgian only rested for a minute or two, then he climbed the high palm-trees and brought down coconuts. We quenched our burning thirst and had only just finished when to our great astonishment we saw two Legionaries appear in front of us. They had swum ashore too. Three Dutchmen had made the same plans—quite independently of us—and had jumped overboard. Only two came ashore—a shark had had a good dinner that night.

'Two hours later we were seen by a Dutch patrol vessel. She took us on board and brought us to Sabang, where we are under arrest. We don't know yet what's going to happen to us, but we hope for the best,' the Dane concluded.

We should have liked to take the Dane with us if it had been possible. The police sergeant thought it would be too dangerous both for us and for him. He had no papers, and we could not call at British or French ports without considerable risk of his being arrested and our having unpleasantness. The Dutchman, however, guaranteed that no harm would be done to the deserters. They would not be handed over to the French: the affair would be smoothed over and work got for them.

The Dutch authorities kept their word. I met the Dane later in Copenhagen. The Dutch had helped him to get to Denmark, and he was eternally grateful to them.

We agreed with our friends from *Alk* to have a sailing race from Sabang to Ceylon, across the Bay of Bengal, a distance of over 1,000 miles.

We cast off our moorings on the morning of Saturday, December 6. It was 6 a.m. *Alk* was to sail an hour later. We should be in Colombo before the 10th, as the East Asiatic Company's motor ship *Lalandia* was to arrive at that time. She was bringing Christmas presents from Denmark, and we had messages and Christmas presents for some of her passengers from people in Singapore.

We expected to be able to make the passage in seven or eight days, trusting to the north-easterly monsoon which had just begun

—or ought to have begun—at that time of year. We had several exciting days.

We sailed in cloudy weather and rain, and as soon as we were outside the rocky harbour we set sail and got well away from the land before setting our proper course. We started with an easterly wind and filled sails, but in a couple of hours the wind went right over into the west and became variable in force. A sailing craft was in sight close in to the coast, and a look through our glasses identified her as *Alk*. She was on a level with us and had overtaken us by her tactics of hugging the coast.

But she could not pass us.

Late in the afternoon the wind freshened and shifted northward. We hauled in the sheets and began to tack. We steered WSW, three points off our course. *Alk* fell farther astern. We kept on the same course, and when the dawn came *Alk* was out of sight.

On the days which followed immediately there was cloudy weather and rain, and we could take no observations. There was a steady head wind, and we had to sail close-hauled all the time, mainly on the port tack and in a southerly direction. This was the bow sailing on which kept us nearest to our proper course, and we hoped that the north-easterly monsoon would soon set in and put things right.

On the third day the sun came out once or twice, and Knud took the opportunity to shoot it. It proved that we had come 50 miles too far south. According to his calculations the current was responsible for 25 of them.

But what had become of the north-easterly monsoon? We expected it every moment. According to the account of these waters and the wind charts it should have been there long ago.

Perhaps it would be better to go about and to the north, right into the Bay of Bengal. The wind conditions might possibly be better there. We discussed the matter and agreed to go about.

We had been sailing on the starboard tack for perhaps an hour, when the wind veered farther into the north. It was idiotic to sail six or seven points off our course when two would have been enough, so the boat was put about again. We tried to get farther north whenever we had an opportunity, but time after time the wind had a game with us. We were naïve enough to think that the monsoon would come and put everything right.

Despite these annoyances, and the rain, it was pleasant to be doing some deep sea sailing again. The heavy swells and long seas were better than the choppy waters of the straits. There was water enough on all sides here—and under our keel. The deck was covered with flying fish every morning, and Isa Lei gorged herself on the delicacies thus provided. The cat achieved a record for the voyage by putting away eight well-grown flying fish in one day—though she was unable to keep them all down.

When we left Denmark we had four-hour watches, but now we changed over to three hours. It could be a hard and depressing job to be on night watch for four hours on end, especially in stormy weather. Poul, who had become cook again, grew more efficient every day. Not many people realize what being cook in a small boat like *Nordkaperen* really means, when he has to take his turn at the wheel as well. I silently admired him. Both Knud and I hated cooking.

Sunday, December 14, had arrived. There had been no wind for two days. The weather was oppressive, the heat stifling and the barometer low. Now and then a rain squall brought us a refreshing breath of air, but it was seldom long before the rain stopped and the wind died away. Sleep was made impossible, partly by the oppressive weather, partly by annoyance at our bad position and anxiety as to whether we should arrive at the proper time.

But after I had taken over the wheel from Poul there were two minor squalls from the north-west, and *Nordkaperen* got a buffet now and again. Even if we were not going the right way, it was better than standing still. Every squall contained wind enough for ten minutes' sailing. After that the weather became oppressive and still again. The tiniest dark cloud which appeared in the north-western sky was welcomed—even if it gave us rain too. My attention was turned to the quarters from which the wind came, and it was quite by chance that I had a look out to leeward. What I saw there more than astonished me. We were sailing in the middle of the Indian Ocean and the nearest land to the south should have been thousands of miles away, but I saw land clearly all the same—and quite close to us.

Along almost the whole length of the southern horizon lay a mountain chain. Great black mountains had grown up out of the water. I moved a little way out of the baulking light of the binacle to have a closer look at the phenomenon.

Of course they were not mountains. They were coal-black clouds that grew rapidly. A storm coming from the leeward demanded caution, especially when its colour, speed and size were abnormal. It looked as if it was moving in a north-easterly direction, and there was a faint possibility of our escaping it. I did not think there was any reason for taking a pessimistic view and waking Poul and Knud.

Again and again I took bearings on the western edge of the black cloud formation, and by degrees it came to look as if we should get a bit of a buffeting. Luckily we had no headsails up, so I was still not at all uneasy, but how incredibly fast those clouds moved!

I was so taken up with the southern sky that I had not thought of the northern and when at last I looked out on to the weather side, I had a bit of a shock. Deep black clouds came rushing towards us—long, ragged arms of cloud whirled along ahead of them like smoke in a storm. We were suddenly surrounded.

I leapt down into the cockpit and rang the alarm-bell. For the first and only time on our world voyage it did not work. I wanted to jump to the companion and call the boys up, but I could not. *Nordkaperen* was simply thrown on her head. So suddenly that I was nearly flung out of the cockpit the boat was thrown broadside on to the water so that the port bulwarks disappeared altogether. I worked my way with difficulty up to the weather coaming of the cockpit and took up my position at the wheel.

*Nordkaperen* was turned cautiously into the wind. The boat was to have a foot in both camps. If she was turned too quickly, and ran right into the wind, her sails and rigging would be shaken into the sea in an instant. There was, however, a danger of our losing our rigging if we let the boat lie broadside on to the sea.

Then the rain came thundering upon us. It came like a wall, cascades of water were hurled through the air, and everything round us grew pitch-black. I thought the force of the rain and wind had now reached its maximum, but it became still more violent. The mast and the surface of the water formed an angle of twenty degrees, the wind rushed by above the sails, and the water ran up inside my rubber boots, which were pressed against the lee coaming of the cockpit.

Poul and Knud tumbled out of their bunks at the first gust of wind. They realized at once what was happening, but it was impossible to take in a sail. It gave me a pleasant feeling of security to see the light in the cabin turned on. I felt myself freed of a little of the responsibility.

Fresh gusts of wind flew over us with the force of a tornado: the rain drummed as violently on deck, sails and oilskins. When I put the boat close to the wind, she shuddered from keel to topmast.

I caught sight of Knud's head in the hatchway and behind him Poul in the lamp-light. He had oilskins on, ready to come on deck.

Knud shouted something to me. I made signs to him that I could not hear him. He shouted louder.

'What the hell is this mess you've got into?'

'Don't ask me, but can you see if we've still got all the sails up?'

I could not see very far through the rain and darkness.

'They're all down,' he shouted, grinning.

I took his meaning. No, it was indeed not very far from the masthead to the water. Incredible that sails and rigging could stand that pressure. *Nordkaperen's* building and the heavy lead keel prevented her from capsizing so long as the sails were not under water. So we had nothing to fear in that direction. It was the rigging we were most anxious about. Poul and Knud made several attempts to take in a sail, but it proved to be hopeless. Twenty able-bodied men all working at once could not have done anything.

When the storm had lasted a good half-hour, there was a lightening of the atmosphere round us. I discovered that the northern horizon was growing lighter—a joyful sight—and the starry ceiling larger and larger. One last violent gust as a farewell, and the wind and rain disappeared as though by magic. Oh, how delightful it was! Off with the wet oilskins and out with the cigarettes. Now the air was clear again.

'You may as well turn in again,' I said to Poul and Knud, 'it doesn't look as if there will be anything more. Next time I'll call you a bit earlier.'

'Yes, I should, if you want to keep the sails,' grunted Knud as he disappeared below. I had just sat down in the cockpit with a cigarette, when the wind came back, but from a different quarter. Luckily there was no rain this time, and the wind was not so strong, so that it was real pleasure sailing. Moreover, we could keep a course. But it only lasted half an hour, then it was over. That was the last wind we had till we reached the coast of Ceylon.

The sails were inspected next morning. They were a deplorable sight. The canvas of both foresail and mainsail was rent in many places. The jib had been torn right across in a squall on the previous day. So there was plenty of work.

'This isn't much like pleasure sailing,' sighed Poul.

We could not reach Colombo before the 18th unless something extraordinary was done. We had not much petrol left. If we put in spirits and petroleum, we should still be without fuel for the last hundred miles.

We might get help from a chance breeze. We had quite given up the faithless north-easterly monsoon. The engine was started, and we steered straight for Ceylon over a sea which grew calmer and calmer.

At midday we were 170 miles from port—not much, if there

had been any wind. In the evening the engine stopped. It had consumed all the petrol!

It grew dead quiet on board; all life came to a standstill. *Nordkaperen* stopped moving, her wake died away; and she lay turning round with no way on her.

We felt it was still a long way to Ceylon.

We got help from a quarter from which we least expected it.

The Indian Ocean is a most mysterious sea—at any rate it was when we were there. That infernal northerly current should have been there long before. The little wind that came—from all quarters—disappeared again as quickly as it had come. The strong current, which should run along the eastern coasts of Ceylon and India and force us south, was running the other way. This was a pleasant surprise.

We thought we were drifting rapidly towards the South Pole; so great was our astonishment when next morning we discovered the mountains of Ceylon to the northward. It was December 16. Our spirits rose, though we still had a long way to go. *Nordkaperen* was sailing sideways and backwards towards Ceylon, and towards night the first light appeared. The strong current helped us all the time, but it was being a bit too smart by taking us close in to the coast, where there is a string of dangerous reefs and a swarm of isolated rocks.

We had to sacrifice some of our precious reserve petrol to get out into deep water again. Next morning we had drifted the right way again, up along the coast towards Colombo.

Then came the last squall of the passage, and it proved our salvation. It gave us wind from astern and held till we were almost in port. Once more we heard the clucking of the bow-wave—a delightful sound—and the sails spread proudly despite tears and holes.

Just outside the harbour we took in the sails and started the engine, and we entered Colombo harbour with our very last drops of petrol at 10 a.m. on December 17.

We had got right into the harbour when the pilot climbed on

board. There was compulsory pilotage, but he took a broad view of it.

The first question we asked was: 'Has *Alk* arrived?'

'Yes, an hour ago.'

'Has *Lalandia* arrived?'

'No, they've been delayed and won't be here till the 23rd.'

The devil! we could have saved a lot of our precious petrol!

We laid ourselves alongside *Alk* and congratulated them on their victory, at which they were delighted. The three grand fellows promised us a chance of revenge later, on the passage to Aden in Arabia.

We had thought *Alk* had gone north of us, but received the astonishing information that they had been much farther south than we. They too had tried to get up northward, but had given it up. At last they had had to start their powerful engine to work their way north. The curious thing was that they had had the finest north-easterly wind for the last two days, on which we had had at most one or two chance cat's paws. They had seen nothing at all of our storm.

Considering that we had been about fifty miles apart, this confirms our impression that the Indian Ocean is a strange sea.

We had a talk with a man from an East Asiatic Company's ship which was homeward bound. He asked what sort of a passage we had had, and we told him that we had had unfavourable weather. We regretted that we had not gone straight north into the Bay of Bengal, where the weather conditions would certainly have been better.

He gave us a horrified look.

'Are you crazy? We're come from the Bay of Bengal and had to change course three times because of typhoons which were reported on the wireless. We only just escaped the last one.'

Really! . . . We wondered if the gale on December 14 could have been an arm of a typhoon.

And we agreed that we certainly had not much to complain of.

CHAPTER XVIII

# *Colombo to Port Sudan*

COLOMBO harbour was as busy and interesting as that of Singapore—crowded with ships of all types. Big, heavy, barge-like sailing craft with enormous sails like birds' wings tacked boldly and smartly in the narrow passages through the crowd.

*Alk* and *Nordkaperen* were lying side by side at a buoy in the western part of the harbour, under the shelter of a high mole. But at once an invitation came to lie in the area of the Royal Colombo Yacht Club at the other end of the harbour. We accepted with pleasure, but regretted it soon afterwards. It was in the disturbed part of the harbour. When a strong wind blew straight in through the mouth of the harbour—and it often did—the sea rose sharply and set both boats dancing. We got into difficulties the very first evening, but *Alk* came off worst. The boats were lying at anchor with a couple of long mooring-ropes from us to the land. We dared not go within ten yards of the quay. Soon after sunset it came on to blow hard: we had the wind and sea from due ahead, and both *Alk* and *Nordkaperen* pitched violently. Our bowsprit was under water several times, and it was something of an achievement to get ashore in the dinghy. The seas thundered against the quay and flung clouds of spray high up in the air.

*Alk's* anchor could not hold. She drifted nearer the quay, while all hands were hard at work trying to meet the danger. The ships' boats in which we were working leapt about in the sea like porpoises. We got out a new anchor with a strong hawser, but halfway through our work a crowd of small boats near by suddenly went adrift. They drifted straight on to *Alk* and ran into her. We had a lot of trouble to pick them up and take them back to their berth. When everything seemed to be all right a big 100-ton lighter came drifting along the quay. She bumped against the mole time after time, while two coolies ran about on board in confusion and tried to fend her off the land with long poles. She could not possibly pass outside us, so we hastened to slacken *Nordkaperen's* and *Alk's* stern moorings. The barge with her yelling crew passed just clear of the two circumnavigators, and we were able to moor our boats again.

We had laid out *Nordkaperen's* big 'hurricane anchor' with masses of heavy chain, so that it did not move an inch. We had some difficulty in getting on board again. Poul went ahead with our own ship's boat. She went too close to *Nordkaperen's* stern, was forced down under water and capsized, but Poul got on board undamaged if only just dry. Knud and I borrowed a dinghy and we fared better, even if we filled the boat to the bulwarks.

The Danish Consul in Colombo, Mr Knudsen, was a splendid fellow. He at once invited us to spend Christmas in his home—and more than that, we were to stay with him in general and make ourselves at home. It was a grand time.

On Christmas Eve we were a party of twelve Danes in the Consul's house, and though it was hard to capture the real Christmas atmosphere, it was a pleasant evening.

One of the guests, Mr Blichfeldt, was the manager of some large tea plantations up in the mountains of central Ceylon. He invited me up there for a few days. We set off for Glentaffe in his car on the morning of December 26. For four hours we wound our way up narrow, steep mountain roads with yawning abysses a few inches from the wheels. Sometimes the bends could not be taken all at once, and we had to back before we could get round. Once the road was blocked by four huge tame elephants, but a small boy of ten got them in to the side of the road with authority and certainty. We climbed to a height of about 5,000 feet, and at last we were at Blichfeldt's fine large bungalow.

I spent five pleasant days there writing and going for long walks in the plantations. There were no mosquitoes, and one could be as cold as at home in Denmark. We came from Colombo's stifling 95° F. to the pure air of the mountains and a temperature of 60°. I had to sleep with two blankets over me at night, and the first morning, when I rushed under the shower-bath, I dashed out again with a howl. The water was icy cold.

From the house, which was almost at the top of a mountain, there was a wonderful view over the magnificent Ceylon scenery. In the distance rose Adams' Peak with its tall slender cone, with a light veil of mist over it, and deep below me a river ran curving through the valley like a shining silver thread.

There were high green mountains on every side, and thin banks of mist clung fast to the slopes. A reverential silence filled the immeasurable spaces. Only now and again distant voices forced themselves on the ear. They came from the workers in the plantations farther down the mountain-side. One single fruity melodious whistle from a bird joined the chorus.

On New Year's Eve I was driven to the nearest town which had a station, Hatton, to take the train back to Colombo. I did not want to miss the experience of an eight hours' train journey. I was the only white person on the platform among several hundred coloured people. I got a place by a window with a richly dressed young couple opposite to me. Their fingers flashed with diamonds; the woman's dress was embroidered with gold and with beautiful colours in the Indian style, while the man wore European clothes. They were newly married.

I had looked forward to an enjoyable trip, looking out of the window at the scenery, but my pleasure was to some extent spoilt by a young Indian who sat down beside me.

'Mr Nielsen?' He looked at me questioningly and at the same time triumphantly.

I looked at him in astonishment: I could not remember having seen him before.

'Yes, I met you in Colombo—it's you who have the sailing-boat *Nordkaperen*—you're Danish—I was on board your boat the first day for my paper.'

He asked endless questions, offered me cigarettes and prattled. After an hour he began to bore me. I read and pretended not to notice him. At last he gave it up and fell asleep.

We rumbled through tunnels for minutes on end; along dizzy precipices, from which gleaming rivers and green rice-fields could be seen thousands of feet below; over high, long, frail-looking bridges, which trembled on the posts they stood on. As we gradually approached the plain the heat became noticeable—some of my mountain clothing had to come off. At last darkness fell and destroyed the view.

At 8 p.m. we rolled into Colombo station, and I took a rickshaw down to the harbour. Here one drove in a rickshaw in the correct manner—with a coolie running in front between the shafts. His bare feet beat on the pavement in a monotonous rhythm.

When I had got on board *Nordkaperen* with some trouble—the sea was calm—Poul and Knud were not at home, but I caught sight of their white yachting caps up on the balcony of the yacht club. They had begun to celebrate the New Year, and it was not long before I was with them. Two of our Dutch friends were there too. The skipper, Allan, was on board the boat. He had an attack of malaria. A number of yachtsmen were assembled round a table which bent under the weight of much foaming iced Carlsberg beer. One of the party was an English sergeant stationed in Colombo. His name was Don.

He came to play a part in *Nordkaperen's* history. He was a man one could not help looking up to—6 ft. 4 in.—a fellow with a good-natured, winning character.

When the traditional New Year toasts had been drunk, we laid in a stock in the club-house bar and arrived on board *Alk* safe and sound. We wanted to drink a glass of wine with the skipper.

The Old Year's departure was celebrated, while good resolutions swirled around in the cabin till they were stifled by the spirituous vapours. When I woke up next morning it was eleven o'clock, and I was lying on the cushioned seat in *Alk's* cabin.

We had heard that a shop in the native quarter was having a sale of old stores from an abandoned naval base. Various things were going cheap, from boots and sugar to compasses and binoculars, and there were oilskins, in which we were specially interested.

The quarter round the harbour did not bear a particularly Oriental stamp. It consisted of high buildings of good appearance. In the middle of the town, in the middle of a street we came upon Ceylon's lighthouse. The traffic divided itself into two streams at the foot of the tower. As we came by degrees into the old quarter of the town, the walk became more and more amusing and exciting. There was swarming life in the narrow streets, and we had difficulty in keeping away pavement traders and people offering us services of some kind. Ragged beggars, coolies and richly dressed upper-class Indians passed in an unceasing stream. The smell was rank—especially round the market-place—and all the time we had to step carefully over large red puddles of juice, left by the many betel-chewers.

As we passed along a row of traders sitting on the pavement, our trousers were plucked at and tempting offers were yelled after us. Some queer goods were offered to us: bits of broken looking-glass, old rusty, bent nails, an odd boot, a broken comb, a knife with half a blade, a nut, and so on. All this stuff was spread out on a mat, in the most meticulous order, as if it were jewels.

At last we found the shop for which we were bound. We had taken various things to do some barter trade, and we returned with a good set of oilskins each, besides other things, including a pair of prismatic glasses. We thought ourselves we had done a good deal. Let us go on thinking so!

Don was going to England in June to continue his twelve years' service in the army—he had done seven!

'I'd like to sail to England with you, if I might—and could,' he said to me one day.

'You're welcome,' I said. I meant it, but thought it was an impossibility, as we were sailing in a few days.

But all the same he got permission from his colonel and six months' leave for the journey.

We had been to drinks with the hospitable soldiers several times in Don's quarters and, moreover, the colonel having given Don leave was worth many good turns to him and us.

*Nordkaperen's* rigging and sails had one more thorough overhaul. We worked hard in the time we lay at Colombo. We painted the boat above water and put new rope-ladders up to the crosstrees. The old ones had become too unsafe. They had been indispensable to us when we wanted to look out for reefs or land, or when we had to take in a caught-up sail.

We were overrun all day by energetic traders, who wanted to sell us provisions and stores, do sail-maker's work, wash clothes, act as watchmen, sell souvenirs, etc.—cheeky, pushing fellows, whom we found it hard to get rid of again.

*Alk* sailed on Saturday, January 3. Her skipper preferred to leave port on a Saturday; he would never sail on a Friday or Monday, and on the 13th of every month he was a quivering bundle of nerves. Curiously enough he did have trouble later on the thirteenth of a month.

We waved good-bye. We were to meet again at Aden: but this was the last time we saw *Alk*. We were to sail ourselves on the 6th, and we counted on being able to overtake them.

We had been told that Colombo harbour was one of the worst for getting a ship's bottom foul. Barnacles and long-necks simply sprang up from the bottom, and when we took hold of the anchor chain on Tuesday the 6th to weigh anchor we were full of nervous anticipation. And the chain was absolutely stiff with barnacles. A slip was fantastically dear in Colombo like everything else. It should and must be done without. *Nordkaperen* would hardly move when we stood out of harbour, although the engine was going full speed ahead. The screw must be covered with barnacles, unless we had got a bit of rope in it. We stopped for a moment and sent a couple of natives down to examine the screw, but they declared that they could not find any rope. Members of the yacht club, who were accompanying us in a couple of boats, began to grow impatient. Several of them had taken time off to be able to say good-bye to us. We did not, therefore, want to put back to look into the matter, and went on crawling out of the harbour.

When we got outside a westerly wind was waiting for us, so we had to start tacking at once. This was a bad beginning to a passage of over 2,000 miles. In our optimism we had reckoned with eighteen days' sailing to Aden at the most. Despite everything we had faith in the north-east monsoon. And the passage could not be much longer if we were to get through the Red Sea in anything like decent weather.

In the very first hour we made a mistake which caused us much annoyance and a great deal of trouble—which could, indeed, have had disastrous consequences for us all. We had agreed to steer south, out into the open sea, instead of keeping north along the coast of India. We knew that *Alk* was going along the Indian coast, but we thought that we should get on more quickly if we went out to sea and caught the fierce monsoon. So we steered south-west.

The very first night the wind changed and we got a fresh easterly breeze. We had good reason to congratulate one another that we had not made the great detour, as *Alk* was doing. The first day we did 112 miles, the second 115, in spite of our foul bottom. Our spirits rose, but on the third day the wind dropped and we did only 52 miles. The days that followed were utter misery.

Don got over the pains of sea-sickness, but it was a long time before he could settle down to the daily round. When he moved about on deck he hung on fast to everything, and when the boat was rolling very much, he crawled on all fours.

He was a hundred per cent British in his self-control. He never showed the least sign of nervousness and never interfered with our arrangements. There was no berth on board that was long enough for Don. He slept in the fore cabin in a bunk that was about a foot too short, and when he slept his unusually long arms and legs stuck out on all sides. His appetite was enormous. Where we could manage with one helping of porridge, he wanted three. We did not grudge it him in the least, but as he was only paying a quarter of the expenses he did not come off badly.

Clamps and objects standing on the deck were torment to him. He always fell over them in the dark, and he asked if we would mind his painting them white. We gave him a pot of paint and a brush, and Don began to develop a traffic security programme. He was one of those dangerous people who will go on painting furiously so long as they have a drop left. He painted sheets and clamps, he painted ventilators, he painted the capstan, but when he seriously wanted to paint Isa Lei white, because he fell over her at night, we took the paint and brush away from him. One day, when we sent him up the mast to paint the new rope-ladder, we discovered that he had a bad head. He would never go farther up than the seventh rung, and hung on fast there by his arms and legs, sending down looks of despair to us below. After that he was trained in going aloft every day, and he climbed a rung higher every time. At last the great moment arrived when he sat up in the crosstrees. Thenceforward he sat there all day uttering wild Tarzan-like yells, and could not be induced to come down. Only when Poul summoned us to a meal did he come down, and then he came at top speed.

Once more we were approaching colder regions, and days were spent in the Indian Ocean in overhauling and mending our 'winter clothes'. And as soon as we had thread and needle in our hands, we sewed our pennants and Danish ensign. It was impossible to get such things in those parts, and the large reserve supply we had brought from Denmark was used up. There was time too, to make a large, solid sea anchor. Yes, there was indeed time . . . more than enough!

The wind was light, but we went steadily on, though the sails thrashed about—and we always had a bit of bow-wave. It was therefore something of a shock for us when on the fourth day our observations showed an advance of only five miles in a day, with a northward drift of twenty miles.

Everything tallied—chronometers and calculations. And Knud guaranteed his sun-shooting. We had reckoned on a run of fifty or sixty miles, so there was disappointment on board.

Next day's observations gave us something to think about. We had gone back fifteen miles and a further twenty miles north, although we had a faint bow-wave as we headed west. At 4 p.m. the same day we had gone back ten miles and five north. Something must be done. If we were to drift, we would help the process ourselves. We would try to get out of the doldrums by steering north. And so we altered course. It was Sunday, January 11.

Knud thought we had got into a gigantic eddy, and time proved that he was right. The next day's observations were eagerly awaited. They were ready at noon. We had gone twelve miles east and thirty-one miles *south*. Knud had been right, and our attempt to break out had failed. When the monsoon changes the current turns, and it was possible that the old eastward current was having a tussle with the new westward current, and that, combined with the geographical situation of the waters we were in—about 200 miles east of the Laccadives and Maldives, whose islands and reefs form a barrier—was making the water move in circles or wander. At least that was our theory, and we have not yet had it refuted—nor, I admit, confirmed.

On the 13th we got a nice breeze from the east, and we changed course to westward again. About midday the wind grew light again, and our observations showed that we had gone twenty-eight miles the right way. The engine was started to make the most of our chances. We must get out of the tangle as quickly as possible.

Although *Nordkaperen* was not sailing fast, our spirits had risen again. We had been afraid of our very scanty rations running out. We had bought as little as possible in Colombo, where the prices did not invite hoarding. We were particularly short of cigarettes.

Our attempt to break out northward had failed, but now we had a chance of getting out, and to it we devoted what petrol we still had. At midnight the engine stopped, and we had only half a gallon or so left for use in the direst necessity.

At noon the next day, the 14th, we had gone nineteen miles to the eastward—i.e. back, and our second attempt to break out had also failed.

On the 15th there was not much wind: we drifted forty-six miles east and thirteen west, heading west all the time.

At noon on the 16th we were nine miles farther south, and at 6 p.m. that day we logged a further drift to the south-east of sixteen miles.

A light easterly breeze put a little life into *Nordkaperen* that evening, and we turned our head south to make our third attempt to escape. If we freed ourselves, we would make a wide curve to eastward, outside the danger zone, and make our way back to Ceylon or to some place on the coast of India to provision ship again. We might there have an opporunity of scraping and inspecting *Nordkaperen's* bottom. We went south all night, and next day, the 17th, we had advanced forty miles on our new course. It looked as if we should succeed this time, but we were 120 miles from the place at which we had attempted to break out the first time. So we turned our head east, and on the 18th we had really made twenty-two miles to the east. Not much, but we were delighted. The mere fact that we were masters of the situation again, even if we had a long road before us, drove away uncertainty and put new life into us.

At last, on Sunday the 18th, a fresh breeze sprang up from the east. It looked like lasting. We changed course to north-east and sailed close-hauled. During the afternoon the wind freshened and moved a few points northward. We had to take in the topsail and changed course to NNE. The sea got up and white crests appeared, so that we soon had to fall off a point again. As so often before we had been sceptical about the wind lasting and showed only qualified pleasure. What was worse, we scorned to batten down the hatches, and when the slowly increasing wind was at last something like half a gale, there was hardly a dry place on board the boat. Huge mountains of water rolled to meet us, and a big sea somehow or other lifted the skylight up, so that fifty buckets of water poured down into the cabin. Wild yells were heard from below, where cushions, charts and humans were floating about. After that the skylight was battened down.

The wind veered farther northward and increased in strength, and it looked as if this was the beginning of the fierce monsoon. If only we could have gone with the wind towards Aden! but we dared not with our small supplies. We might run the risk of getting into the 'roundabout' again.

We were carrying too much sail, but doubt as to the wind lasting made us reluctant to take in sail. Don was to take over the wheel from Poul at 10 p.m., and when Poul came down in his dripping oilskins, he proposed that we should take in the flying jib. Before we had agreed what to do, there came a shout from Don on deck.

'Hullo! we've lost a headsail!'

The flying jib had blown into the water. We thought at first that it had gone altogether, but it was fixed firmly to the sheet and was trailing behind us in the water. The damage done had been slight.

The rest of us turned in, while Don remained alone up in the darkness. It was hard to sleep. I listened to the wind's howling in the rigging and the noise of the seas breaking over the boat. It sounded as if wind and sea were rising. I clearly remembered what it had been like the first time I sat at the wheel at night in the dark and in rough weather; I recalled the feeling of loneliness that took possession of one, and inwardly pitied the inexperienced Don. It was not long before I turned out and put on my oilskins to go up and keep him company. I had to relieve him later on anyhow . . .

The wind had increased. We had to fall off a few points again and let the sheets well out. *Nordkaperen* went through the seas well and steadily, but nearly every one left its card in the shape of several tons of water on the deck. It was clear that we were carrying too much sail, but our prolonged sufferings in the charmed circle made us ignore all other considerations and simply try to get on.

Don and I had a pleasant chat and tried to smoke a cigarette. The hours passed, but the weather became worse. When a huge sea had nearly upset the boat, I decided to wake Poul and Knud. We must have some of the sails down.

While Poul and Knud were putting on their oilskins a series of sharp cracks from the fore-deck were heard, and the rigging all over the boat shook. I knew what had happened before I got there. Our beautiful great jib was done for. Half of it had blown away into the darkness, and the remains clung to the luff-ropes like a row of white flags and thrashed about.

Poul and Knud took in the remnants of the jib while Don held a light for them. I myself took the wheel to keep the fore part of the boat dry as long as work was going on there. The mizen sail also was taken in. This lightened *Nordkaperen*. We let out the mainsail and foresail more and fell off one or two more points. It was high time. The wind was gradually becoming something like a gale, and the fierce monsoon seas flung us about mercilessly. It was in fact idiocy to tack against the heavy sea—it would have been a good deal more pleasant to leave the boat hove to and go below and sleep, but we had gradually fallen off so much that we were sailing right through the charmed circle, and we were not going to do that again—on that we were movingly in agreement.

Poul, Knud and I took tricks at the wheel all through the night, and all three of us had the same fear: if only the sails hold out!

It was horrible down below. Everything was wet; all night long one of us was running round with a wet cloth under his arm trying to find a fairly dry place to sleep in. Another thing was that the rolling of the boat made sleep almost impossible.

But *Nordkaperen* continued her wild chase, and in the ten hours the storm lasted we sailed about 100 miles. Next morning the

Impudent and provocative Indians follow in our wake

PLATE XIV

Warm clothes in the Mediterranean—45 degrees after 90 degrees in the Red Sea

A friendly chat and a drink—always effective in dealing with authorities

PLATE XV

Arrival at Copenhagen

wind died away suddenly and left behind it a high, white-crested, unpleasant sea, which continued throughout the day.

In the evening of the 20th we got a north-westerly breeze, and we set our course towards the coast of Southern India. We were anxious next day to know what our position was, but fortunately we had come thirty-five miles in the right direction and were apparently out of the 'roundabout'. In the afternoon we could make out land. India appeared on the north-eastern horizon.

We decided to call at the port of Cochin, which was about 100 miles north of us, and in the course of the 22nd we had sailed half-way. But *Nordkaperen* would do no more!

The wind grew light, and we met a fairly strong current. We crept right in to the coast to escape the current—almost right in under the palms, but we did not advance more than ten miles that day.

All along the coast not a house was to be seen. Now and again a temple rose among the palms, but round about us were many fishermen in their little outrigger canoes.

In the morning a party of ragged black Indians came rowing after us. They became bolder and bolder, rowed up alongside the boat and clung to the bulwarks. If their behaviour had been dictated by inquisitiveness or mendicancy, we should not have been uneasy, but there was something else in the atmosphere.

The fellows were becoming dangerously insolent, and Don, who was accustomed to take a high line in talking to the natives in Ceylon, nearly caused an explosion by abusing them in the most sulphurous terms.

I went quietly down into the cabin and got hold of the rifle, took it up on deck with me and began to fiddle with it. I looked through the barrel, cleaned it, and put in a cartridge, all as if it was an every-day procedure. However, it had an incredible effect on the Indians. They let go of the bulwarks at once and the chorus of yells subsided. The canoes slid away one by one, and we were soon alone again.

About midday we sighted some houses ahead; it was the town

of Alleppey. At long last we had worked our way to a point just off it. It had no harbour, only a bit of a landing-stage running out into the water. It might take us many days to reach Cochin at the pace we were going. It might be worth while to try our luck at Alleppey. A small steamer was lying at anchor some way out. We hailed a man on her bridge and asked if he knew anything about the possibility of getting provisions in the town.

'Yes—five fathoms,' he yelled. The conversation was broken off by our drifting away. We had not asked about the depth of water, but, of course, it was very nice to be informed about that. So we crept in towards the coast to spy out the land. Long low white warehouses and a lighthouse dominated the town from the eastern side, and a few big lighters and barges lay anchored close to the landing-stage. It was impossible to lie there. The great on-shore rollers from the ocean created a heavy sea. But we were tired of sailing and decided to land and investigate local conditions instead of wasting several days in getting to Cochin. Moreover, we should not have to pay harbour dues at Alleppey. We dropped the big anchor in four or five fathoms at 3 p.m. on January 23. The water was disturbed and it was a bad anchorage; two men had always to stay on board to be ready to weigh anchor if the weather became unfavourable. Two hundred yards away the breakers were thundering on the shore.

Don and I went ashore in the ship's boat and reached the landing-stage safe and sound. Alleppey was a part of old India. It did not bear a European stamp. The town consisted of long low windowless houses, and everywhere in the streets oxen and goats were grazing. Our first greeting was a procession which approached us: all young people and children, who mingled their voices in a chorus of speech and at intervals raised clenched fists in the air. A gigantic red flag bearing a hammer and sickle waved at the head of the column. Most of them thought it great fun, especially the children, who forgot to keep time. Ahead of us walked three dignified elderly Indians with some books under their arms. Three black umbrellas gave them shade against the sun. They steered straight towards the leader of the procession and stopped in the middle of the road to continue their profound discussion—and lo! the procession turned respectfully aside, and the chorus of speech gave place to almost complete silence. But we had not the courage to try the same method.

Along the shore the poor section of the population lived in huts made of straw mats and clay. They looked so ramshackle that we dared not sneeze for fear of their collapsing on the heads of those inside.

It was a deadly dull town for a sailor: no shops, no restaurants, though it had over 100,000 inhabitants. Of these only 27 were white.

At last we found the highest port authority, an Indian with a dashing moustache and a shining white uniform. I had taken the ship's papers with me to report in proper style, but he was quite indifferent—not even the passport interested him. He asked if there was anything he could do for us, and I asked him for permission to go ashore.

'But you *are* ashore!' he replied in astonishment. So there was nothing to thank him for and we left him. It was the easiest admission to a foreign country we had yet obtained.

An Englishman living in the place recommended an Indian merchant for the supply of provisions, and we found him after a long search. He promised to come on board to get the orders.

'But there are limits to the amount I can provide,' he said, shrugging his shoulders.

Petrol was one of the things he could not get, but we got into touch with the captain of the steamer that was lying at anchor, and he gave us fourteen gallons: it only cost £2, and curiously enough he was afraid of his owners finding out there was not enough in the ship's boats. Normally we could have arranged all the provisioning in a few hours, but four precious days were to pass before everything was fixed up as well as it ever could be at Alleppey.

The provision merchant did not come on board till next day. We made a long list of the things we should want, and he promised to bring them next day. We could not pronounce his name, but we called him Albert, at which he was obviously flattered. He was a Buddhist and a particularly pleasant fellow, although so dilatory.

While Albert was working for us ashore, we set about the scraping of the boat's bottom. But setting about it was as far as we got. Don and I had jumped overboard to scrape off the worst of it, but the current was strong, and we had the greatest difficulty in resisting it. The big seas made *Nordkaperen* jump up and down like a pavement beetle. It was dangerous to dive under water, when stern or bow was coming crashing down from a height of ten or twelve feet. We did not want to lose our heads and gave up the work after a short time.

Albert came on board with the sad news that many of the things we needed would have to be got from another town. He had a holiday on Saturday and on Sunday the people from whom he was going to buy had a holiday, so two days would be lost over that. Our disappointment was slightly mitigated by his having fresh vegetables and fruit for us, besides a box of Virginia cigarettes.

'What are you in such a hurry for?' said Albert. 'You've got all your life left. The more you think the slower you act, and the fewer follies you commit!'

It was easy for Albert to give advice; he was not going through the Red Sea. On Monday morning he returned, his four rowers struggling with an overloaded canoe. Unfortunately it was not provisions that were on board—or only half what we wanted. On the other hand there were mats and various other things he wanted to try to sell to us. He could not have the rest of the provisions there before next day, but he faithfully promised to bring them before noon (we forgot to make him swear by Buddha). We were not interested in his carpets, although they were cheap, but he gave us a lot of things as farewell presents.

At twelve o'clock next day we were looking landward hoping to see Albert and his canoe, but neither of them was in sight. Not till after 8 p.m. did his canoe appear out of the darkness. We were furious, but, as I have said, Albert was a nice fellow, and in two minutes he had the upper hand again. Some of the goods he had forgotten, others he had been unable to get, but now we could not wait any longer. When we were to settle with him, he began to make a list of the things we had had from memory. There were more than a hundred things, so this took just two hours more. Then Albert set his rowers to work to lift *Nordkaperen's* anchor, and all unauthorized persons were put over the side.

We glided out into the brilliance of a full moon, followed by Albert's good wishes. This was at 10 p.m. on Tuesday, January 22.

All hands were on deck to enjoy the moonlight, and we began to talk of the nineteen days we had wasted. If we had sailed straight from Ceylon to Alleppey—about 260 miles—we could have made the passage in two days. Now we had taken seventeen days, plus four days in India.

An offshore breeze took us out gently, and a short fifteen miles from land we detected a dark shadow in the water. It was a large canoe with ten men in it, rowing across our bows at full speed. For safety's sake we altered course, and steered to pass astern of them. They immediately stopped rowing. We had to change course again and go ahead of them. This made them just start rowing again.

Well, if they wanted war, they should have it! We steered straight for the canoe, which was only a good ship's length away from us, and now they were in a hurry to get away. We all four stood on deck and shouted at them threateningly as we passed close by. Suddenly they were standing in a row in the narrow canoe, fishing and looking comparatively innocent. As soon as we had passed them, however, a hail of abuse came back to us.

We were soon back in the daily round of life at sea. The continual search for wind began afresh. On the first day we went forty miles in the right direction, and in the first four days we sailed 200 miles. We passed the advanced post of the Laccadives, Kalpeni, at night without seeing it, although we were only ten miles away, and continued towards Nine Degrees Channel, a passage through the string of islands.

We could save a detour by cutting off a corner of the passage and going inside the island Suheli Par. It was dark when we had the island almost on our port beam, but the wind rose violently, and we could not keep a course with certainty. We had to pay off vigorously, and there was danger of our being unable to clear the island and its insidious reef. If it had been light I think we should have tried it, but the darkness did not encourage an adventure of that kind. We had to go back and get on to our old course again. Thus we lost a couple of hours instead of gaining them.

On February 1 we had just got clear of the group of islands, when a strong current drove us more than thirty miles south. We were afraid of getting into the 'roundabout' again, but the next day's observations showed that we had no cause for worry. We were still thirty miles south. Our daily runs from Alleppey had been from forty to forty-five miles, but on February 3 we caught the north-east monsoon properly, and now we had daily runs of 140–150 miles.

To counteract the foul bottom we set all the sail we owned. In additional to topsail, flying jib, jib, mizen, mizen staysail, foresail and mainsail we set studding-sails under the boom and small square sails below and above the crosstrees. Not the smallest breath might be wasted. A number of days with little change followed, and the monsoon held till we had got across and under the African coast. On February 10 we had Socotra on our port beam, and the wind dropped noticeably.

We had three or four days of idle wind which only had an attack of energy now and again, and our daily runs became small again. We had a feeling that our average daily runs from India to Aden had been miserably small, but when the figures were counted up they came to a higher total than expected—like a hotel bill.

Everything breathed peace on board—we had just enjoyed our Sunday afternoon coffee and were reading or dozing. Don was at the wheel. It was Sunday weather; the sun shone from a blinding blue sky, the temperature was agreeable, and we had a light breeze on our starboard quarter.

The idyll was disturbed by Don yelling:

'Help! quick! Isa Lei's fallen overboard!'

This had happened before, but we jumped up, because a persistent shark had been following the ship for several days and defying both hook and rifle bullets.

Isa Lei had got into the habit of jumping up on to the starboard light bracket to enjoy the view. This time she had not jumped straight and had fallen into the water. Don had made desperate efforts to save her, but *Nordkaperen* was sailing too fast.

Our fear that the shark might snap up Isa Lei made us work our utmost, but it was not so easy to turn *Nordkaperen*.

We had spinnakers and braces on, so it took some minutes to turn, and Isa Lei, who was swimming round with her tail straight up in the air and mewing, dropped farther and farther astern. Everything went wrong when we tried to take in the spinnaker boomkin and braces. Knud hurriedly started the engine, as we should not have time to tack back. At last we were able to bear down on Isa Lei, who was hard to see in the high waves. The shark had not been on the look-out, so we reached the cat before it did and hauled her on board. Half an hour later, having received a reprimand and dried herself, she was again sitting on the light bracket.

Poul got the shark later with a lucky shot, when it carelessly showed its fin above water a little too long.

On the last day before we reached Aden the wind freshened again, and we were able to enter the harbour on the night of February 15. The entrance to the harbour was admirably marked, and we had no hesitation about entering while it was dark. We went slowly in, using the engine, and at 4 a.m. we had found an anchorage with the help of soundings. The Indian Ocean was behind us, and we relaxed over a cup of coffee and a cigarette, while we looked at the coloured lights over the harbour and town; and then it was time to turn in.

We were awakened by the arrival of a messenger with post from the Consul, and we devoured our home letters in our bunks. We had had no news since we were in Colombo. While we were reading them the harbour-master arrived and we asked him at once if we could get a slip. Unfortunately there was none, but the rise and fall of the tide round Aden was 5 or 6 ft., and he promised to show us a place where we could careen the boat. He would tow us there himself. It would cost nothing, he said.

There was nothing else about Aden that invited a long stay. It was a dismal, dry stone desert, with the houses built on naked grey rocks without any kind of vegetation. It never rained at Aden. The Arabs had recently murdered thousands of Jews, and British soldiers were still to be seen on guard over certain houses where the rest of the Jews were collected.

It was not merely difficult for us to keep the busy, impudent Arabs at a distance; it was simply impossible. They swarmed on board the ship from all sides and on every pretext to sell or steal. Aden was the only place where we took a strong line with the inhabitants, but it was necessary. Agreed prices for provisions and petrol rose by 50 per cent before we got them on board. We protested and made representations, and finally complained to the Danish Consul, but in vain.

'It's like that in Aden,' he said.

About midnight, the day after our arrival, the harbour-master towed us in to a quay where the depth of water was suitable for careening. He assured us that there were no rocks in the shallow water, but all the same *Nordkaperen's* bottom came to rest on a rock. Nor was the depth of water right: we had to push and drag the boat up to the wharf.

Towards morning, when the water had fallen, we set about scraping and greasing the bottom. We could do nothing with the lowest part of the keel.

The harbour-master promised to tow us off with his powerful boat at 1 a.m. the next morning, when the tide was highest, but he did not come till 2 a.m., and then an extra boat had to help him.

This boat and her crew belonged to a British destroyer whose personnel had become good friends of ours. The two boats toiled for some time to get *Nordkaperen* off, and at last they succeeded. We felt anxious about the rudder, which had come into violent contact with a stone during the operation, but were reassured by its working normally.

We presented the harbour-master with a bottle of gin for the service he had done us—it was not too much for putting a boat on a slip. *Alk* had given up waiting for us and had sailed three days before we arrived. The good fellows had telegraphed to Ceylon to hear whether we had sailed, and anxious inquiries from our friends in Ceylon had reached Aden. Although we had wasted nineteen days on the passage, and *Alk* had left Colombo three days before we did, she had arrived at Aden only ten days before us. We had counted on leaving again on the 23rd—we were very tired of sailing and needed a week's rest—but we decided to leave as early as the 19th. Aden was an intolerable place to stay at, and we were worried all the time by thoughts of the deterioration in the weather in the Red Sea. We received a typical farewell greeting from Aden just before we sailed. An Arab came with a bill from the harbour-master for help in putting *Nordkaperen* ashore and towing her off again. We had given him a bottle of gin and tipped his men because he had promised to help us free of charge. And he was not an Arab!

But we had still not done with Aden. The anchor was weighed and we had just begun to move, when an Arab climbed on board. It was our washerman. He had delivered some washing earlier in the day. It was only washed and not dried, and he had demanded twice the agreed payment. With the Consul's approval I had paid the Arab only the sum agreed in advance and ignored his lamentations, and at last he disappeared. Now, presumably, he had heard from another Arab that money was being paid out on board *Nordkaperen*, and he could not refrain from a last attempt at extortion.

We let him talk, and steered out towards the entrance to the harbour as if he was not there. He sat down on the bulwarks and alternately threatened and begged.

Poul went up to him and asked: 'Do you want your money? That's where it is,' and pushed him backwards into the water. He yelled and raved after us and threatened us with clenched fists.

'You damned sons of dogs, may you be wrecked and drowned!' he screamed in his harbour English, followed by a string of Arabic oaths. We waved him good-bye and saw him picked up by a rowing boat which hurried to the spot.

So we were off again, and this time a passage of from 1,400 to 1,500 miles awaited us, which would consist mainly of tacking. *Alk's* crew had left a message that we were to wait for one another at Suez. We did, but under different circumstances from what we had expected.

Our course was set for the Straits of Bab-el-Mandeb, the southern gateway to the Red Sea, and next morning we had put behind us the last bit of the Gulf of Aden. We got a very strong wind behind us as soon as we got into the strait. The first day we did 165 miles, and the wind remained fresh for the following three or four days. We were already beginning to calculate when we could be at Suez.

In ignorance of the excitement and hardships that lay before us, we enjoyed life and caught plenty of fish. On the fifth day at sea the wind dropped steadily and finally disappeared. We had entered a belt of dead calm over which the engine was to help us. *Nordkaperen* glided forward over the glassy sea, with the engine working faultlessly. We had thought the windless belt was about 600 miles wide, but when we had covered a couple of hundred miles we were already meeting light northerly winds. These came before we had expected them, which was ominous.

The wind freshened steadily, and as early as Wednesday the 6th we recorded wind force 5—and dead ahead. We were not yet half way through the Red Sea.

The following days were tough, with unbroken hard tacking. We sailed eighty to ninety miles a day, but only made thirty to forty miles on our course. Hatches and skylight had to be battened down all the time, and the heavy list, combined with the boat's continual trembling in the seas, made us, if not sea-sick, at any rate uncomfortable. No more work was done on board than was absolutely necessary.

Beside the hard life that sailing close-hauled involved we had other troubles to contend with. We were never sure if our position was correct! The refraction in the Red Sea was very great—which means that one does not see a heavenly body where it actually is. It can be forty minutes wrong, and irregular cross-currents did not make things any easier for a navigator in a small boat. We tacked from one side of the Red Sea to the other, but never sighted land, for the reefs stretched as much as twenty miles out into the sea.

On Saturday the 28th the wind really took command and at midday it was strong. *Nordkaperen* crawled over one watery mountain after another, and now and again we had to pay off vigorously for an unusually high sea—otherwise the boat would have been flung aside like a match-box. We realized clearly that we had come three weeks too late.

It was a bit of luck that we had cracked the boom in the Torres Strait—but for this it would never have occurred to us to cut down the mainsail. This was an advantage to us now, when the boat was holding her own with full sails. We had taken a ton of water and a ton of petrol on board at Aden, and this made the boat very stable, but still there were limits to the amount of sail we could carry.

The sunset on Saturday evening was unusually beautiful. The sky over Africa was glowing red and threw a golden light from horizon to horizon. It was a fascinating sight, but at the same time disquieting. There was savagery in those colours.

Yet the night passed without excitement, although the wind increased steadily in force. The jib needed to be set tauter. The water, which was continually splashing up on to it, had made it slack. Knud and Don went on to the fore-deck to attend to it.

Knud hauled and Don made fast—or should have made fast, but the sheet slipped away from him and the jib was blown to tatters in a twinkling. It was almost dangerous to take in the thrashing remnants of the sail and sheets: we had to let the jib go into the water first. This slightly reduced our spread of canvas, but the boat became hard to steer.

Don was at the wheel: he was sitting enveloped in oilskins and dodging down to avoid the seas. Suddenly he ran the boat close to the wind, so that the sails flapped.

'Hi, Don! pay off, you're keeping her too close,' we yelled from the cabin below. We thought he was having a nap.

'I can't! I can't!' he shouted back.

We all hurried on deck. Don was sitting at the wheel and turning it furiously—first one way, then the other, but *Nordkaperen* did not answer her helm. We all tried to turn the wheel, one after the other. The wheel offered no resistance at all.

'It's only the wheel-chain snapped,' said Knud, and dived down to survey the damage. He climbed up through the hatch rather puzzled: both chain and quadrant were intact. I chanced to detect a shadow in the water close to the port quarter. I thought at first that it was a fish, but it was *Nordkaperen's* rudder. It was hanging as it were by a thread, dangling uselessly to and fro.

This was a catastrophe in the existing conditions. We realized the seriousness of the situation slowly, but with appalling clarity. The boat lay bumping in the heavy seas. We let out the mainsail and mizen, and backed the foresail, so that she came to lie a few points from the wind. Knud and Poul set to work to get the smashed rudder on board, whilst I collected materials for an emergency rudder. We sacrificed the spinnaker boomkin and some teak planks for this purpose.

The rudder could not be salved. Our stern was just as often under as above water, and every time Poul and Knud had got a wire round the rudder and were about to haul it in, *Nordkaperen* plunged into a sea, so that it was all they could do to hold on. So the rudder had to remain hanging where it was, if it would.

Trying to make an emergency rudder proved to be a waste of time. The lashings snapped again and again. It swayed to and fro about ten or fifteen feet up in the air, then fell on to the surface of the water with a crash, and all the ropes snapped like threads, We tried many expedients, but the timber was simply torn out of our hands in the raging sea. After more than an hour's work we gave up trying to make an emergency rudder, We must hit on something else.

According to our calculations we were more than fifty miles from the nearest land or reef, so there was no immediate danger.

We took in the mainsail, set the storm trysail as a jib, let the mizen right out and put a brace on, and waited anxiously to see what would happen. *Nordkaperen* did not really know what she wanted. The jib was backed, and the boat began to come up. A sea that struck the bows helped her on her way, and soon she was lying broadside on to the sea. The strong wind made her list heavily. The headsails were slackened again, and *Nordkaperen* now turned round and headed back along almost the same course that we had followed.

If she had not been built in such a way that the mainmast was a long way forward, towards the bows—and she had a long bowsprit—this manoeuvre would not have succeeded.

Now we were going south with the foresail and storm trysail stretched and bellying in the bows, while the mizen was used as a spinnaker.

*Nordkaperen* zigzagged on towards an unknown destination. Sometimes we were on the point of jibing. Next moment she straightened up, so that the headsails flapped. We quickly discovered that she could look after herself, and that we could direct her course to a certain extent by trimming the sails. To that extent we were safe, but we wanted to get into port.

Our course was almost parallel with the African coast with the wind on our starboard quarter. It was an uncertain course; the boat yawed over eight points. We carefully studied the chart, but the information we got from it was cheerless. The nearest harbour was Port Sudan, a good 200 miles back, and we had no detailed chart of the waters in that region. The general chart only showed that many reefs stretched out into the sea round the harbour. In other words, it would be a difficult place to approach. But we had no other choice, and if we made a mess of the landfall —if, for example, we sailed past without sighting land—we should have to go on for a further 700 miles, right back to Aden.

If the wind had not been so strong and the sea so rough, we should have taken a brighter view of the situation, but as it was we were grave and depressed. It had become dangerous to take *Nordkaperen* into port. I felt very sad about it all—the voyage round the world was over! Even if there was a slip at Port Sudan, I could not pay the cost of the repairs.

About midnight we saw the lights of a large ship to north-westward of us. Her masthead lights showed that she was bearing straight down on us. We were carrying lights and counted on the ship seeing them, but when she steered straight for *Nordkaperen* we began to have our doubts. All four of us were on deck watching the big ship. We thought we could get in ahead of her, but she was going faster than we calculated, and passed just ahead of us. She had seen us; a very strong searchlight was turned on us, and she stopped. When we were down in the trough of the waves we could not see her, but when we came up on to the summit of a water mountain, we were quite dazzled by the powerful light.

I tried to read the others' thoughts. I had no doubt about Poul and Knud, but Don had really not the same interest as ourselves in concluding the business with our honour intact.

'I'll stay with you—you can be sure of that,' he replied, when I put the direct question to him.

I waved my hand in a gesture of refusal and signed to the steamer to proceed; we did not want help. She disappeared southward. Her lights were soon out of sight, and we were alone again...

I took over the watch at 2 a.m. on Monday morning. The helm was out of action, but nevertheless I sat—a slave of habit—with my hand on the wheel. I shall always remember the hours of that night as the most melancholy in my life.

The facts of the case gave my brain no rest as I sat there in solitude; the voyage round the world ended so near the goal—four years' work wasted—our plan upset by a broken rudder. I could not help thinking of the Arab's curses at Aden.

At 3.30 a.m. something happened. I began to feel uneasy. What the danger was, and where it came from, I did not know, but there *was* danger. I worked my way on to the fore-deck and peered out into the darkness.

Nothing unusual was to be seen—only a strip of moonlight ahead to break the monotony of the billowy surface. I felt it must be that my nerves were on edge. I crawled back to the cockpit and lit a cigarette. We had been short of sleep of late . . . I was sure it was the same with the others.

But the uneasiness did not leave me. I looked at the sky, as if I could find the reason there—and I did!

There was no moon—had not been for many hours—but that being so, what was it ahead that I had taken for a strip of moonlight? I was on the fore-deck again in a twinkling. My suspicions were confirmed. The 'strip of moonlight', which now had come unpleasantly near, revealed itself as a boiling, foaming reef, whose white surf shone like phosphorus in the darkness.

I remember the minutes that followed as one recalls a feverish nightmare.

I stood in the cockpit and pressed the alarm bell, whose sharp tones rang through the ship.

'All hands on deck—quick—reef close ahead—quick, for God's sake, never mind about dressing!'

The moment the first head appeared in the hatchway, I ran aft and loosened the brace on the mizen. Don came to my help. We wanted the mizen forced over to the other side. Poul had rushed to the fore-deck at once to try to back the headsails. We wanted to have the wind on our port side—that was necessary if we were to get clear of the reef.

Knud had immediately set about starting the engine, which would help us clear when—and if—*Nordkaperen* was turned round. There was great risk of the dangling rudder, if it was still there, impeding or damaging the screw, but we had to chance that; the attempt must be made. The seas rolled over us, boiling and roaring, and the boat approached the reef at a sharp angle. Poul's manoeuvre on the fore-deck made *Nordkaperen* fall off a few points, and that was enough for the mizen, which Don and I had hauled amidships, to begin to flap with the wind dead astern. A few tense seconds followed, then the wind caught us on the right side and the sail ran out with a crash. At the same time several loud reports came from forward. Poul also had got the wind into the sails on the port side, and *Nordkaperen* changed course. Then the blessed sound of the engine was heard; it had started up at the first attempt. Knud, with his usual coolness, had not overlooked one cock or screw. While waiting for the almost inevitable crash he worked away, calm and collected, down in the bottom of the boat. The engine-power was of immense help. Instead of sailing along the thundering reef and being flung towards it by the seas, we could now at last, slowly but surely, get away from the strip of foam, which was visible on both sides as far as the eye could reach.

Later, when we were sitting over a cup of coffee, we all showed visible signs of reaction, and the others said how thankful they were that I had become alive to the danger in time. I would not accept their thanks. Alive was just what I had not been.

I had reckoned, as we all did, that we had had the nearest reef at least forty miles away on our starboard beam, and I had, therefore, not kept as sharp a look-out as I ought to have done. On the other hand, a feeling of uneasiness, which only those can have who have been for a long time in close contact with the sea, had been our salvation.

Looking back on it all, I was able to analyse the causes of my feeling of uneasiness. The sound of the sea had acquired a different tone; the noise from the reef had blended itself in the melody. The lighting round me had changed; the long foaming reef had shone up in the night. The rhythm of the waves had altered; the solid barrier created submarine currents and tidal movements. These factors all taken together had made me uneasy.

We ascertained later that the reef—Shab Kommoros—which had nearly been our fate, lay ten miles from the African coast.

We kept an extra sharp look-out for the rest of that night, as we did not then know where we were. We might sight land next day, but this was problematic in those waters, where the reefs stretched so far out to sea. We zigzagged with the greatest care in towards the coast, nearer and nearer, but it was not till evening that we descried faint outlines of the African mountains. This did not tell us much, but in all probability we should have an exciting night. We counted on reaching Port Sudan before daybreak, but there were many reefs between us and the safety of the harbour. Our only hope was to sight the light on Sanganeb Reef, which marked the approach to Port Sudan: if that failed, we should have to go on to Aden. We could not sail against the wind. Also, the Red Sea was poor in harbours, and we had no charts of the small harbours which at last we found. They were doubtless more tightly packed away among reefs than Port Sudan.

There was no sign of a change in the weather. *Nordkaperen* was continually washed by big seas, and the wind was cold, which was irritating.

The atmosphere on board was charged with excitement: what would the night bring? Just after sunset something happened which raised our spirits. I had climbed up into the rigging to look out for reefs and immediately caught sight of Sanganeb lighthouse winking at us cheerfully, much earlier than we had expected. Now we knew where we were. We just missed a reef between us and the lighthouse. A couple of hours later we could see the lights of the town winking and flickering faintly on the horizon. It was a joyful sight.

Soon after midnight we were able to stand in towards Port Sudan. We changed course by working with the sails and got the sea on our beam—a persistently aggressive sea, furious at seeing a certain prey slip through its fingers. We were soon in shelter behind a reef, which ran close to us to starboard. The smooth water was a relief to us. It was difficult to keep our course, but now we were able to help with a steering oar. The engine was started, but it did not work: the rudder had fouled the screw.

It was our intention to remain lying outside the harbour till it grew light. The unknown entrance—and in a boat which could not be steered—frightened us. But we could not remain lying where we liked. We continually had to turn round, sail to and fro, tumble about and work with the sails without respite. An anchorage would undeniably have made things easier, but here there were 100 fathoms close up to the reefs which closed us in on three sides.

However, Knud found a Port Sudan light list, and we agreed to try to enter harbour. It could surely not be more dangerous than lying outside in the way we were doing. The light list nearly cost us *Nordkaperen*!

We should have a lighthouse, that stood on the northern mole of the harbour, to starboard. So the list said, and we held our course boldly. The boat was cautiously guided in towards the light. We then detected small eddies in the water a few ship's lengths ahead. Poul thought it was a reef. It looked queer. They must be made by the current, for the description of the lights could not lie. On the other hand, we could not see more than one light. There was a swarm of red and green lights inside the harbour and perhaps there were a couple of lights marking the channel among them, but we could not find a way out of the confusion.

Poul climbed up to the crosstrees, and when he came down again he was more emphatic than before. He would eat his hat, he would live a celibate for the rest of his life, we could call him a Dutchman, we were stone-blind, etc., if there was not a reef ahead.

Knud maintained the opposite. I went down into the cabin again and studied the book thoroughly. There was no doubt about it, Knud was right. I climbed up to the crosstrees.

It was the deuce and all! It looked from there as if Poul was right. Of course they could not both of them be right, but in any case the landing was off. About 4 a.m. the wind dropped, and the danger of running on a reef became much less. The weather conditions were quite friendly when it at last began to grow light. At the same time we discovered that Poul had been right. There was really a reef where there should have been a channel leading into the harbour.

## CHAPTER XIX

# *Suez*

THE pilot boat came out to us before it was really light. The pilot perceived our difficulties and saw that a stout line was passed to us from the pilot boat, which towed us into harbour.

Here we obtained the solution of the lighthouse puzzle. The mole lighthouse had been moved from the northern to the southern entrance in 1947; our list dated from 1946. The pilot told us that three months earlier a 30-ton yacht had run on to the reef, her people, like ourselves, not knowing that the light had been moved. She was still lying outside as a wreck.

The pilot told us at the same time that *Alk* had been in Port Sudan to oil. She had sailed two days before, so that we had crossed one another.

So we were in harbour. Our lives and the boat were saved, but our joy at this quickly evaporated at the thought of *Nordkaperen* and what was in store for ourselves.

The kind and understanding harbour-master could give us no consolation; on the contrary. There was only one slip at Port Sudan which could take *Nordkaperen*, and that would be occupied for the first three or four months of the year. If we were willing to wait, we could get the boat up, but we might not repair the damage ourselves. The yard workmen would have to do that, and it would cost the equivalent of over £200.

Our last hope now seemed to be extinguished. We had no funds left after visiting five continents. Everyone showed understanding of and sympathy for us in our situation, but that could not help us. A couple of shipping agents came on board. *Nordkaperen* was handed over to them for sale at once. When they asked what the price of the boat was, I said to them:

'So long as you get enough to pay our fares home, that'll be all right.'

Then the harbour-master brought us an exciting piece of news.

'It's curious,' he said, 'one Danish ship calls here every six months at the most, and today we shall have two.'

'What do you mean? Tell us!'

'Yes, there's a ship called *Lalandia* coming; she'll be here in a couple of hours—I'll give you a hail!'

The Eastern Asiatic Company's *Lalandia* with our friends on board! We had had some unforgettable days together in Ceylon. We knew that fine fellow Captain Kjaer Jepsen would help us if it was in his power. The shipping agents came on board to get some information, and I told them to hold up the sale of *Nordkaperen* for a day.

Some time after midday *Lalandia's* white hull appeared on the horizon. When she had berthed we were the first on board. I briefly explained the situation to the captain, and the first question was whether *Lalandie* had a derrick which could lift *Nordkaperen* up on the deck, and whether there was room. That side of the matter could be arranged, and the captain would also allow us to repair the rudder in the few days before *Lalandia* reached Port Said, but there was a snag. The ship was much overdue already; she was to sail again next morning, and the captain could not take the boat on deck without permission from the head office at Copenhagen.

Our hope disappeared again. We could not get a telegram to Copenhagen before the office closed, and would the people there with whom the decision lay understand us? There were limits to what one could say in a telegram. Perhaps it would get to the bottom of the pile like any business message—while *Lalandia* sailed away.

The captain and I were talking things over at some length, when an idea occurred to me. The president of the Royal Danish Yacht Club, Mr Niels Benzon, the chemist, had shown some interest in us earlier. He was the man who could help us. An express telegram in curt phrases was dispatched. I did not remember the address, but wrote simply 'Niels Benzon, Copenhagen.'

The reply could not arrive before next morning at the earliest. We must just wait!

The captain shortened the time of waiting for us by inviting us to supper on board, and we were entertained in princely style. Afterwards we looked into the officers' mess to kill time. Although we had not slept for two days, we could not close an eye now for nervous excitement. We smoked one cigarette after another all through the night. We felt as if we were awaiting a death sentence. Poul and Don had remained on board *Lalandia*.

At 8 a.m. neither of us had slept yet. Knud was sitting in the midships cabin, and I was lying in my bunk in the after-cabin fully dressed.

A man came tramping along the deck. He came down into the cabin and mumbled a few words.

'Calle,' Knud called, 'it's a telegram!'

'You can open it yourself!' I answered. I dared not.

A few painful moments passed while Knud fumbled with the paper. Then another moment of silence.

'It's good enough!' I heard Knud say in a low voice. He could not altogether conceal his emotion.

What does one do in such moments? Does one jump up and shout hurrah? No, the moment was too great for that. We felt as if a vast burden had been removed from us, we felt ourselves lifted up into the pure, clear, sunshiny blue air. A few tears rolled down our cheeks. Yes indeed, our nerves were out of order.

Thanks, all powers of good—thanks, Niels Benzon, thanks, Eastern Asiatic—thanks, *Lalandia* . . . A miracle had happened.

Now we must get to work. The captain had made certain demands, supposing that an affirmative answer was received.

Everything was to be taken out of *Nordkaperen*: masts, rigging, water, petrol, ballast, reserve supplies, provisions, etc. The boat must be lightened as much as possible, as the crane could only take 15 tons.

Poul and Don put their backs into it. It all had to be done in three hours. We did it, although Captain Kjaer Jepsen was doubtful and nervous. The captain had asked me what *Nordkaperen* weighed, and I had replied, to the best of my conviction, that she weighed a little over 15 tons! Nevertheless the derrick had difficulty in lifting the boat. Spars and wires creaked and groaned, and the engine stopped twice. A later measurement showed that *Nordkaperen* weighed over 22 tons. It was a hard job to get her up on to the *Lalandia's* deck. She had to be eased and turned many times before her fifty-two feet stood where we should be. The stowing of the boat on deck was directed and supervised by both the captain and first officer, and was followed with great interest by passengers and crew. We were all standing on the *Lalandia's* deck when the derrick began to work

When the boat was at last on the big ship's deck, the damage to the rudder was inspected. It appeared that it had broken above the groove for the screw. Officers and crew declared themselves astonished at our having got into harbour unaided with such damage, especially in those waters, and the weather we had had. We had certainly had luck, nor did we deny it.

It was an almost hopeless task to repair the broken rudder in the short time at our disposal. The engineers shook their heads. It was impossible, they said. They did not realize that we ourselves had reconstructed the boat. We were not quite green.

Unfortunately there were no cutting tools on board. We had to remove a piece of the iron rudder by boring a series of holes and carving our way through. A few iron plates which were placed at our disposal were to be used as a strengthening. We had to chisel them into shape. We borrowed a little drilling machine to make the smaller holes with; all the larger had to be bored by hand. The strengthenings were bolted on each side of the rudder. Knud and I looked after the rudder, while Poul and Don put *Nordkaperen's* bottom in order. We worked all round the clock. At night we stood below decks in *Lalandia* with our boring machine and vice. We carried on till about 5 a.m., then we had a cup of coffee, rested a little and began again at 8 a.m. This went on for three days and nights. During that time we never washed. Bumps and scratches were a part of the daily round and Knud got emery in his eye, which made him nearly blind for a long time despite medical treatment.

The captain followed our work with great interest. He was very nervous about our not getting it finished in time—almost more nervous than we were ourselves.

The rudder was finished in time. It was as good as new, and it was long since *Nordkaperen* had had such a smart bottom as she got on board the *Lalandia*. It goes without saying that we did not see much of Suez or the Canal. We had other things to think about. While we were working Isa Lei had struck up a friendship with a little monkey which belonged to the crew aft. They outdid one another in comical pranks to the great amusement of everyone. When we reached Suez we were met by hailstorms which turned the deck white. The temperature fell from 82° F one day to 45° F the next. Isa Lei's playmate the monkey could not stand this. It died the evening before we arrived at Port Said.

We were busy that evening cleaning up and washing, and when we at last had a little time to look at our surroundings, it had grown dark. We had to content ourselves with the sight of the lights ashore and the many-coloured signal lights in the Canal.

The *Lalandia* dropped anchor at 10 p.m. on Saturday March 6, and an hour later *Nordkaperen* was in her proper element again. Masts, stores and gear had to wait till next day, and we took it in turns to keep guard over our property, which lay on the *Lalandia's* after-hatch. Arabs swarmed round it like flies. But despite our care and the sharp look-out we kept many of our things disappeared; the Arabs, so to speak, charmed them away under our very eyes.

We had been entered by mistake on the *Lalandia's* passenger list, which caused a lot of trouble with the Egyptian authorities. Of course passengers might not go ashore in Egypt without visas, and the police sergeant maintained that we were passengers. We protested vigorously, saying that we had come in our own boat.

'Well then, let me see your Canal pass,' he said.

'We haven't sailed through the Canal. We haven't any pass.'

'Where do you come from then?'

'From the Red Sea.'

'Have you been dropped from the air, then?'

'No, we've got our own boat with us.'

He was completely bewildered.

We took him out on deck and showed him *Nordkaperen*, which had then not yet been let down into the water. Then we showed him our ship's papers, which were in the most perfect order.

Now he was in utter confusion. He had no idea how to deal with the matter and said he would seek directions from his superior. He went away mumbling: 'passenger by *Lalandia*—no, crew, but in *Nordkaperen*—no Canal pass, but come from the Red Sea and been through the Canal—ship's papers from a boat which isn't in the harbour . . . Allah help me!'

He came back—his superior could not solve the problem either —and the discussion began again from the beginning.

I gradually became annoyed at the sergeant's lack of manners, but later found him to be a decent, pleasant man, and he did us a good turn on another occasion. At last the matter was settled, but when the time came for us to leave Egypt the trouble began afresh. *Nordkaperen* had come as cargo on board the *Lalandia*. They had papers to that effect, but one could not remove cargo from Port Said then and there without further formalities: and that would cost money.

This matter too was settled—though not without difficulty— by the East Asiatic Company's agent. At 6 a.m. on Sunday we began to move masts, ballast, etc., down on to *Nordkaperen's* deck. There was no time to stow it out of the way, and things got into a hopeless muddle on board.

The *Lalandia* weighed anchor soon after. She took our thanks and farewells with her—besides the consciousness of having played a decisive part in our voyage round the world. We gazed after the miracle-working ship till she disappeared from view.

We were allotted a berth in the harbour and at once began to clear up. We would not sleep till we had done this. We had literally not slept for five or six days, but if we left all that stuff lying about loose on the deck, it would disappear into thin air. It took four days to get it all stowed away, and after that the boat was to be painted and varnished above water, and the engine overhauled: the sails wanted patching too.

Although we kept a careful watch over our things, a great deal disappeared: among other things a sack of sand which stood on the after-deck. It was Isa Lei's 'toilet sand'. The Arabs must have thought it was sugar or something of the kind.

It was difficult to avoid the Port Said army of shoeblack boys, who, for that matter, made their living in every way except by cleaning shoes. They were little gangsters who did not shrink from the basest crimes.

If one paid without haggling the sum one of these shoeblacks asked, he was struck dumb for a moment and then demanded another coin for the other shoe. Of course one refused to pay over again; and the whole thing ended in his fetching a crowd of his colleagues, who stood round one with a threatening air. So one had to be diplomatic, especially at night. It frequently happened that a sailor came on board his ship stripped to the skin—and he had been lucky that it was nothing worse. People seeking information about dubious enterprises could be sure of getting it from an Arab shoeblack boy, but not for nothing.

On one of our first days in Port Said we were taken charge of by an old Arab—or Egyptian, as he called himself—and that was an acquaintance we did not regret. He was entrusted with the provisioning of *Nordkaperen*, and we have not met a more honourable Arab. His name was Khalil-El-Kasseify, and he was also called 'the King of Port Said'.

He had built his own private mosque in the harbour quarter, and all the inhabitants of the quarter, rich and poor alike, were allowed to use it. In other ways he had supported different undertakings of a social kind. He was a very rich man. He was also full of wisdom and prophetic utterances, but the background of all his good deeds was not purely altruistic love of his fellow men.

'I hope to get a place with Allah,' he said, quite seriously, 'for a mosque like this is expensive to run.'

We honestly shared his hopes.

One day when we were working on board two men came out to us—a Dane and a Swede, both Canal pilots. They invited us to berth the boat over on the other side of the Canal at the landing stage of a sailing club of which they were members. We accepted the offer with pleasure, as we were exposed to thieving where we now lay. Soon *Nordkaperen* was lying at the landing-stage at Port Fuad, the Canal Company's administrative town, which consisted exclusively of villas.

The Danish pilot, Jens Haunstrup, did what he could to make life as agreeable and lively for us as possible. Among the pleasures he had in store for us was a drive in his car to the Pyramids. The distance to Cairo was over 150 miles. We drove over 300 miles in one day, along the Suez Canal, through stretches of desert, past Arab country towns where the houses were built of mud—through landscapes in which tall bird's-wing sails towered up over green meadows. These were the sails of the cargo barges which travelled along the narrow canals, invisible at a distance. We drove through the amazing noise and traffic of Cairo and at last reached the Pyramids and the Sphinx. We waded for hours through soft sand blinding to the eye, dried the sweat from our foreheads, and chased away importunate Arab boys. We grew thirsty on the old Egyptians' behalf at the thought of the grind it had been for them to drag all those stones out into the desert. Then we returned to Cairo to quench our thirst and get a bite of food.

When we returned to Port Fuad late in the evening, a note was lying on the cabin table. It was a greeting from Uncle Hermann and Aunt Martha whom we had known in Australia. They were on their way home to Denmark and thought they would use a stay of two hours in Port Said to pay a call on us—and we had not been at home. We consoled ourselves with the thought that we should see them in Copenhagen.

We grew daily more anxious about *Alk*, which should have been at Port Said long before. We made inquiries on board all ships coming from the Red Sea, we telegraphed to various shipping agents and consuls; but no one had heard anything. At last, one day, there came a letter from the Dutch Consul at Suez. *Alk* had been wrecked. She had run upon a reef at 4 a.m. on March 13, about three miles from land—only 120 miles from their destination, Suez. But the Consul was glad to be able to tell us that all three Dutchmen were saved.

Later a letter came from William, who described the shipwreck in detail. At 4 a.m. March 13 William had taken over the wheel from Allan, the skipper. Allan was suffering from malaria and done up for want of sleep. Their engine had broken down, and they were tacking in fresh, rainy weather. William was to call Allan at 5 a.m., but at 4.15 *Alk* was flung fifty yards up on a reef and ripped up her bottom at once. The water rose in the cabin to the level of the table, and they hastened to save what could be saved of their belongings and instruments. The boat was a complete wreck, but luckily remained on the reef. When it grew light, a native fisherman happened to come past with his boat behind the reef. They established contact with him, and after some laborious salvage work they all got ashore safe and sound. Next day the sea had gone down, and they got more stuff ashore with the fisherman's help. They had to ride seventy-five miles through the desert on camels to reach civilized places, and were now going straight home to Holland by steamer. William wanted to sail home with us. They would like to come and see us when they passed through Port Said, he added.

Their steamer arrived a few days later, Unfortunately William's documents could not be put in order in the short time the ship was in harbour. Poul and I hurried from consulate to consulate, to shipping agents, to the chief of police—but all was in vain. Egyptian authorities are strict—especially towards white men. Allan, who was still William's captain, could perhaps have helped us to put the thing through, but the matter did not seem to interest him.

'We've all three shared bad luck and good luck for three years,' he said, 'so I think it's best we should share the disgrace when we get home.'

I said to him that I could not see that there was any disgrace in being wrecked: but on thinking the matter over more closely I understood him well. Allan's hand shook as he said:

'Here's to a happy finish to your voyage round the world! My very best wishes! Now you're the last of this year's circumnavigators. You shall and must get home!'

That was a fact to which I had not given a thought—that we were the last in the lists. Of the four or five boats which had started from Denmark to sail round the world the same year as ourselves, one had been lost. The others had dropped out in different ways. One just reached America—and there was a split among the crew. The American *Alone* was lost with all hands, another American stopped at Tahiti, and now last of all *Alk* had been wrecked.

Allan gave me a lot of charts and navigation tables.

'And here—take these too. I shall have no use for them anyway!'

He pressed a bundle of dollar notes into my hand.

I protested, but the disappointment in his face weakened my protest.

'Well,' I said at last, 'but you must let me do something for you when you come to Copenhagen.'

Heaven knows that the money came where it was needed, and I pocketed the ninety dollars.

William had got Allan's permission to salve a mainsail and a jib from *Alk* when she was wrecked—with the sole object of presenting them to us. They had brought the sails the whole way through the desert, and we received the gift when we took leave of them.

A last handshake, and we jumped down into the dinghy. We rowed round the stern to the other side of the steamer, where the sacks containing the sails were passed down to us. The Egyptian Customs official had been bribed.

## CHAPTER XX

# *Through the Mediterranean*

*Nordkaperen's* sailing date was fixed for Easter Sunday, March 28. It was rather early in the year to sail in the Mediterranean in a boat of her size, but we were racked with impatience to get home. We were advised to wait for three or four weeks, advice which had no effect whatever. Rather a little bad weather than three weeks more in Port Said.

We regretted our decision later.

During our short stay at Port Said we came into contact with a Danish crew. Their ship was a tanker owned in Panama, but they were pure Danish from captain to ship's boy. All the time the tanker was in harbour the whole crew spoilt us. The captain asked us to dinner every day, and when we took leave of our countrymen they filled up *Nordkaperen* with provisions. When our sailing date arrived, various friends came on board to say good-bye. Our Egyptian friend Khalil-El-Kasseify brought several boxes of chocolates and a whole roast duck, plus any number of wishes for our good luck and happiness. Allah be with you! Other Arabs brought flowers. In this respect there was a difference between Aden and Port Said.

We were to have sailed at 5 p.m., but in the forenoon the barometer began to fall heavily. The sky became yellow and misty, and millions of insects from ashore came swarming over the ship. Jens Haunstrup had come on board to say good-bye. Having been a Canal pilot for many years he knew the weather conditions round Port Said. We asked him what he thought.

'There's going to be a sandstorm,' he said.

'How long will it be before it comes?'

'I expect it'll be here in three or four hours.'

He said that a sandstorm might last two or three days, and when we asked him if it was possible for us to escape it if we sailed at once, he replied that we should certainly be so far away that we should not get it badly.

We made ready for sea at top speed, the visitors were put overboard and the anchor weighed.

Our Swedish friend, the Canal pilot Schölin, escorted us in his boat, with Haunstrup on board and a number of the seamen from the Panamian tanker. When we came out of harbour the sun was just a veiled shining disc, and many small fishing-boats were coming in. Schölin thought best to turn back before the weather changed. We continued with a level, steady southerly breeze. Gradually the air became oppressive and the sun vanished altogether into the thick yellow haze. Then the wind dropped, all bird life disappeared—only one hawk flew over going northward—and all around us on the sea was still. *Nordkaperen* sailed on north-westward with her engine at full speed. The haze grew thicker. At 6 p.m. still nothing had happened.

Then the sandstorm came!

A white-bordered vapour came rolling towards us over the water from the south-west. We had the mainsail in in a twinkling, and when the first gust of wind struck the boat, she pitched violently under only mizen, foresail and jib.

But the gusts were not so severe as we had expected. We were now about twenty-five to thirty miles from land, and the storm had certainly lost some of its strength, but nevertheless the sand reached us. Luckily we had a pair of dust-glasses on board. The man at the wheel put them on. We ground sand between our teeth. There were traces of the sandstorm everywhere on board.

When we had got over the worst we straightened up on to a north-westerly course again—we had let *Nordkaperen* fall off before the storm. We were delighted to have got over it with comparatively little trouble. 'Good Lord, was that all?' we thought.

But it was not all. There was still a surprise in store for us. At

8 p.m. the wind turned westward and increased in strength steadily and malignantly. By degrees the wind veered into the north-east, the sea grew high and white crests appeared on it. We had not expected that two storms would come directly after one another, and so we had been a bit careless about battening down. Hatches and skylights had just been opened after the sandstorm and the tarpaulins removed, and we saw no point in beginning from the beginning again. When at last we became alive to the facts, there was not a dry spot in the whole ship. At the same time the temperature fell sharply—to only 44.3° F.

Add to this that we were all four of us suffering from food poisoning from the magnificent farewell dinner that had been held for us the evening before on board the Panamanian tanker. This, combined with the cold and damp, was a severe tax on our powers of endurance, but, as so often before in a tight place, we called grim humour to our aid.

At 10 p.m. we had a regular gale. The jib had long ago been struck; we were now carrying only foresail and mizen, but none the less *Nordkaperen* was swung round in the high sea, which had the whole length of the Mediterranean in which to gather strength. In the coloured light of the sidelights we could see the spray flying across the fore-deck in the screaming gusts. *Nordkaperen* was continually buried in water. When she was up on top of a sea the wind forced her on to her beam-ends. The night was pitch dark. We could not see a thing. It was a trying job for the man at the wheel.

It was, indeed, the first regular gale we had experienced, and we would have hove to if we could. But we were too near the coast of Palestine. If the gale went on for a few days we should drift quickly towards the land. There was nothing to do but to hold on. At midnight the sea was one huge sheet of foam. One impudent roller got a grip under the skylight, lifted it and sent hundreds of buckets of water down into the cabin. The falling water was greeted with oaths and curses, and at last we got together to lay a tarpaulin over the skylight. It was hard work.

Three men were wanted for it, and they were under water most of the time.

There was nothing whatever to do but to hold tight. Before the water had run off the deck a fresh sea filled the boat, and anything that was not firmly lashed was swept overboard. Fortunately we had left the ship's boat behind at Port Said, so we had not that to think of. A couple of old sails that were lashed tight on the after-deck were washed overboard in the course of the night, one or two fenders as well, and the big anchor jumped up out of its bed on the deck when the boat put her nose into a sea. It slipped down to the lee side of the boat and smashed a foot and a half of planking. The lashings of the lifeboat were broken and it was washed down from its place on top of the deckhouse, but luckily caught in a clamp on the after-deck.

Watches were reduced to an hour. It was hell being on deck. About 3 a.m. *Nordkaperen* was swept by a particularly violent sea. Don was at the wheel and was almost washed out of the cockpit. It was too much for the usually imperturbable Don.

'It's no good—it's no good!' he yelled through the noise.

I stuck my head out of the cabin.

'What's no good?'

'This isn't—something must be done!' he said, visibly nervous.

'Very good—you're in charge. What shall we do?'

'I don't know, but we can't go on like this!'

He had hardly finished his sentence when a fresh sea made him cling to the wheel. I explained to him that we were too near land to be able to heave to and tried to console him by telling him that *Nordkaperen* was a well-found boat; her hull and rigging would be all right in the open sea, but not on a reef. Soon afterwards the watch was changed. It was Poul's turn, and Don crawled down below, obviously relieved.

The night passed, and a grey miserable day began. The wind showed no sign of moderating; the sea raged more fiercely than before.

In the course of the afternoon of Easter Monday came a series of fierce, swift seas. Knud was at the wheel and was sitting under the shelter of a big tarpaulin, which was rigged round the cockpit on heavy planking supports. A sea struck the tarpaulin a terrific blow, smashed the inch-thick supports like matches and buried the whole after part of the boat in water. Fortunately Knud was still hanging on to the wheel when the water began to run off the deck.

We agreed to pay off a few points.

Later in the day we nearly lost Isa Lei.

I was at the wheel and was fully occupied in avoiding the worst seas, when Isa Lei appeared on the cabin ladder. She was going to her sand on the after-deck and was only waiting for a favourable moment. At last she plucked up courage and raced to the after-deck. I followed her anxiously with my eyes. If only a sea did not come before she had finished! In readiness for all eventualities I unfastened the strap with which I was lashed to the wheel.

Then a big sea came. Isa Lei shot like lightning towards the safety of the cabin, but too late. Before she had got halfway she was buried under masses of water. She was washed down towards the lee bulwarks, which were under water. I was afraid of her going overboard and let go the wheel to save the cat. But when I was bending down to pick her up, the boat was struck by a fresh sea. I lost my balance and forced Isa Lei down under the water with my whole weight. Luckily we both kept inside the bulwarks, and I laboriously worked my way up to the wheel, holding Isa Lei. From the cockpit I flung the cat several yards through the air and down through the cabin hatchway, where Don caught her, by now half dead. She was severely reprimanded which was really unjust; she was only doing what we had taught her to do. Later on the voyage through the treacherous Mediterranean she learnt to use the regular lavatory. The fact is that Isa Lei was no ordinary cat.

The weather looked like changing. We had to pay off again a few points, and there was some danger that we might not clear the western point of Cyprus. When it grew dark that evening we agreed to seek shelter under the east coast of the island. Again we paid off a few points, and in the course of the night we should see if Knud's calculations had been correct.

We had the engine going to make our sailing steadier. It began to miss, and it was found that a packing round the exhaust had become loose. The water was running into the bottom of the boat. It had already reached the level of the fly-wheel and was flung up on to the magneto, which became wet. Now we had to pump every hour, while Knud set about repairing the damage to the magneto.

Knud's calculations proved to be right enough. We sighted the light on Cape Kiti, and at 1.30 a.m. we had it on our port beam 13 miles away. We decided to seek shelter behind a point on the south-eastern tip of Cyprus, Cape Greco. Our spirits were rising again, the effects of the poisoning had passed off, and it was more comfortable sailing now, with the seas astern of us.

At 4.30 a.m. we had the light on Cape Greco abeam, and we perceived that we were getting shelter. The seas were losing their violence, and the wind was hardly as unpleasant. We rounded the point at dawn, and it was easy sailing up the east coast. We arrived at Famagusta about 10 a.m.

We had not meant to call at Cyprus and therefore had no special chart of the waters and harbour conditions of the island, but fortunately a large British steamer was lying in the roads, and a string of motor-boats was hurrying to and fro between her and the harbour. We followed in their wake and slipped in safely between the sandbank and reefs. On the big steamer's deck we saw some netting barricades, behind which thousands of Jews were crowded together. They were to be landed on Cyprus, where thousands more Jews were living in internment camps.

So we were in harbour, dead beat. Sails, clothes, and cabin equipment would now be aired and dried, and then we should get some sleep.

*Nordkaperen* was berthed in Famagusta's pleasant provincial harbour alongside a large black pleasure schooner called *Black Joe*.

The caretaker on board *Black Joe*, a negro, also looked after *Nordkaperen* when we were ashore, but for that matter the native population of Cyprus were the most honest people we ever met. Our negro cooked cuttle-fish soup for us and became very friendly with Isa Lei who spent most of her time on board *Black Joe*.

The harbour lay outside old Famagusta, whose ruins, dating from the palmy days in the Middle Ages, were surrounded by a high and well-preserved town wall—a protection against Turkish expansion in former times. Only a few people lived in old Famagusta. The new town, however, which had grown up outside the wall, did not bear a very modern stamp with its narrow winding streets.

We found in Cyprus an abundance of foodstuffs at incredibly low prices. We gave 60 öre (a few pence) for a litre of Cyprus wine. It was a regular holiday for us to be there. The inhabitants of Famagusta were friendly and helpful.

We were anxious to sail again as quickly as possible, but day after day unfavourable weather reports came. The Mediterranean must have run amok that spring and a fortnight—a delightful time—passed before we put to sea again.

A Danish ship which called at the port was kind enough to adopt *Nordkaperen's* crew during her stay. We had several tremendous days with them. When the ship sailed, the American marine research ship *Atlantis* arrived in her place, with a large crew and many scientists on board. *Atlantis*, a pretty two-masted vessel with the lines of a pleasure yacht, was, by the way, built in Denmark. For the last two days at Famagusta we laid *Nordkaperen* alongside *Atlantis* and had a pleasant time with the Americans. The boatswain was a Dane. He had deserted from the training ship *København* shortly before she was missing.

Day after day a fierce north-west wind swept over the Mediterranean with force 7-8, but at last, on April 13, there was an improvement, and at 3 p.m. we weighed anchor and put to sea.

We tacked uninterruptedly along the south-east coast and about

7 p.m. we had Cape Greco on our starboard beam four miles away. On the following days we had light westerly winds, and we sailed close-hauled till we were almost past Crete.

At 2 a.m. on the 17th a violent thunderstorm came up from Crete. Its violent gusts of wind from astern made *Nordkaperen* fly over the water.

This was a turning-point in our weather conditions. The long thunderstorm had left an easterly breeze behind it, and next morning the snow-covered mountains of Crete were out of sight.

The east wind persisted for a couple of days with a high sky and fine weather.

We had been warned against the wind conditions off the coasts of Crete, but apart from the thunderstorm we had no unpleasant experiences with that island.

According to the wind chart and sailing directions for the Mediterranean we should get fifty per cent of east winds and these with a maximum force of 5. We should, in other words, thoroughly enjoy the trip, but all calculations and rules were disproved that spring. The trip through those waters will live in our memories as one of the hardest jobs we have tackled. Besides the contrary weather, sails and rigging were worn almost to scrapping point. There were signs of boredom among us, our nerves were wearing very thin—and the cigarette ration was severely cut down.

It looked as if the Mediterranean was going to prevent our reaching home on the date we had fixed ever since the voyage began—June 23. We had made it a point of honour to keep this date. Taken all round everything had gone according to programme. We had kept to our itinerary but for seeking shelter once or twice, but now our chances were ruined. The distance from Cyprus to Malta, at least 900 miles, was covered in fairly good weather, but the rest of the way was a severe trial to us.

Isa Lei fell overboard for the seventh—and last—time, and this time she was practically drowned. She was usually a good swimmer, but in this case she was handicapped by her 'interesting condition'. On that anxious night at Port Sudan she had sneaked ashore without our noticing her and had been escorted on board next morning by a smart black and white admirer. A souvenir of Africa was the result.

Isa Lei was sitting sunning herself on the bulwarks aft, and Knud went up to her to play with her. Isa Lei was ready for a game. She leapt high into the air, but when she came down again the boat had gone.

Knud dashed down to start the engine, and the rest of us set to work to take in spinnakers and spinnaker boomkins. At last we were able to turn, and we steered back towards Isa Lei, but the cat was nowhere to be seen. The choppy sea handicapped our look-out, and Don went up to the crosstrees. We tacked to and fro searching wider and wider areas, but in vain. After a quarter of an hour we had given up hope of finding our little friend again, but nevertheless, we circled round once more, and Poul caught sight of something to the north of us which could be Isa Lei. It *was* the cat, drifting along with all four legs in the air. She righted herself just once, and then turned over again. We took the drowning cat on board and began to pour the water out of her. At last she uttered a hoarse little mew. She was dried and wrapped in hot blankets, and next day she was all right—so much so that she staged an athletic performance of which we had never seen the like.

Many birds came to visit us, and it was hard to keep Isa Lei away from them. It led to trouble in the end.

A swallow flew down into the cabin, and the cat, which to all appearances was lying asleep, shot up to the deck like a projectile and caught the swallow. There was nothing to be done about it; the bird was dead, and we threw it overboard and gave Isa Lei a severe telling-off.

Half an hour later the cat was on deck, eagerly following the flight of one or two swallows which were playing round the ship, We did not think there was any danger, but suddenly Isa Lei leapt six feet into the air, and when she came down she had a swallow between her paws. This was something only a South Seas cat could do. The swallow was dead, and we let her eat it.

A couple of windless days followed, in which we had to rely on the engine. We blessed the warmth of the sun: we mended and darned our own clothing and the old mainsail was patched up for the *n*th time. Unfortunately the sail we had got from the Dutchmen did not fit *Nordkaperen*: it was much too narrow and too tall, but by the agency of good friends a foresail and a mizen had been sent to us at Port Said. This was a piece of luck for us, for the Mediterranean cost us four sails in all. We sighted Malta on the morning of the 24th, ten miles farther north than we had expected. The current had probably taken us out of our course during the night.

The wind grew steadily fresher, and by degrees we got quite a stiff little breeze dead ahead. At last we reached the southern point of the island and began to tack up along the coast. There was deep water right up to the coast of the rocky island. There were reefs and single rocks here and there, but we kept clear of them.

Small turtles swarmed in the water round *Nordkaperen*. They resembled at a distance their brothers in the South Seas.

When we were near Valetta, the chief town of Malta, we were hailed by a British torpedo-boat which wanted to know who we were, where we came from, etc. We were then allowed to pass the fortress.

At 2 a.m. we sailed into the entrance of the harbour, and a pilot jumped on board. We thought there was compulsory pilotage, as there usually is in British ports, and accordingly made no protest. If only we had! He was a private pilot, and we had a bill for nearly £4 for the five minutes it took to allot us a berth.

Valetta harbour was a busy scene: it was a naval harbour well concealed and protected by high hills. Warships of every kind, from speedboats to battleships, were continually going in and out of the harbour. We saw obvious traces of the war. The whole of the southern part of the town was in ruins, and the work of the German bombers could be seen on the northern side of the harbour also. But the holes and caves in the hillsides were intact. On looking at them we could understand how the population had been able to withstand the German bombing for many months.

All the streets were full of marines. We went up into the town by a lift. This was the easiest way at any rate. Our winds were not good enough for the many steps, and we did not like the idea of a skinny cab-horse dragging us up by a steep roundabout route. In the evening the main streets swarmed with people, walking about or sitting at tables enjoying orchestral music or having a final drink. Unfortunately we did not see as much of Malta as we wished, for our time was occupied with work of various kinds on board the boat.

Moreover, a sharp eye was kept on us. The authorities seemed to see a spy in every visitor. They nearly took Don away from us. They did not believe his statement that he had got permission to sail with us while a serving soldier. He was taken off for interrogation time after time. and not till telegrams confirming what he told them arrived from Ceylon and England was he left in peace. He was made to wear uniform all the time we were in Malta.

Our call at Malta was to have been only for two days, but the weather reports were bad, and it was not suitable for us till the 28th—not because the wind had dropped, but because it had shifted into the east. We cast off our moorings and moved out into the middle of the harbour to take in fresh water. When this was over, and we were standing out towards the harbour mouth, we passed a British cruiser at anchor. The White Ensign was dipped in our honour; fortunately we were prepared for this, and the Danish flag was dipped simultaneously with the British.

Outside there was a fresh wind and a sea running, but when we had got clear of the land it was only a couple of hours before we were well away from Malta, so that we could set a course for Gibraltar.

We had in mind to go straight to Madeira, about 1,600 miles, but this was not to be. The fresh easterly wind held till 11 a.m.

next day; then it disappeared, and *Nordkaperen* lay rolling in the same old rough sea.

We took in the sails—it was important to spare them—and started the engine. We had cloudy weather with rain and haze for a couple of days. There was no wind, and our precious store of petrol had to bear the brunt. We sighted Sardinia on May 1. We ran along the south coast at a distance of thirty miles.

In Malta we had been warned against the weather conditions between Cap Bon, a point on the North African coast, and Sardinia. Sudden and violent north-westerly gales might be expected there. We tried, therefore, to get close in under the lee of the Sardinian coast.

We were clear of Sardinia on the night of Sunday the 2nd, and we congratulated one another on having come safely through those treacherous waters. But it was too soon!

Towards morning the sky assumed a blue-black colour, and a violent thunderstorm with furious gusts of wind fell upon us. The thunderstorm continued hour after hour, and it went on blowing hard from the north-west. We began to suspect that it was not quite an ordinary thunderstorm, and kept going with only small sails and no mainsail.

On Monday morning we had to take in the mizen and jib—to be exact, the jib took itself in, in three pieces.

The sea had risen violently, and we made hardly any progress. In the afternoon we could only just maintain our position. At 6 p.m. the wind had become so strong and the sea so high that there was no longer any question of sailing close-hauled; we had to heave to.

We cursed the treacherous Mediterranean from the bottom of our hearts. We were losing precious time there.

We had difficulty in getting in the foresail. We kept the mizen and flung out a sea anchor—an admirable sea anchor which had cost me a week's work in the Indian Ocean. Five minutes after it had been flung out a sea swept *Nordkaperen* from bow to stern. The boat put her nose very hard into the sea with the result that the sea anchor broke loose. It appeared later that the cross, which was made of heavy planks, had not been strong enough.

Then we rigged a storm foresail on a spar and used it as a sea anchor, but half an hour later a heavy iron ring was torn out as if by a gaint's hands, and the sea anchor was flapping about—unresisting and useless.

We found, however, that the boat would lie hove to very well without a sea anchor, so we did not trouble any more about that. *Nordkaperen* did indeed sometimes get broadside on to the seas through inadvertence, but then we were snug down below. We had battened down everywhere, hung up a powerful, clear light, and once in every hour the man on watch poked his head up to see if there was anything particular to be noticed. We were most anxious about the Sardinian coast, but we proved to be clear of it.

We passed the time in reading and sleeping, and in contrast to what had happened in the gale off Cyprus we were now quite dry below decks. We were perfectly comfortable and hugged ourselves when we heard a sea sweep the deck.

The night passed, and the next day brought no improvement in the weather. On the contrary, in the afternoon the gale reached its height. Mountains of water rolled towards us, and grey ragged clouds swept over the sky, so low that they seemed to touch our masthead.

Ugh, how cold and wet it was on deck—down into the cabin again! We not only lost our sea anchor and had our jib torn to pieces, but the engine became flooded and the chains of the jib-boom and the outrigger aft were both snapped.

On Wednesday morning the wind dropped a little, but the seas were still high and swift. We lay hove-to for forty-two hours—forty-two wasted hours. Our chances of getting home to Denmark before June 23 were becoming very small. About 7 a.m. we began to clear up, the sea anchor was taken in, and we repaired the minor damage of different kinds which the boat had sustained. At mid-day *Nordkaperen* was under control and heading south-west. The sea became moderate again, but the wind kept steadily in the west.

Next day we were close to the African coast, and at dusk we went about and headed out to sea again. In the middle of this Isa Lei had two kittens. She had them in Poul's bunk, and Poul dutifully moved his things into the midships cabin. The weather became very uncertain, fresh contrary winds alternating with almost complete calm. We made hardly any progress at all.

Coffee, sugar and butter were almost used up, and cigarettes too were running very low. I sounded the atmosphere on board and realized that the east wind must not keep us waiting long if the morale of the crew was to be maintained. We could no longer derive any consolation from the fact that we should soon have been round the world. On the evening of Saturday, the 8th, we passed Algiers. It would have been very pleasant to have a couple of days' rest there and replenish our stores, but money was very short, and if we once got into harbour it was difficult to get out again quickly. Algiers disappeared from sight, but we were soon to see it again.

About 8 p.m. we were attacked by a few violent squalls. A sudden furious gust forced *Nordkaperen* on to her beam ends, and the alarm bell shrilled ominously from end to end of the boat. Don was at the wheel, and the storm had taken him by surprise. While we were hurrying into some clothes a few sharp cracks were heard from above, while the boat shivered from masthead to keel.

When we came on deck we saw that it was the topsail that had been in trouble. Before we could begin to take it in it blew out into the darkness; only a few torn fragments fell on to our heads.

We had to take in the rest of the headsails in a hurry. The rain and thunder followed soon after. The storm passed over comparatively quickly, but we found that the mainsail was torn in several places. Long rents threatened to divide it into several pieces. That thunderstorm was the signal for a change in our programme.

The voyage from Denmark to Australia had been child's play, but homeward bound from Australia we had had a hard time, especially quite recently. We must be careful in the last lap—so near the goal. It was like a game of bricks; the last arches and gables must be laid on cautiously, or the splendid building will collapse.

We went back to Algiers.

When we were about to have a cup of 'thunderstorm coffee' we found that the paraffin tank was empty—one reason more for putting back. The self-starter broke clean off when we set the machine going.

On our way in to the coast we saw that the barometer was falling steadily. On the other hand, our spirits were rising. The decision to put back had swept away the taciturn, irritable, surly, unfriendly spirit which had prevailed on board. Soon we got a bearing on the lighthouses on Cape Matifau and Caxine, and not long after the harbour light of Algiers appeared on the horizon right ahead. We approached the lighted town and were very soon to land on the coast of Africa for the third time. Behind us coal-black clouds were rolling up in the north-western sky, but we should be in before they could reach us.

We crept in through the harbour entrance and made our way into the western part of the harbour, keeping a sharp look-out for a place to anchor. We could not see a ship's length ahead of us and at last dropped anchor at random. It was beginning to blow outside, and all night the wind howled in the rigging, but we were warm and comfortable.

We found next morning that we had dropped anchor just where we should have—among the pleasure craft, which had their berths in this part of the harbour. The sun was shining over a white town lying picturesquely on the hill-sides. Above the two-tiered promenade along the harbour high modern houses stood; a Danish flag caught the eye and showed us where our Consul lived. Farther uphill lay the Arab quarter. It was Sunday; pleasure boats and fishing parties were on their way out of harbour with lunch packets and rods.

French sailing men came to visit us. When they heard we were on a voyage round the world they began to give us good advice, We must be careful in going through the Red Sea, keep our eyes open in the waters round Australia, and so on, quite interminably.

It is not easy to interrupt a Frenchman, but when at last we got a word in and explained that we had been round the world, they looked rather sheepish.

Had we a sextant and chronometer?—Good God! For that matter we had been asked other curious questions, for example: did we sail at night or anchor?

Some Danes in Algiers gave us a good time. A big Danish wine-merchant sent us his delicious products, and many Danes came and went and made themselves at home on board *Nordkaperen*. One of then, Claude Winther by name, got me out of a difficult position later on, when we were about to sail. Two men from the local wireless station came on board and absolutely insisted on my saying a few words to their listeners. My French was more than defective, and I refused emphatically, but the men were inexorable. Winther saved the situation for me by driving up to the studio with me and saying what had to be said.

We needed petrol for *Nordkaperen*. The Danish Consul advised me to ask for three times as many petrol coupons as I could use, for as a rule only a third of the quantity applied for was allowed.

The gentleman who determined the size of the ration, however, proved to be most interested in circumnavigation. He gave me, without making any objection, coupons for the 175 gallons I asked for. We had only money enough to pay for sixty-five gallons. I now had a regular fortune in my hands, as in the free (black) market the coupons were several times the cost of the petrol. I did not sell the surplus coupons, but saw that we obtained other advantages through them. It was impossible to feel oneself a law-breaker in Algiers.

We had intended to sail on May 15, but a troublesome Customs official put a spoke in our wheel. We could only get petrol from a particular tank in the harbour, and it was only open on weekdays between 8 and 10 a.m. At 9 a.m. we were ready to go alongside the little landing-stage where the tank was, but were afraid of coming into collision with the many small boats which also had come in to fill their tanks, so we circled round outside till the way was clear. At five minutes past ten there was room to get in, and we laid ourselves alongside by the tank. The man in charge of the tank was willing enough to sell us the petrol, but the Customs man who had to superintend the sale made trouble, muttering that he was now off duty. I could have bought him with a small bribe, but I was furious. Before my fury could find expression the fellow had locked up the tank and sneaked off with the keys.

I was pleased to learn later on that a complaint—through the local yacht club—had earned the disobliging Customs official a most severe reprimand from his superiors, as well as the loudly expressed disapproval of all the people in the harbour.

The worst of it was that the tank was closed the next day—Sunday—and Monday was a holiday, so that we should not get our tank filled before Tuesday morning. Thus the Customs man, now so regretting his action, cost us three days' delay.

We were to sail at 5 p.m., but thanks to the broadcast we did not leave till 8 p.m.

There was a very light westerly wind, and the engine had to bear the brunt. It was calm all night and next day, but on the morning of the 20th the wind freshened and we got an awkward head sea. We stopped the engine, set sail, and before long we were tacking.

Despite the cloudless sky the wind rose steadily and it grew colder. The barometer gave no indication that anything particular was to be expected. None the less the wind increased in force to a stiff breeze. The mistral was upon us—the cold hard wind that swept out of the Gulf of Genoa.

We held steadily out to sea, but *Nordkaperen* lost speed in the rising sea. Mizen, mizen staysail and jib were taken in—we no longer had anything that could be called a topsail—and we hammered on through the seas with only foresail and mainsail.

It was enough to make one scream with rage. Day after day,

week after week, all possible hidden forces combined to work against us.

Hatches and skylights had been battened down. One day we were struck by a cross sea. Tons of water were flung up on to the mainsail, which was rent in five or six places and had to come down. We set the mizen, went about and steered in towards Africa.

We agreed to seek shelter in a little bay we had passed the day before. We fell off and got the wind and sea on our starboard quarter. The wind increased and the seas grew swifter as we approached the coast. Chenoua Bay was well protected by high mountains to the north-west. We made our way forward, using the lead, to a good anchorage. Not till we were about fifty yards from the shore did we drop anchor in from twenty-five to thirty feet of water. Two hours later the wind force was up to over 8, and we did not regret our decision to run for shelter, although we had made only thirty-nine to forty miles in the right direction in two days.

We dried sails and clothes and patched the torn mainsail. A few fishermen from the little town of Tipazo came rowing out to us with some fish. Don and Poul went ashore, but soon came back, as there was nothing particularly interesting to look at.

We kept an extra sharp look-out all through the night. We could easily get into a dangerous situation if the wind should change suddenly. Towards night the wind decreased, but fortunately we did not rely on it, for at sunrise it began again with renewed violence—always from the west. Not till the wind dropped late in the afternoon and then shifted into the south, did we trust it. We weighed anchor at 7 p.m., with the engine going. It was not long before the wind was westerly again, but it was not particularly strong, and we worked our way north-westward through what was left of the previous day's sea and swell. It was a long way to Gibraltar, and we made only forty miles in the day. On Saturday we had a dead calm and had to use our precious petrol to the full.

On Sunday morning a light north-easterly wind made a tentative appearance. We took hope. At 10 a.m. heavy clouds came up from the east, and soon there was wind enough. All sail was set and the engine stopped. Now we should get some sailing. We were now only 290 miles from Gilbraltar. We flew along. We were in tremendous spirits, and made a big hole in our scanty cigarette and coffee rations. The arrival of the east wind was further celebrated with a couple of bottles of wine. The ceremonial welcome was hardly over when the wind died away altogether. Two hours later we had the wind from the south-west. Our course was set towards the Spanish coast, and the boat sailed at a good speed. Hour after hour the wind increased in force, and at sunset we were no longer pressing her. It did not serve any reasonable purpose to lie messing about in cold and water to gain a very few miles in a day and get the sails torn to ribbons. We should have to use them in going home through the Atlantic.

We therefore tacked to and fro for a little while along the south-east coast of Spain and found a little bay which looked inviting—San Pedro it was called. We dropped anchor close to the land without any misadventure.

I was awakened about five o'clock by hearing voices close to *Nordkaperen*. When I came on deck a small fishing-boat was lying alongside us. The two Spanish fishermen offered us delicious fish, which we obtained in exchange for a little tobacco and rice.

We had been a week covering the distance of rather over 200 miles from Algiers—a disgraceful result when our record distance was 222 miles in a day. We weighed anchor a little after dawn and crept carefully out of the bay to continue the eternal tacking.

Our daily runs kept steadily around forty miles for a week. We had now a sharp current to contend with as well. Our petrol was almost used up. We were also out of bread, margarine, butter and potatoes; we were living on pancakes and rice porridge. These are not dishes to be despised, but when one has had them for breakfast, dinner and supper every day, it tends to promote ill-humour.

Our preserves had been finished long before; only the cat's food was left.

We reached Gibraltar on the twelfth day after leaving Algiers. We had been sixty-two days sailing through the Mediterranean, twice the time we had allowed for the passage.

We cheered up when we sighted the Rock of Gibraltar in the distance on Sunday, May 30. When we had finished with the Mediterranean but for twenty miles, the north-easterly wind came sweeping down. It was ironical.

CHAPTER XXI

# *The Last Lap Home*

WE sailed out of the Straits of Gibraltar before a fresh breeze in mist, with rain about, and in pitch darkness. At 3.30 a.m. we had the light on Cape Tarifa on our beam. We were now in the Atlantic again. Madeira lay 600 miles out in the ocean, waiting for us.

The first day in the Atlantic was not good—no wind and a day's run of only thirty-two miles—but the rest of the days averaged over 120. The wind veered from north-east to north-west. The wind on our quarter suited us best, then the ship could steer herself, without our being on the rack all the time. There was cloudy weather and rain every day, but on board the sun was shining. Our talk was cheerful with an undertone of quivering excitement. We should soon have reached our goal now. We were washing and ironing. Our shore clothes were pressed and the boat scrubbed and polished. We were a little worried by the fact that the mainsail was beginning to split again: but it held! On the other hand, the screw of the port foresail stay was broken in a gust of wind. It nearly destroyed the foresail, and not long afterwards a bolt in the outrigger aft gave way, and the mizen ran out and thrashed about in the wind. Everything was repaired at once.

At 4 a.m. on the morning of Saturday, June 5, we sighted the Porto Santo light, and we counted on being in port that evening. So we were, but we were first to have a hard tussle with a cross-current and sudden gusts of wind at a point close to Funchal. The seas came foaming from all sides, and the strong gusts attacked us from every quarter. At one moment the sails were beating and thrashing about, at the next the boat lay on her beam ends. When at last we had trimmed the sails to a fresh direction of the wind, the gusts suddenly came from the lee side. Knud turned to to start the engine, but it would not go. Poul and I gave up fiddling with the helm and the sails, but Don kept on running about and changing the headsails. We could not help laughing at him. At last the engine started, and we were soon out of the eddies of wind and current. About 10 p.m. we crept into Funchal harbour, to the familiar panorama with the thousand lights running up the hillsides.

We found the same anchorage as two years before, and at 10.20 the anchor chain rattled out of the hawse-hole. We had sailed round the world and crossed our own course.

A bottle of Algerian wine was brought up, that we might meetly celebrate the solemn moment.

We supposed that we had entered the harbour unnoticed, well covered by the darkness, but all the same a Portuguese found his way out to us. He remembered us from our previous visit and offered his services. Anthonus, as he was called, was sent ashore to despatch a few telegrams. We knew there were people in Denmark anxiously awaiting news, and when he came back he had some bottles of Madeira wine with him. But our carouse did not last long. We were tired and turned in.

Next day *Nordkaperen* was dressed with signal flags, and people began to come on board to congratulate us. We were cordially received by the authorities, who got nearly as drunk as the time before, and a mass of telegrams began to come in from our families and friends. Letters from friends and sailing clubs all the world over were waiting for us, and in the days that followed greetings came from people who we thought had long forgotten us, but who nevertheless had found out in peculiar ways that the voyage round the world had been successfully completed.

But we could not live in transports of joy all the time. If we were to get home across the Atlantic with whole skins, there was work to be done. The mainsail must be strengthened, and the rest of the sails and rigging thoroughly surveyed. We must also provision ship, and the whole thing cost money. We took a sad farewell of various personal possessions, but that did not bring in anything worth speaking of. Money had to be raised, a lot of money, for Funchal was a very dear place to provision ship in. We had to have petrol too. The Danish and Swedish Consuls arranged several delightful parties for us, car drives in the mountains, lunches, etc., but they had little idea of our real necessities. Time after time we had had refusals to our applications from the currency office at home—of which in itself we could not complain. I had another try, however, and got the Danish Consul to support my telegraphed request. Of course, there was another refusal from the currency office, but at the same time they had sent the request on to the Foreign Ministry, and we had the sum we needed advanced to us through the Legation clearing office.

This made the outlook much brighter. Even if there was nothing to shout hurrah about, we could manage all right by provisioning meagrely and carefully.

On June 22 we were able to clear ship for sea and take in petrol. We could not afford more than twenty-two gallons: we hoped the sails would hold for the 2,200 miles to the nearest port of call, Dover in England. If the weather were unfavourable it might be a six weeks' voyage—and we only had cigarettes for three. There was not the same atmosphere about our sailing as there usually was. No one uttered the word 'worries', but it could be read in our faces.

We were to have sailed at 10 p.m., but the police official who was to have come with our passes did not appear. When it was nearly midnight, we sent Don and Anthonus ashore to look for him.

After a long search they found him in the Casanova, a dance restaurant. At last he rolled on board very drunk, with the passports in his hand. In the meantime it had become my birthday and the second anniversary of our start from Copenhagen. This had to be celebrated with an extra glass. Anthonus and a couple of our Portuguese friends were of the party and held their own well. About two o'clock we began to weigh anchor. There was something wrong with the capstan. Anthonus wanted to help, but was not as careful as he should have been; the little finger of his right hand was caught in the capstan and torn off. It was an unpleasant sight, and seemed to us a bad omen. I was afraid we should have trouble with the authorities, but the police officer settled matters for us. Anthonus was bandaged and had another glass to keep him going, after which our police friend had him taken to hospital. Anthonus sent greetings to us from the dinghy as he was rowed away.

'You mustn't worry,' he called, 'it was my fault. Good luck!'

The police official gave us to understand that we could go, and as we could keep ourselves informed by letter of how things were going, we had no scruples about leaving harbour.

The sea was calm, and the engine had to do the work. We sailed along the coast towards Pto. de Barlavento, and at 7 a.m. we began to tack to the eastward.

Before this the engine broke down. There were indications that this time the defect was serious. Meanwhile we had caught a light north-easterly breeze and when we were clear of Madeira set a course towards the Azores.

Isa Lei was recovering her spirits. She had been upset for several days because we had taken away her big kittens and left them to be brought up at Madeira.

For the first twenty-four hours the wind was undependable, and we sometimes lay for hours on end rolling in the high seas, without a breath of air. This was bad for the sails. On the second day the wind freshened, and we hauled the sheets taut and steered north-west. Mizen, jib and mizen staysail had to be taken in, but the boat still heeled over sharply to port. It was a tiring sail. It was impossible to stand on our legs; we had to crawl about and hold on tight. The boat leapt and bumped in the sea till the guts were nearly twisted out of us. The seas gradually became as high as houses, but they were more comfortable to sail in, for she kept her speed up and down them. But if she was at last struck by a cross sea a corresponding amount of damage was done on board.

We were sailing without lights. It seemed to us unthinkable that we could come into collision with a ship far out in the Atlantic and away from all shipping routes. The night when I was going on watch, I went up on deck a short time before I was to take over to see if everything was all right. *Nordkaperen* was sailing without a steersman. There was not a light to be seen all round the horizon.

Five minutes later I called Knud. While he was dressing I heard him say in his quiet way:

'Didn't you see her before?'

'See what?'

He nodded up towards the open hatchway.

The masthead lights of a ship, and the light from her bridge, were gliding past our stern, horribly close. We could see it all from down in the cabin. I shot up on deck again. A gigantic liner was ploughing through the seas at right angles to our course. We heard the thumping of her engines distinctly.

'Well, I'm damned—I was up on deck not more than five minutes ago, and I didn't see a sign of a ship!'

'Don't you think we'd better have the lights?' said Knud.

After that the lighting regulations were scrupulously observed.

On the following days the wind was somewhere near half a gale. We recorded wind force 6, and it was uncomfortable to be on deck. We had had cloudy weather and rain since we left Madeira, and everything was beginning to be damp and sodden. We had not touched the wheel for several days. *Nordkaperen* was working her way steadily over the water mountains with the port bulwarks under water. Three bottles of wine were smashed through her pitching, and one morning the boat smelt of the most splendid cognac. I had a feeling that my fine presentation cognac from Madeira had had it. It was lying in my locker in a straw covering. When I pulled the bottle out it was empty. A rent had been made in its bottom, and all its noble contents had disappeared down into the locker below.

According to our reckoning we should be level with the Azores on June 27-28, 120 miles away. We had been unable to take observations on account of the weather. At last the sun came out for a couple of hours on the 28th. There was joy on board when Knud established that our position was much better than we expected. We were 625 miles from Madeira. It turned out later that the log had played us a trick: it had gradually become worn out. The wind dropped somewhat again, and we used the opportunity to repair the jib, which again had been blown into several sections. One evening, when all the wind had disappeared, we took the mainsail, rigged up a light and began to repair the many small rents which were beginning to appear. We had nearly finished when the wind began to stir again.

On the 30th we had a whole day of delightful sunshine, but the price was—no wind. Blankets, clothing and sails were laid out on deck to dry. We had got some split cod from Madeira; they should be dried too. That was Knud's job. He would have the cows out to grass, he said.

There was, as I have said, not much change in our diet. We had no preserves. It consisted mainly of porridge, potatoes and split cod. Only an egg now and then gave a little colour to the bill of fare. Poul discovered that split cod baked in pancakes was a delicacy. We greeted every variation in our food with pleasure and readily agreed with him.

There was a dead calm for several days. The Atlantic was as quiet as a church. The old grey Atlantic was having a nap. We profited by the opportunity to take down the engine. It was found that the valves were worn. It would be difficult to put them right in the open sea. Knud hunted and poked about in lockers and drawers and at last got an apparatus together which could be used for grinding in valves. We started work under Knud's guidance.

On July 3 there was fine weather again. The wind returned, and with it came rain and cold. The first airs came from the south-west, but as it increased in force it gradually veered north. On the following day we raced along with a fresh breeze and did 160 miles with the wind on our port side. We were only about 750 miles from Dover and had sailed about 1,500.

We enjoyed the short nights. It was beginning to get light now as early as three o'clock. For a long time we had had twelve hours of darkness. The cold became more noticeable; it was all we could do to keep warm in the cabins.

We made good progress with the repairing of the engine, and we had time to clean and grease the boat's bottom on the inside.

On the 6th a grey steamer flying the Panamanian flag came up with us from astern. She stopped her engines, glided close up to us and sounded her siren three times. There was waving and calling to us from up on her deck. There were obviously people there who had seen us before, but the distance was too great for us to recognize them. One of the officers leaned out over the rail, made a trumpet of his hands and shouted:

'Haven't you got any farther than this?'

'What are you talking about? We're on the second round,' we shouted back.

He waved his hand incredulously and roared with laughter.

We had the wind almost dead ahead for two or three days in succession—a cold, bitter wind, and we tacked laboriously towards England. Low clouds drove swiftly over us, and there was a ceaseless drizzle. At last, on the 10th, the wind shifted into the north, and we had a good run towards the Channel. The wind backed farther over into the north-west visibly and the next day it was blowing heard. We entered the Channel at a speed of over eight knots. The Atlantic took a respectful farewell of us and helped us along with a puff of wind at the last moment.

The engine had been put in order at last, and a trial passed off satisfactorily. We passed a number of large French sea-going fishing-boats. They made quite a homelike impression—the first sign that we were close to land. On July 13 we sighted the faint outline of England to the north, and towards afternoon cliffs and headlands appeared out of the mist. We were only 135 miles from Dover.

The wind was changeable, and we were worried by a strong current. We had counted on being in port on Wednesday the 14th, but it was pitch dark before we were there, and as we were not sure about the currents in the neighbourhood of Dover harbour, we decided to wait till next day.

At 7 a.m. we steered for the mouth of the harbour. The current was very strong, and we almost had to sail sideways. Just outside the entrance the engine began to miss, but luckily it waited to stop until we had just got inside. We were allowed to moor alongside a large fishing-boat, so we avoided having to struggle with moorings in the fierce tide. Our neighbour had no less than thirty-seven persons on board—Estonian refugees, women and children, who wanted to go to Canada to start a new life there.

We took a cordial farewell of Don, who had now shared our ups and downs for half a year. He had been fully equal to his job. We saw him disappear down the road along the cliffs in the pouring English rain. His long body was bent under the weight of his bedding as he went back to seven years of a soldier's life.

We took a new passenger home from England with us. This was one of our Danish sailing men, Helmut Sörensen, called Smut. He had sailed with us on the first stage of our voyage from Copenhagen to Fredrikshavn, and now he wanted to sail with us for the last stage home—for which we were glad. We had sailed the 2,200 miles from Madeira in twenty-one days. It could just as well have taken forty, but Smut had calculated in some curious manner that we should be in England on July 15 and had therefore come over to meet us. He had arrived the day before.

'It wasn't so hard to calculate,' he said, 'You usually sail 100 miles a day.'

It was a wonderful feeling to be able once more to take up a telephone receiver after two long years and ring up my wife at home, and it was delightful to be in a European town again, even if it was cold and damp.

Our papers were quickly in order, and we were able to buy some provisions as well. Petrol was the greatest difficulty, and we got that only thanks to the circumstance that we were circumnavigators. We were shown many applications, including one from the Danish yacht *Atlantide*, and afterwards copies of the refusals: the authorities regretted that it was impossible.

'I'm sick of this,' I said. 'It's the first time we've been refused in a British port. Our sails are worn, and we can hardly manage without petrol.'

'How many British ports have you been in?'

'Many—in the Pacific and elsewhere.'

'Is it you who have been round the world?'

'Yes.'

'I'll try to get the head office in London on the telephone—one moment.'

The official who had thawed to this extent asked me many questions about the voyage while waiting for the telephone call, and when the conversation with London was over, there was a note of triumph in his voice as he said:

'That's good enough. The consent will be here in three hours. But before you go—what was it like in Tahiti . . .?'

Smut and I had a busy time getting everything ready for our sailing. We spent the whole day rushing from one end of the town to the other, while Poul and Knud set to work to patch up *Nordkaperen's* defects for the last time.

We were able to leave Dover, its historic cliffs and the front-line fortress Dover Castle, whose massive towers stood out against the bright blue sky, as early as Sunday morning, July 18. We got a fresh westerly wind at once and set our course for the Kiel Canal.

We followed the Goodwins route and fell into the busy traffic. During the night the wind jumped round from north-west to south, but it was all the same to us—so long as we were going towards Denmark. Smut took over Don's duties, but old yachtsman though he was, he could not stand *Nordkaperen's* unexpected movements. He was sea-sick.

On Tuesday we sighted the P2 buoy and turned into the Humber-Elbe route. We had had cloudy and rainy weather all the time, but we did not notice it. Our hearts and minds were full of other things. Large and small ships passed us, and now and then a Dane sent us a greeting. About 11 p.m. a thick bank of fog suddenly rolled over us from the south-west. It was not pleasant to lie embedded in the fog in the heavy traffic, and we thought best to move a mile north of the route, but there too we had to have the fog-horn ready. Once a hideous deep hoot came from somewhere astern of us. Knud and I were on deck, but we could not see anything. I sounded the horn too for safety's sake. At the same moment the masthead lights of a big steamer appeared almost over our heads. Knud put the helm hard-a-starboard, and the great shadow glided past us.

'So one can't be in peace even outside the channel,' Knud grumbled.

A couple of hours later the fog lifted as suddenly as it had come, and we slipped into the traffic lane again, passed one buoy after another and noted a strong northward current.

On Wednesday evening we received a last greeting from the open sea. A hard south-westerly wind made us take in sail a bit, and the man at the wheel got a dousing. We passed a string of lightships, and at 2 a.m. on Thursday we were off Cuxhaven and approaching Brunsbüttel.

We entered the lock about 8 a.m. It was a slow proceeding: a very strong current held us up. We were in the lock with several ships. The gates were shut behind us; we were in the Kiel Canal.

There was still one surprise in store for us. Our papers were not in order. We should have sought permission to pass through the canal from our last port, but no one had told us. What would happen now?

The British officer scratched his head. It was something new to him for a boat to sail boldly into the lock without the right papers.

'You must come out of the lock for the time being and tie up inside. Then I'll look into the matter,' he said.

He went off to telephone. We needed some infernal military permit stamps on our passports. Smut was the only one of us who had them.

The pleasant Englishman came back.

'I can't get the man who deals with these things. He's at Holtenau, at the other end of the canal.'

'Can't we sail along and talk to him?' we cunningly suggested.

'Well, there can't be any harm in that,' replied the officer. 'Perhaps I'll be able to fix the matter up for you before you get there.'

We wanted to sail without a pilot, but were not allowed to. The boat was too big. An old German pilot came on board, a nice fellow, who could speak Swedish. He made an enormous hole in our stock of coffee and butter and told us a lot of tall stories in return. To make our petrol last we set all sail, and the pilot, as an old sailing ship man, was delighted at being allowed to steer a ship under sail again. Down-draughts between the hills sometimes worried us, but the engine got us through. At several places along the canal people waved to us and shouted: 'Love to Denmark.'

We were to change pilots on the way. The old one was sent off with a few victuals in his pockets.

'For my grandchildren,' he said, and wanted to kiss us.

The new pilot was young and strong. He disposed of the whole frying-pan of kedgeree Poul had made for him. Afterwards he smoked cigarettes till he had an attack of asthma. The stumps were carefully hidden away.

'They're for my wife,' he said, with an embarrassed smile.

At 9.30 p.m. we entered the lock at Holtenau and the gates were shut behind us.

Now the same performance began as at Brunsbüttel. How had we been able to come through without a permit? The people at Brunsbüttel had evidently forgotten to report our arrival. We explained what had happened, and the two Englishmen were really very nice, but the law was the law, and the law must be obeyed.

The commanding officer would decide the matter next day. Would we tie up outside the lock and wait till next day before sailing? 'You'd better not go ashore,' the officers said kindly. We then adopted a more private footing and emptied two bottles of Madeira.

Big and small children stood on the quay begging for scraps of bread, and we took the opportunity to empty *Nordkaperen* of all emergency provisions.

Although we had been forbidden to land Poul went to a dance on shore with the crew of a Dutch motor sailing vessel which was lying alongside us. No one took any notice of it. The pleasant Dutchmen asked Knud and me over to drink a bottle or two of gin, and we agreed that they should give us a tow up to Svendborgsund.

Next day a serious gentleman in uniform came on board *Nordkaperen*. It was he who decided our fate.

'It's very unfortunate, but you cannot get permission to sail through the canal. You must sail back to Copenhagen and get your passports stamped by a British authority.'

We had difficulty in keeping our faces. Was his decision based on a misunderstanding, or was he a good sportsman who was solving a difficult problem with real diplomatic flair? We think so.

When his elegant figure had gone out of earshot, Knud said:

'We must remember this for next time. If we haven't a stamp on our passports, we'll just sail through backwards!'

On Saturday afternoon the Dutch motor vessel *Necton* towed us away. We had a regular spring cleaning above and below decks, while our excitement rose from hour to hour.

The first glimpse of Denmark, the outlines of Als, appeared in the west. The weather was brilliant, but there was not a breath of wind. At 9 p.m. we cast off the tow-rope between buoys three and four and waved good-bye to the Dutchman. We went on with our engine in the lowest gear. We did not want to be in harbour till next day. We glided slowly into Svendborgsund. It grew dark, the lights flashed around us and the stars above us. Denmark was giving us a wonderful welcome.

I tried to get a couple of hours' sleep like the others, but it was impossible. A two years' old dream would be fulfilled in a few hours' time—a moment dreamt of in long solitary night watches —on brilliant moonlight nights and in raging storms: a moment that had given us strength in difficult times, the moment that had drawn us back to the far north again. That moment would soon have come!

I slipped out of my bunk and made a cup of coffee, which I drank with Smut up in the cockpit. We enjoyed the night. I shaved, and asked Smut if I might take what remained of his watch. I could not rest. It was I who had wife and children waiting over there—somewhere behind the dark trees.

Slowly it grew light, the trees began to have colour. Isa Lei came for a walk on deck. She stood with her forepaws on the bulwarks and studied her new country.

The sun came out. Knud and Poul would soon be called. Knud and Poul—I could not have chosen better comrades for my journey. Poul—a dare-devil figure with the spray flying round him, Knud—safe and self-controlled, immersed in his calculations.

They came on deck. We were now close to Svendborg harbour and decided to enjoy the lovely morning and drop anchor a little way out. It was just on six o'clock.

The pilot from Tankefuld came on board with the news that my wife and children had arrived the evening before. He was going to fetch them now and sail them out to us.

I could not do anything—only wait. Wait for Mimi, whose hundreds of letters had cheered me in the remotest corners of the world; Mimi, who had taken care of the business and children while her egoistical husband was wandering about the oceans.

I could see several figures about to enter the pilot's boat. Now the boat had pushed off from the landing-stage and was making for *Nordkaperen*. . . .

We were sitting in the Café Niklasson over a glass of beer—at the same table where the plan had been hatched four years earlier. No one had said a word for a long time. Poul was fiddling with a box of matches, Knud thoughtfully studying the surface of his beer.

'Well, so the adventure's over,' I said with a sigh which had in it an undertone of relief.

'We've become richer by a few experiences and poorer by a few illusions,' muttered Knud. 'If we can only get into the old rut again!'

'But what we've experienced is something no one can take from us,' Poul put in.

'No, perhaps not,' said Knud, 'but one never gets anything without giving up something in return!'

I understood what he meant. There was a bill to be paid.

'Hallo, waitress! Three more beers!'

The circle was complete.

GEORGE ALLEN & UNWIN LTD
*London: 40 Museum Street, WC1*

*Auckland: 24 Wyndham Street*
*Bombay: 15 Graham Road, Ballard Estate, Bombay 1*
*Calcutta: 17 Chittaranjan Avenue, Calcutta 13*
*Cape Town: 109 Long Street*
*Karachi: 254 Ingle Road*
*New Delhi: 13–14 Ajmeri Gate Extension, New Delhi 1*
*São Paulo: Avenida 9 de Julho 1138–Ap. 51*
*Sydney, N.S.W.: Bradbury House, 55 York Street*
*Toronto: 91 Wellington Street West*

## THE NAKED AUCAS

### by Rolf Blomberg

Deep in the swamps and jungle of Ecuador live a savage tribe of Indians—the Aucas. Feared by their neighbours, they do not hesitate to attack any party entering their territory. They appear to kill for the pleasure of killing and become gloomy and depressed if many days pass without bloodshed. But, according to a captured native woman who eventually managed to escape, 'when they had captured me and run their spears through the other two they laughed and howled and bellowed. At home, too, there was laughter and joy.'

Rolf Blomberg determined to make peaceful contact with the Aucas after he had collected all the information he could glean from those who had survived their attacks. The first part of his book records the information he amassed, including the stories of the early Jesuit missionaries. The second part tells of his own expedition in 1949. Blomberg; David Cooper, an American missionary; Robinson, a brilliant photographer; and six Yumbo Indians made their way up the River Napo. They advanced slowly, plagued by sandflies, torrential rain, and aware that they were being watched and that the gifts left for the Aucas had been ignored. Suddenly, a hail of spears flew across the river. Ideas of making peaceful contact were quickly abandoned and the party, with only one casualty, retreated.

*Demy 8vo* *21s. net*

## MAN-EATERS AND JUNGLE KILLERS

### by Kenneth Anderson

The author is not at all a hunter of big game, but because he has so great an understanding of how the animals think, he is frequently called in to handle situations where a locality has to be freed of the menace of the man-eater at large. Step by step he takes one through each adventure, explaining his methods and precautions, and building up the intense excitement of each dangerous situation as he experienced it himself.

A book for all who are fascinated by jungle life and by adventures in remote places.

*Demy 8vo* *About 16s. net*

## FROM THE BACK STREETS OF BENGAL

### by Bernard Llewellyn

Whether he is talking to fellow passengers, riding pillion on a policeman's motorcycle, or fighting for a place in a crowded bus or train, he is always enjoying the adventure. His enjoyment and his love of people, even when they smell worst, is passed to the readers completely and his story is as fascinating as it is graphic.

'Mr Llewellyn wields so lively a pen, and has produced so eminently readable a narrative. . . . The narrative of his journey through certain parts of India is no less engaging than his account of his travels in Pakistan . . . he writes with a broad pen, and gets his effects with vivid touches. . . . How well it is written.' *Times Literary Supplement.*

'He writes vividly and gives a convincing picture of the life of the ordinary man.' *Manchester Guardian.*

'A work of heroism, interspersed with "good humour, laughter, patience and kindness".' *Church Times.*

*Demy 8vo* *18s. net*

## TIGERMEN OF ANAI

### by Ton Schilling

It was many years ago, when the islands of the Dutch East Indies were still full of wild and remote forests, that the author lived and worked there as a surveyor and a builder of roads. In this isolated life his one diversion was the pursuit of big game and in this book he relates not only his thrilling and unique experiences in hunting tigers, crocodiles, elephants, boars, panthers, buffaloes, stags and many other beasts, but his immense and intimate knowledge of the wild life of the jungles.

The book takes its title from the widespread legend of men who can turn themselves into tigers at will. When in human shape, they may ask a villager for shelter, but if he does so only his bones will be found in the morning and his guest will have disappeared.

This is a book of romance and excitement and the thrill of wild life in exotic places in days long passed away.

*Demy 8vo* *About 18s. net*

## WORLDS BEYOND THE HORIZON

### by Joachim G. Leithäuser

This is a history of discovery and adventure from the days of Columbus to the preparations for interplanetary travel. In it are traced the fabulous careers of all those impassioned men whose lives were expended upon the exploration of the world's remotest parts: pathfinders like Columbus, Magellan and Vasco da Gama; conquerors like Cortez and Pizaro, who destroyed civilizations and built empires; trappers and hunters like Champlain and de la Salle; explorers like Livingstone, Stanley and Humboldt; polar discoverers like Peary, Amundsen and Byrd. Whatever the form his passion took, each of these contributed to enlarging the boundaries of the known world and giving to the earth its real shape and dimension. Having conquered his own earth, man now looks out into space, and the book ends with a full and unfanciful account of what is actually being done in preparing for the exploration of the universe.

'Despite the tremendous scope of the book, the pace never flags; the translation by Hugh Merrick excellently serves the material. This book will enrich the home: it will stimulate many a discussion, it will answer many a question.' *Books of the Month.*

*Sm. Roy 8vo* *40s. net*

## THE LAST KINGS OF THULE

### by Jean Malaurie

Thule—*Ultima Thule*, the most northerly point in the world—was, when Jean Malaurie arrived there in 1950, still a mere settlement of unspoilt Eskimo hunters, and beyond it lay the Arctic wilderness as far as the Pole. But when he returned there, many months later, after the most strenuous journeys in the icy wastes, it was a settlement no longer: thousands of American engineers had landed there and were building one of the biggest air bases in the world. A little while later the remaining Eskimos left and migrated north; the advance of 'civilization' was driving the 'Last Kings of Thule' even closer to the Pole.

*Demy 8vo* *21s. net*

GEORGE ALLEN & UNWIN LTD